2007 **Saint Paul ALMANAC**

Cover designer, Kevin R. Brown
Editor, Kimberly Nightingale
History facts researcher, Brie Goellner
Saint Paul Almanac photography © 2006 Patricia Bour-Schilla
Capitol image on backcover © 2006 Patricia Bour-Schilla

Other photography credits: page 22 © John A. Weide, Minnesota Historical Society; pages 23 and 148 © Minnesota Historical Society; page 80 © Cheu Lee/*Hmong Times;* page 184 © Jerry Hass; pages 225 and 266 © Kelsey Bour-Schilla; page 244 © Sao Sue Jurewitsch; page 259 © Mark Connor

Photo illustrations pages 10, 21, 48, 55, 58, 94, 158, 208, 218 © Allen Zumach. For more information visit www.zumach.net.

Saint Paul city map on pages vi–vii used by permission of Big Stick Inc. © 2003. Purchase maps from Big Stick at 1-888-507-0058 or www.bigstickinc.com. Saint Paul downtown map on pages viii–ix © SaintPaul RiverCentre Convention and Visitors Authority. Used with permission.

ISBN 10-digit: 0-9772651-0-2
ISBN 13-digit: 978-0-9772651-0-7

Manufactured in Canada

Saint Paul Almanac
PO Box 16243
Saint Paul, MN 55116
saintpaulalmanac.com

Saint Paul Almanac is a nonprofit corporation.
Our books are published by Arcata Press.

ARCATA
PRESS

Table of Contents

Acknowledgments

It's been great fun putting this first *Saint Paul Almanac* together, and many people have helped in its creation.

Thanks to Brie, Kai, Mom, Dad, Kelly, Chris, Val, Susie, Anna, Drew, Lea, Quinn, Rachel, Mitchell, Henry, Wendy, Chloe, Mogeni, Kyah, Katie, Mandy, Matt, Gunnar, Kahlil, Helen, Ane, Zora, Isabelle, and Denise Fosse, Jami and Julie Shoemaker, Maria Manske, Christine Snow, Patty Bour-Schilla, Larry Schilla, Joci Tilsen, Ken Tilsen, Connie Goldman, Kate Cavett, Jim Bour, Kim Keller, Kimberly Buell, Barbara Schmidt, Blake Taylor, Betsy Peterson, Jenny Gehlhar, Michael Maupin, Karin Simoneau, Kevin Brown, R. Eli Boyum, Lisa Tabor, Amy Martin, Kathleen Walek, Zimena Ortiz Zamora, Brett Kahnke, Mai Neng Moua, Dennis Presley, Brenda Fong, Dara Syrkin, Phuong Dao, Kathryn Lynden, Bergen Papka, Cathy Lue, Leah S. Harvey, Jessica Hubley, Janet Bertok, Gretchen Williams, Sara Reller, Eileen McCormack, Roberta Sladky, Tricia Mattes, Pat Laurel, Jackie Jones, Brad Toll, Herta Pitman, Lisa Haller, Joshua Becerra, Kara Beckman, Holly Hinman, Gordon Slobaugh, Jason Michaelson, Cheu Lee, Heatherjo Gilbertson, John Feustel, John Crawford, Elise McHugh, Sara Remke, Austin Tripp, Mark Jung, Beth Northcutt, Andy Wilson, Pat Benson, Nicole Lucas, Mick Sterling, Devin Halden, Ruth Hayden, Beth Kainz, Shelley Johnson, Marsha Lynn, Liz Tufte, Theresa May, Robyn Erickson, Krin Berntson, Adam Kocinski, Richard Aguilar, Robyn Beth Priestley, Cynthia Bet, Kathy Ross, Marjorie Nugent, Nicole Lucas, Marianne D'Angelo, Antoinette S. Williams, Elizabeth Cleveland, Christopher E. Crutchfield, Art Weddington, Jill Waterhouse, Chris at Big Stick Inc., Allen Zumach, and all the almanac writers. And especially to Dan—thanks for everything.

Lastly, thank you to all Saint Paulites for telling and sharing your stories and allowing our indulgence in printing some of them. For it's the telling of stories that bridges us to place, to time, and connects us to each other.

Introduction

The *Saint Paul Almanac* is an annual book about our city that goes beyond shopping, styles, and restaurant reviews, and digs up from the grassroots the energy of the people of Saint Paul. It is our belief that stories make a city and those stories bind us together and weave within each of us a sense of belonging.

The almanac embraces the quiet disorder of our Saint Paul lives—our dreams, our everyday living, our birthing, our dying, our generosity, our denial, our understanding, our history, our successes, and our failures.

Katrina's devastation of New Orleans and the gritty determination to rebuild it cry out the true love we have for our cities as places of tremendous mythology and spirit. Saint Paul has shaped the lives of our writers and artists, and the almanac hopes to make that connection between place and art. We publish excerpts from books by Saint Paulites to encourage you to read, buy, and support local writers' work and to share the stories of our city.

Included is a datebook for the year with Saint Paul happenings listed in the calendar. You can get more detailed information about these happenings in Event Listings, starting on page 278. There are also health and fitness events listed in the back to keep you active around the year. We've tried to be as accurate as possible with dates, but sometimes they change, so double-check before you head out.

Dig in and read and write in your almanac. Make a grand mess of it. And please send us your stories at editor@saintpaulalmanac.com.

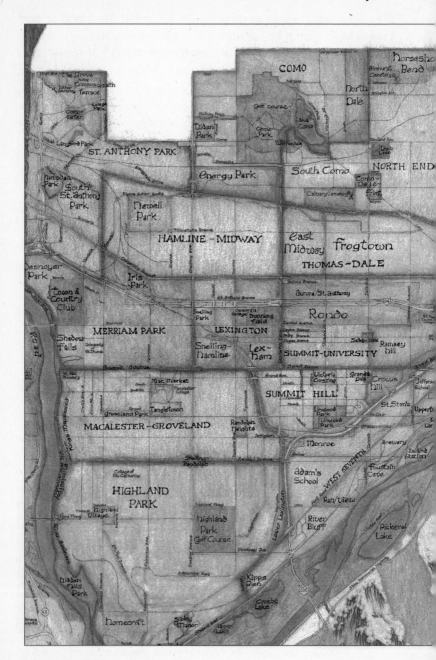

Saint Paul

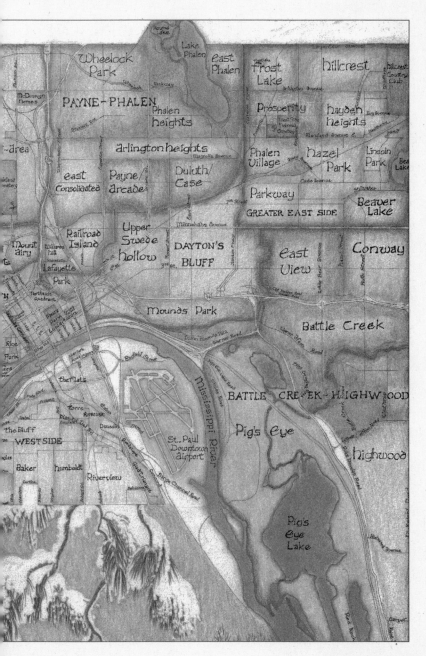

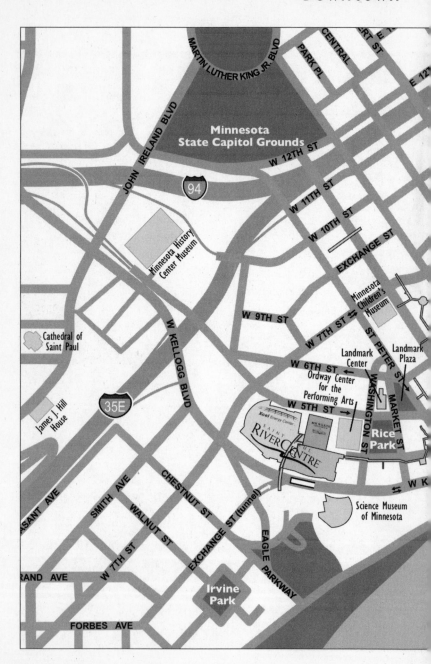

Minnesota
State Capitol Grounds

Minnesota History
Center Museum

Cathedral of
Saint Paul

James J. Hill
House

Minnesota
Children's
Museum

Landmark
Center

Landmark
Plaza

Ordway Center
for the
Performing Arts

Xcel Energy Center

SAINT
RiverCentre

Rice
Park

Science Museum
of Minnesota

Irvine
Park

Saint Paul

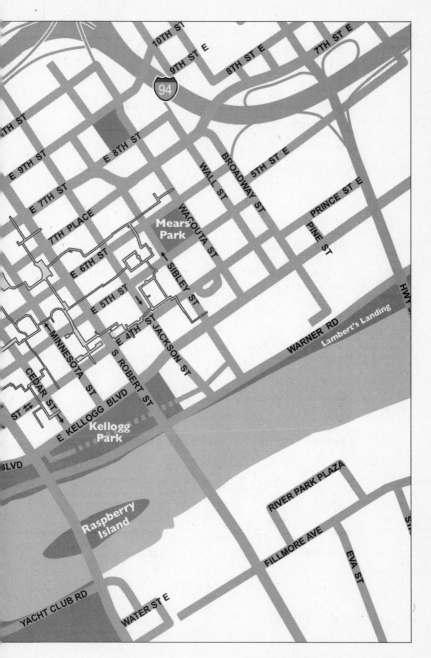

2007

JANUARY

S	M	T	W	T	F	S
	1	2	3	4	5	6
7	8	9	10	11	12	13
14	15	16	17	18	19	20
21	22	23	24	25	26	27
28	29	30	31			

FEBRUARY

S	M	T	W	T	F	S
				1	2	3
4	5	6	7	8	9	10
11	12	13	14	15	16	17
18	19	20	21	22	23	24
25	26	27	28			

MARCH

S	M	T	W	T	F	S
				1	2	3
4	5	6	7	8	9	10
11	12	13	14	15	16	17
18	19	20	21	22	23	24
25	26	27	28	29	30	31

APRIL

S	M	T	W	T	F	S
1	2	3	4	5	6	7
8	9	10	11	12	13	14
15	16	17	18	19	20	21
22	23	24	25	26	27	28
29	30					

MAY

S	M	T	W	T	F	S
		1	2	3	4	5
6	7	8	9	10	11	12
13	14	15	16	17	18	19
20	21	22	23	24	25	26
27	28	29	30	31		

JUNE

S	M	T	W	T	F	S
					1	2
3	4	5	6	7	8	9
10	11	12	13	14	15	16
17	18	19	20	21	22	23
24	25	26	27	28	29	30

JULY

S	M	T	W	T	F	S
1	2	3	4	5	6	7
8	9	10	11	12	13	14
15	16	17	18	19	20	21
22	23	24	25	26	27	28
29	30	31				

AUGUST

S	M	T	W	T	F	S
			1	2	3	4
5	6	7	8	9	10	11
12	13	14	15	16	17	18
19	20	21	22	23	24	25
26	27	28	29	30	31	

SEPTEMBER

S	M	T	W	T	F	S
						1
2	3	4	5	6	7	8
9	10	11	12	13	14	15
16	17	18	19	20	21	22
23/30	24	25	26	27	28	29

OCTOBER

S	M	T	W	T	F	S
	1	2	3	4	5	6
7	8	9	10	11	12	13
14	15	16	17	18	19	20
21	22	23	24	25	26	27
28	29	30	31			

NOVEMBER

S	M	T	W	T	F	S
				1	2	3
4	5	6	7	8	9	10
11	12	13	14	15	16	17
18	19	20	21	22	23	24
25	26	27	28	29	30	

DECEMBER

S	M	T	W	T	F	S
						1
2	3	4	5	6	7	8
9	10	11	12	13	14	15
16	17	18	19	20	21	22
23/30	24/31	25	26	27	28	29

Calendar

Plus Saint Paul Stories, Articles, and Poems

2007 Year Planner

	JANUARY	FEBRUARY	MARCH
1	M NEW YEAR'S DAY	TH	TH
2	T	F GROUNDHOG DAY	F
3	W	SA	SA
4	TH	SU	SU
5	F	M	M
6	SA	T	T
7	SU	W	W
8	M	TH	TH INTERNATIONAL WOMEN'S DAY
9	T	F	F
10	W	SA	SA
11	TH	SU	SU DAYLIGHT SAVING TIME BEGINS
12	F	M	M
13	SA	T	T
14	SU	W VALENTINE'S DAY	W
15	M MARTIN L. KING JR. DAY	TH	TH
16	T	F	F
17	W	SA	SA SAINT PATRICK'S DAY
18	TH	SU TET CHINESE NEW YEAR	SU
19	F	M PRESIDENTS' DAY	M
20	SA MUHARRAM	T MARDI GRAS	T
21	SU	W ASH WEDNESDAY	W SPRING EQUINOX
22	M	TH	TH
23	T	F	F
24	W	SA	SA
25	TH	SU	SU
26	F	M	M
27	SA	T	T
28	SU	W	W
29	M		TH
30	T		F
31	W		SA MAWLID AL-NABI CESAR CHAVEZ'S BIRTHDAY

2007 Year Planner

	APRIL		MAY		JUNE	
1	SU	PALM SUNDAY APRIL FOOL'S DAY	T		F	
2	M		W		SA	
3	T	FIRST DAY OF PASSOVER	TH		SU	
4	W		F		M	
5	TH		SA	CINCO DE MAYO	T	
6	F	GOOD FRIDAY	SU		W	
7	SA		M		TH	
8	SU	EASTER	T		F	
9	M		W		SA	
10	T	LAST DAY OF PASSOVER	TH		SU	
11	W		F		M	
12	TH		SA		T	
13	F		SU	MOTHER'S DAY	W	
14	SA		M		TH	
15	SU		T		F	
16	M		W		SA	
17	T		TH		SU	FATHER'S DAY
18	W		F		M	
19	TH		SA		T	JUNETEENTH
20	F		SU		W	
21	SA		M		TH	SUMMER SOLSTICE
22	SU	EARTH DAY	T		F	
23	M		W		SA	
24	T		TH		SU	
25	W		F		M	
26	TH		SA		T	
27	F		SU		W	
28	SA		M	MEMORIAL DAY (OBS.)	TH	
29	SU		T		F	
30	M		W		SA	
31			TH			

2007 Year Planner

	JULY	AUGUST	SEPTEMBER
1	SU	W	SA
2	M	TH	SU
3	T	F	M LABOR DAY
4	W INDEPENDENCE DAY	SA	T
5	TH	SU	W
6	F	M	TH
7	SA	T	F
8	SU	W	SA
9	M	TH	SU
10	T	F	M
11	W	SA	T
12	TH	SU	W
13	F	M	TH ROSH HASHANAH RAMADAN
14	SA	T	F
15	SU	W	SA
16	M	TH	SU
17	T	F	M
18	W	SA	T
19	TH	SU	W
20	F	M	TH
21	SA	T	F UN INTERNALTIONAL DAY OF PEACE
22	SU	W	SA YOM KIPPUR
23	M	TH	SU FALL EQUINOX
24	T	F	M
25	W	SA	T
26	TH	SU	W
27	F	M	TH
28	SA	T	F
29	SU	W	SA
30	M	TH	SU
31	T	F	

2007 Year Planner

	OCTOBER	NOVEMBER	DECEMBER
1	M	TH ALL SAINTS' DAY	SA
2	T	F DAY OF THE DEAD	SU
3	W	SA	M
4	TH	SU DAYLIGHT SAVING TIME ENDS	T
5	F	M	W HANUKKAH
6	SA	T	TH
7	SU	W	F
8	M LAILAT-UL-QADR, INDIGENOUS PEOPLE'S DAY	TH	SA
9	T	F	SU
10	W	SA	M UN INTERNATIONAL HUMAN RIGHTS DAY
11	TH	SU	T
12	F	M VETERANS DAY (OBS.)	W
13	SA EID-AL-FITR	T	TH
14	SU	W	F
15	M	TH	SA
16	T	F	SU
17	W	SA	M
18	TH	SU	T
19	F	M	W
20	SA	T	TH EID-AL-ADHA
21	SU	W	F
22	M	TH THANKSGIVING DAY	SA WINTER SOLSTICE
23	T	F	SU
24	W UNITED NATIONS DAY	SA	M
25	TH	SU	T CHRISTMAS
26	F	M	W KWANZAA BEGINS
27	SA	T	TH
28	SU	W	F
29	M	TH	SA
30	T	F	SU
31	W HALLOWEEN		M NEW YEAR'S EVE

January

Holiday Flower Show Dec. 2–Jan. 21

Saint Paul Winter Carnival Jan. 26–Feb. 4

Vietnamese Tet New Year Festival Jan. 27

Saint Paul Chamber Orchestra Jan. 12, 13

See page 278 for more information on January events.

Beginning

The moon drops one or two feathers into the fields. | The dark wheat listens. | Be still. | Now. | There they are, the moon's young, trying | Their wings. | Between trees, a slender woman lifts up the lovely shadow | Of her face, and now she steps into the air, now she is gone | Wholly, into the air. | I stand alone by an elder tree, I do not dare breathe | Or move. | I listen. | The wheat leans back toward its own darkness, | And I lean toward mine.

—James Wright

In 1840 Pierre Parrant was forced by the Army to relocate his whiskey-selling business downriver to present-day downtown Saint Paul. A small hub was soon erected and named Pig's Eye after Parrant's nickname.

JANUARY

S	M	T	W	T	F	S
	1	2	3	4	5	6
7	8	9	10	11	12	13
14	15	16	17	18	19	20
21	22	23	24	25	26	27
28	29	30	31			

1 Monday

New Year's Day

2 Tuesday

3 Wednesday

4 Thursday

5 Friday

6 Saturday

7 Sunday

City Daughter

Carol Caouette

Saint Paul beckons me. Sitting high or crouching low along the mighty river, her voluptuous, sculptured hills undulate then flatten on their way out to the city limits. The river seems to stall in her presence, coiling around and through, accommodating her before taking a straighter tack to the Gulf. Saint Paul claims the Mississippi waters for herself in certain springs, inviting the great river onto her flats from time to time. They try more of each other out for a time, but the Mississippi always retreats, never getting more of her than before. It is like this with Saint Paul; it is a city that has its limits but charms you anyway.

I wind around and through past the downtown, eastbound in my car. Saint Paul has never let me stray far from her since I began life as an orphan in a Como Park neighborhood. Like a godmother she meted out firsts to her goddaughter: my first conscious thrill at seeing her bright city lights; my first conscious fear crossing the High Bridge; the first playground for new forays; the first freedoms of adolescence; my first dates, my first apartment, my first look at people another color than me, another sexual persuasion than me, less able-bodied than me, less fortunate than me. A microcosm of the world is the world, after all.

I can't forget the mechanics near Union Depot, where Dad took the family cars. They changed their Jewish name to the Johnson Brothers. Their shop was where I got my first hints about sex through innuendo from the monthly voluptuous calendar girls on the wall. "May is Dairy Month!" "June is busting out all over!" I miss the idea of Frank Murphy's dress shop at Fifth and Saint Peter with its indoor balcony. As a little girl I'd slip between smooth satin or sequined dresses just to feel them on my skin while my mother shopped the sale rack.

Young and single, I squandered some time while living in a shotgun-style brownstone at Lincoln and Grotto. Purportedly, F. Scott Fitzgerald invested some money in that old development. I sure did live it up there, even fell in love there, just like he would have. I danced to disco in the basement at the Commodore Hotel, the same haunt of ghosts who kicked up their heels in life to the sounds of jazz and big band music. My dad's stories of his boyhood on the West Side revealed a Saint Paul once spicier, laced with gangsters, fewer governors, more daring-do. If only I could have experienced the Hollyhock Club,

a 1930s speakeasy. Almost certainly, my mother must have—maybe in something satin. I'm sure I would have been a frequent visitor; I would have worn sequins and feathers.

Like its river, Saint Paul has a strong current that pulls you in.

Discovering *The Hungry Mind* in the early '70s was like finding the Holy Grail. How many books did I leaf through struggling to find myself in the pages? How many familiar authors and friends did I find in the stacks? Sadly, more than I can remember, but I can feel the place just from calling it up. A favorite friend and I ate regularly at the lunch counter of Moudry's Apothecary, northeast corner, Fifth and Saint Peter. The chicken noodle soup was the best comfort food around. We'd browse in Gleason's Specialty Shoppe, where you could buy exotic tea and other goods from the British Isles. The friendly proprietor had an equally exotic English accent. For dinner we'd hit Mei Chu's for egg foo yung, just across Saint Peter. Three-Acre Wood at Seventh and Wabasha was my "head" shop of choice, where you could buy posters, papers, books, jewelry, or even ceramic tea sets. I don't know what history was attached to all of these haunts of mine, but I had my favorites and now they're gone. Some left before their time.

Like its river, Saint Paul has a strong current that pulls you in. I can't stay away long. Something about her doesn't change while other cities reinvent themselves or create color-coordinated façades. Saint Paulites maintain her from the inside out. Warehouses become lofts. Drafty Victorians get gutted and revamped. Neighborhoods once divided or scarred or ostracized claim their streets; the people announce their presence with color and food and culture. That is how Saint Paul draws you in; you only have to open up to her. Like a warm embrace, she wraps herself around and, eventually, through you.

In 1841 the Reverend Lucian Galtier, a Catholic priest, asked for Pig's Eye to be renamed Saint Paul. The name was accepted and has stuck ever since.

JANUARY

S	M	T	W	T	F	S
	1	2	3	4	5	6
7	8	9	10	11	12	13
14	15	16	17	18	19	20
21	22	23	24	25	26	27
28	29	30	31			

8 Monday

9 Tuesday

10 Wednesday

11 Thursday

Mississippi River Bridge No. 15 Built in 1915

12 Friday
Saint Paul Chamber Orchestra
page 278

13 Saturday
Saint Paul Chamber Orchestra
page 278

14 Sunday

Happiness

Daniel Bachhuber

For Deborah Keenan

I called a friend the other day and I was so surprised when she asked if I was happy that I hung up the phone and realized that I was happy, and had been that way since the day I started writing poetry. It was like standing in the middle of a demolished building eating a piece of cantaloupe and loving it. The next morning I read poetry before breakfast which I often do and there was a poem about death and I thought, "It's before breakfast and I'm enjoying a poem about death." I thought about my own poems: baby death, brother death, father death, the death of childhood, flowers, ambition, scrapbooks and dinosaurs; the death of silence and the death of death. I strode to the kitchen and fried two eggs that had wobbled the long tube far from the love of their mother; I punched down the toast that came from the fields that fell beneath the circling blades. I cut the fruit—the apple, the orange, the watermelon—into wet chunks, and I stared at the beauty of what lay before me. All those things cut off from their source about to feed my source which will feed the sources of others. Understanding that it is deeper love, not morbidity, that draws us toward death. I wept as I ate, silently, in happiness.

You can find "Happiness" and other poems in Dan Bachhuber's poetry book Mozart's Carriage, *published by New Rivers Press. Order* Mozart's Carriage *at newriverspress.com.*

Minnesota Heritage Hotdish

Celebrate Minnesota's Favorite Supper

Ronnie Howell

When I first moved to Minnesota from the East Coast, I was introduced to this thing called "hotdish." I learned quickly that it was the staple of all comfort food meals served by every mother and at all church and family gatherings. Here is a basic recipe.

Ronnie's Tater Tot Hotdish

1 lb.	lean ground hamburger, thawed
15 oz.	mini onion Tater Tots, frozen
1 can	condensed cream of mushroom soup
1 can	golden sweet corn, drained
1/3 cup	milk
	salt and pepper to taste

Lightly spray 9" × 9" square baking dish with cooking spray. Press the meat into the bottom of the pan. Next layer the potatoes, then the corn. Leave a slight gap along the sides for overflow of the sauce (to avoid spilling over in the oven). Mix the soup and milk in a separate bowl, and pour it over the layers in the pan. Bake in a preheated 350°F oven for 1 hour. Serve hot. Feeds 3–4 people. Recipe can be doubled by using twice the ingredients in a 9" × 13" pan and increasing baking time by 30 minutes.

Saint Paul was made the Territorial Capital in 1848. In 1857 the legislature passed a bill to move the Territorial Capital to Saint Peter, but a representative ran off with the bill before it could be signed by the governor.

JANUARY

S	M	T	W	T	F	S
	1	2	3	4	5	6
7	8	9	10	11	12	13
14	15	16	17	18	19	20
21	22	23	24	25	26	27
28	29	30	31			

15 Monday

Martin Luther King Jr. Day

16 Tuesday

17 Wednesday

18 Thursday

Ice Fishing on Pickerel Lake

19 Friday

20 Saturday

Muharram

Winter Carnival Medallion Hunt
Last day to register button
pages 18, 278

21 Sunday

Winter Carnival Medallion Hunt begins
First clue in the *Pioneer Press*
pages 18, 278

Treasure Hunt Blues

Kelly LaBrosse
(aka Artemis the Huntress)

It's the thrill of the hunt
the elusive treasure we seek

It's that little bit of rebel
inside us young and old
makes us bundle up, grab our tools
and brave the Minnesota cold

Keeps us runnin' round in circles
tryin' to follow all their clues
But still we keep on diggin'
even though we got the Treasure Hunt Blues

It's that little bit of pirate
that lives inside us all
that sets our minds to flight
with each new midnight call

Keeps us runnin' round in circles
tryin' to follow all their clues
but still we keep on diggin'
even though we got the Treasure Hunt Blues

It's the satisfaction of trying
using our brains and brawn
even if we don't find it this year
next year we might be right on!
Still we keep on diggin' even though

I got the (I got the)
You got the (you got the)
We got the Treasure Hunt Blues

Dig for Buried Treasure
in Saint Paul

What makes Saint Paul one of the best cities in the world to live in? Why, the Treasure Hunt, of course. No other city has buried treasure where you can win ten thousand dollars just by figuring out clues and digging in the snow. So how do you win all that cash?

1. Buy a Saint Paul Winter Carnival button and send in the registration form—must be postmarked no later than January 20, 2007.

2. Clip and save the daily clues in the *Pioneer Press*.

3. Find the *Pioneer Press* Treasure Hunt Medallion.

4. Collect $10,000.

Pioneer Press **Treasure Hunt Hotline**
651.228.5547

The Lost Mittens: Another Treasure Often Buried in Saint Paul Snow

The streets around Rice Park, in the "Uppertown" neighborhood of downtown Saint Paul, aren't set up in grid fashion. When constructed in 1849, the streets were set at a 45-degree angle from Saint Peter Street by the planners, Henry Rice and John Irving.

JANUARY

S	M	T	W	T	F	S
	1	2	3	4	5	6
7	8	9	10	11	12	13
14	15	16	17	18	19	20
21	22	23	24	25	26	27
28	29	30	31			

22 Monday

23 Tuesday

24 Wednesday

25 Thursday

Ice Skating at Landmark Plaza, Corner of Fifth and Market Streets

26 Friday

Saint Paul Winter Carnival
page 278

27 Saturday

Saint Paul Winter Carnival
Grande Day Parade, 1 p.m.

Vietnamese Tet New Year Festival
page 278

28 Sunday

Saint Paul Winter Carnival
page 278

Saint Paul's Winter Party

Moira F. Harris

The most frequently photographed buildings in Saint Paul's history have been those ephemeral edifices erected for the Saint Paul Winter Carnival: its palaces of ice or snow. Usually built in the city's parks, they become the targets of cameras from the first assembly of the frigid blocks to their later demolition by the forces of the Fire King, Vulcanus Rex. Carnival palaces are an icon of the city even though they do not appear every year and last no longer than a few weeks from late January through early February.

The most recent ice palace was built in 2004 on the parking lot opposite Xcel Energy Center, where the All-Star Hockey Game was to be played. An ice wall surrounded an ice rink, ice sculptures, and the palace. On one Carnival evening visitors met Saint Paul's mayor, Randy Kelly, dressed in an old Carnival marching uniform, skating loops on the rink. Like many of its predecessors, the ice palace had towers topped with colorful canvas, a stage in front, and an arch under which visitors could pass. Colored lights played on the glistening sides of the towers. Carnival goers could skate, listen to music, and see displays within two large tents.

2004 Ice Palace

The 1886 Saint Paul Winter Carnival Ice Palace

The concept of the Saint Paul Winter Carnival began in 1885 when city business leaders realized that the only other North American city holding such an event had struck it from the next year's calendar. Montreal was suffering through an outbreak of smallpox and was under quarantine. George Thompson, editor of the Saint Paul *Dispatch,* suggested that Saint Paul become the winter capital of the country. And so it happened. Montreal's ice palace architect provided the drawings and Canadian organizers suggested the types of activities that had appealed to their city.

That first ice palace, a huge structure with a massive central tower and entrance porticos, was surrounded by ice sculptures, evergreen trees, and the tepees of Dakota Indians, who had been invited to show how they coped with winter. Most activities took place either in front or inside the palace, except for parades and the slides erected on several of Saint Paul's hilly streets. Early ice palaces had rooms where concerts, balls, and even weddings took place. Currently, due to safety and insurance concerns, ice palace structures cannot be entered.

To support that first Carnival, residents were encouraged to form groups (especially ski or snowshoe clubs), so that they could march together in the parades, dressed in warm wool jackets and pants. Although curling and skating were already familiar winter pastimes, skiing, ski jumping, and snowshoeing were not, so newspaper writers took care to explain the peculiar techniques employed.

Not only did sports need interpretation, but there also had to be a story, a legend behind the Carnival. As J. H. Hanson wrote in "An Idyll on Ice," the Ice King was feverish and unhappy because the temperature in his realm had already reached zero. Then he had an idea.

> We'll go to Saint Paul
> The Queen of the World.
> The Ice Monarch's banner
> Shall be there unfurled.
> 'Tis a place
> Thricely blessed,
> Climate, commerce, condition,
> All aid to produce
> A great City's Position.

In the poem the Ice King (then called Borealis, but later shortened to Boreas), his Queen of Snows, and his courtiers all go to Saint Paul. They are welcomed at City Hall and parade in horse-drawn floats to the ice palace, built in Central Park (near the location of the present State Capitol). The reign of Borealis lasted two exciting weeks until his enemies, the Fire King and his supporters, attacked the ice palace, symbolically ending winter and heralding spring.

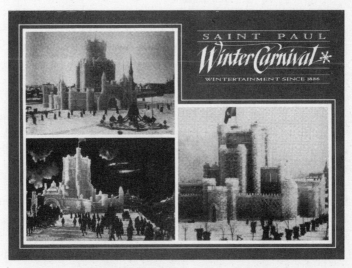

Postcard of Past Winter Carnival Palaces

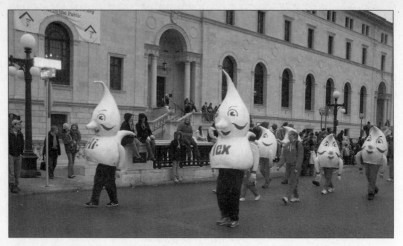

The Hilex Gnomes in the Saint Paul Winter Carnival Parade

The characters of the Carnival legend have had some additions and name changes over the years, but the basic struggle of ice against fire remains the same. Boreas, his Queen, Prime Minister, Princes and Princesses of the Four Winds, and the Royal Guards are only half of the legend roster. The Fire King (Vulcanus Rex) and his red-suited Krewe (General Flameous, the Duke of Klinker, Grand Duke Fertilious, Count Embrious, the Prince of Soot, the Count of Ashes, and Baron Hot Sparkus) are in opposition. Briefly, Fire Kings reigned with Fire Queens, but today Klondike Kate, a saloon singer from the North, is often linked to the rowdy Vulcan Krewe. There is also a Senior and Junior Court with appropriately named attendants and duties lasting after the Carnival is over.

Once the Carnival ends and the ice palace falls, both Boreas and Vulcanus assume their yearlong duties as representatives of the city, visiting hospitals, senior residences, and other festivals. Vulcanus and his Krewe travel, when possible, in their venerable Minnesota-made fire engine to the sound of an appropriate cacophony of horns, bells, and whistles.

At least one daytime and the evening torchlight parade has been part of every Carnival. In the 1880s floats were horse-drawn and marchers represented the newly formed sports clubs.

Saint Paulites are fond of the Hilex gnomes, whose heads are made of fiberglass in the shape of drops of the bleach the company makes. The Lost Mittens and the Saint Paul Bouncing Team are favorites of the parade watchers too.

The Saint Paul Bouncing Team holds a blanket taut so that a very agile and light girl can be bounced in the air. This is supposedly an old Inuit hunting ploy. In early Carnivals passersby were sometimes captured and bounced, but today the role of the bounced is restricted to a member of the troupe.

Many sports events have been part of the Carnivals. Ski jumping, speedskating, ice fishing, snowmobile racing, car racing on ice, curling competitions, hockey matches, and balloon racing have all found their way onto schedules. One of the most famous events—subject of both a book and a film—was the idea of Louis Hill in 1917. His father, James J. Hill, had once traveled from Winnipeg to Saint Paul by dogsled and thus a commemorative dogsled race seemed appropriate. The 522-mile race lasted over a week. Most of the racers were Canadians, but an American named Fred Hartman captured the hearts of those following the race. One of his dogs attacked another, leaving him minus two dogs to pull his sled. One of the missing animals had been the lead dog, so Hartman was forced to take over the role himself and thus run the entire race with his remaining animals. He finished last, by over four hours, yet he was considered the hero of the race and applauded when the racers made vaudeville appearances afterward.

Neither a sport nor a race, the Treasure Hunt is another of the Carnival's favorite events. A Winter Carnival Medallion is hidden somewhere in Saint Paul or Ramsey County by a staff member of the *Pioneer Press*. Clues in rhyme are published in each day's paper. Whoever finds the Medallion, saves the clues, and registers his or her Carnival button can win a ten-thousand-dollar prize. This contest has drawn a cadre of early rising fans eager to read the newspaper's next clue from its very beginning in 1952.

Just as the ice palace is the icon of the Saint Paul Winter Carnival, its symbols and sources of funding have been, from the beginning, commemorative buttons. To gain entry to many of each year's events, one needs to wear a button. The designs change every year, and for many people, buttons become the nucleus of a Winter Carnival collection. Those who portray the legend characters, especially Boreas and Vulcanus, may present other buttons as gifts that become highly collectible.

The Saint Paul Festival and Heritage Foundation runs the Winter Carnival from its headquarters in Landmark Center. Civic events usually utilize the talents of a few paid staff members and a very large number of volunteers.

February

Saint Paul Winter Carnival Jan. 26–Feb. 4

Winter Flower Show Feb. 2–Feb. 18

Saint Paul Chamber Orchestra Feb. 3, 22, 23, and 24

Scottish Ramble Feb. 10–Feb. 11

The Minnesota Opera *Grapes of Wrath*, Feb. 10, 13, 15, 17, and 18

Minnesota Home and Patio Show Feb. 15–Feb. 18

Minnesota State High School Leagues—

   Dance Team Competition Feb. 16–Feb. 17

   Girls' Hockey Tournament Feb. 22–Feb. 24

   Girls' Gymnastics Tournament Feb. 23–Feb. 24

See pages 278–279 for more information on February events.

S	M	T	W	T	F	S
				1	2	3
4	5	6	7	8	9	10
11	12	13	14	15	16	17
18	19	20	21	22	23	24
25	26	27	28			

The ice palace built for the 1888 Saint Paul Winter Carnival was one of the largest buildings in the world, measuring 14 stories high and covering an acre of land.

---

29 Monday

Saint Paul Winter Carnival
page 278

---

30 Tuesday

Saint Paul Winter Carnival
page 278

---

31 Wednesday

Saint Paul Winter Carnival
page 278

---

1 Thursday

Saint Paul Winter Carnival
page 278

A Vulcan in the 2006 3M King Boreas Grande Day Parade

2 Friday

Groundhog Day

Saint Paul Winter Carnival
page 278

3 Saturday

Saint Paul Winter Carnival
Vulcan Victory Torchlight Parade, 6:30 p.m.
page 278

Saint Paul Chamber Orchestra
page 279

4 Sunday

Saint Paul Winter Carnival
page 278

Saint Paul *Pioneer Press*
Winter Carnival Medallion Hunt
Hiding List

Over the years, the Saint Paul *Pioneer Press* Winter Carnival Medallion Hunt has lured people outdoors to face the frigid weather and to search through some of the most scenic spots in the fair capital city to find a modern bit of buried treasure. Here are all the hiding places dating back to 1952.

2005 Crosby Farm Nature Area—underneath a fallen piece of bark from a fallen tree, frozen to the ground

2004 Phalen Park—inside a green donut (in reference to the Archie comic #78 where their local newspaper sponsors a similar hunt), in the area between Phalen and Round Lakes

2003 Como Park—frozen in a chunk of ice under fallen timber and leaves in a wooded area north of the dirt bike course and dutch oven

2002 Merriam Park—taped to the underside of a tortilla chip can liner

2001 Como Park—inside an Iron Man sports sock and tucked into a Dove soap box

2000 Newell Park—inside an Ace brand box of playing cards

1999 Conway Park—wrapped inside a white, crocheted holder

1998 Cherokee Park—placed inside an Old Navy brand sock

1997 Como Park—in a Curad bandage box, wrapped in a red bandanna

1996 Harriet Island Park—inside a Skoal tin

1995 Battle Creek Park—placed inside a knitted yarn pouch

1994 Highland Park—inside a little white box

1993 Hidden Falls Park—stuck inside a diaper

1992 Cherokee Park—inside a white mitten

1991 Langford Park—stuck inside a Hostess brand Sno-Ball

1990 Como Park—wrapped in clay and grass

1989 The Capitol Mall—inside an earmuff

1988 Tony Schmidt Park, Arden Hills—coated with almond bark

1987 Indian Mounds Park—wrapped in clay and grass

1986 Highland Park—inside a pipe

1985 Kellogg Mall Park—glued inside a White Castle hamburger box

1984 Newell Park—attached to a broken 45 rpm record

1983 Lake Phalen Park—substituted as filling in an Oreo cookie

1982 Wakefield Lake Park, Maplewood—wrapped in a newspaper

1981 Acorn Park, Roseville—taped in between leaves

1980 Como Park—inside plaster

1979 Marthaler Park, West Saint Paul—taped to a dead tree

1978 Harriet Island Park—frozen inside a snowball

1977 Irvine Park—inside a cigar box

1976 Keller Lake Park, Maplewood—attached to a piece of wood

1975 Mears Park—inside a Bull Durham sack

1974 Cherokee Park—in a crushed Coke can

1973 Lake Phalen Park—cemented inside a closet bracket

1972 Marydale Park—stuck inside a chunk of drain pipe

1971 Wakefield Lake Park, Maplewood—attached to a baby buggy wheel

1970 Battle Creek Park, Maplewood—attached to a cast-iron vise

1969 Victoria Street and I-35E—in a crevice of two rocks

1968 Highland Park—attached to plasterboard

1967 State Fairgrounds—underneath eight inches of ice

1966 Harriet Island Park—attached to a flatiron

1965 Como Park—attached to a hunk of printing lead

1964 Beaver Lake Park—attached to a gold-colored brick

1963 Caroll, Jefferson, Farrington, and Rondo Street—found in a snowbank without protection

1962 Along Mississippi Street—attached to a disc

1961 Highland Park—in a large clump of grass

1960 Harriet Island Park—in the heel of a boot

1959 Warner Road—under a tree

1958 Under Highway 61 Bridge—in milky ice (first year of Medallion)

1957 Battle Creek Park—in a clump of roots above ground

1956 Como Park—inside a hollow log

1955 Seventh and Robert streets—under a mailbox (chest had been magnetized)

1954 Hidden Falls Park—in a dead, hollow stump

1953 Cherokee Park—in a snowbank; State Fairgrounds—in a large bush near the Poultry Building (there were two chests hidden in 1953)

1952 Highland Park—in a clump of weeds

Saint Paul was first surpassed in population by Minneapolis in 1880. Saint Paul continues to have fewer residents than its twin.

FEBRUARY

S	M	T	W	T	F	S
				1	2	3
4	5	6	7	8	9	10
11	12	13	14	15	16	17
18	19	20	21	22	23	24
25	26	27	28			

5 Monday

6 Tuesday

7 Wednesday

8 Thursday

Saint Paul Bouncing Team Girl

9 Friday	

10 Saturday	Scottish Ramble
	The Minnesota Opera
	Grapes of Wrath
	page 279

| 11 Sunday | Scottish Ramble |
| | *page 279* |

The Turf Club

Jenny Gehlhar

The Turf Club is an historic landmark in the Twin Cities music world. One might wonder how this club set in the Midway—the land between downtown Minneapolis and downtown Saint Paul—amongst porn and pawn shops, liquor stores and Ax Man, maintains a name at all. This is not the hubbub of nightlife; no river views, no skyscrapers, no horse carriages or antique fire trucks, no pretty street lights, no Snoopy. It's University bus stops and Snelling traffic.

But part of the Turf's charm lies in the very fact that it is set apart, an outcast from the rest of the busy modernizing Twin Cities. A hop and skip to one of the numerous venues in Minneapolis is always an enticing option, but Saint Paul has a unique and opposing aesthetic to Minneapolis, one that is captured on the outskirts of downtown, at the Turf. Rich in unpolished history, this is a rock 'n' roll joint that gives everyone what they expect from a Midwest bar: flannels and beer. Sorry, there ain't no chocolate martinis here.

Opening in the '40s as a two-steppin' country bar, mellowing a bit through the folk artsy '60s, morphing with the dance wave of the '70s, then embracing the grunge of the '80s, the club is like a treatise on Minnesota music. And this brings us to the other part of the club's success: its consistent dedication to local and independent music, something this town of ten thousand musicians definitely recognizes and even appreciates enough to maintain loyalty in the face of an adverse location. So much so that the adversity becomes even more reason to frequent the damn place.

When the quirky—or to some, just plain creepy—Clown Lounge opened in the basement to showcase clown memorabilia, it suddenly started to book some of the hottest and most experimental jazz in town, not to mention offering some seriously stiff drinks. Despite the management changes and loss of the Clown Lounge (RIP), the Turf remains one of the few dependable red-eye rock venues in a city that does sleep—like around 11 p.m.—on weeknights. You just never know what will come along next, but you can be sure it's gonna be good. You see, catering to music junkies apparently pays off, especially when they are the ones entranced by rock—rock 'n' roll, classic rock, alternative rock, indie rock, folk rock, punk rock—because those music junkies just don't die, they just don't go away, and some don't sleep.

The Turf Club

The Turf is a perfect setting for rock. The long, prominent bar scales one side of the narrow interior; the stage is at the back; the entire space is enveloped in dark woods; and tinkling Christmas lights make for a cheap strip club ambiance rivaling the best of the local Veteran's Legions. The music is loud, the crowd is devoted. So, just how diverse and representative is this venue for Minnesota music these days?

Well, how many places can claim to have hosted a self-proclaimed punk rock wedding complete with music from the wedding couple's band? How many clubs have let a musician stay on stage for a fifty-two-hours-plus gig? How many places can keep the cover at five dollars? And how many places turn the volume up so loud that the floor bounces? One. The Turf Club. And the local *City Pages* can't resist putting the club on their must-see, gotta-be-there "A-List" again and again. Yeah, we all know Minneapolis would like to claim this one as its own. That's no surprise. It's the dirt-covered diamond in the rough, sure to provide a gem of a night to remember.

Ask anyone from Mark Mallman (the guy responsible for that absurd fifty-two-hour marathon gig) to All the Pretty Horses (who frequent the club clad in bondage-goth ware) if the Turf is the place to be, and you'll get a blank stare. Everyone knows the Turf has that special something. Even musicians tainted by the boys' club method of booking; the chatty, aloof crowd; and the ear-splitting PAs and speakers can't deny the elusive draw to be on that stage. It exudes a mysterious magnetism, but it predominantly stands as a dingy and dirty and loud backbone to Saint Paul—probably with no bar brawls, but several bar stories. Vive le rock 'n' roll at the Turf Club.

In 1880 Saint Paul might have had a smaller population than Minneapolis, but we sure knew how to have a good time. We had more saloons (242 to Minneapolis' 176) and more acknowledged brothels (7 to Minneapolis' 4).

FEBRUARY

S	M	T	W	T	F	S
				1	2	3
4	5	6	7	8	9	10
11	12	13	14	15	16	17
18	19	20	21	22	23	24
25	26	27	28			

12 Monday

13 Tuesday

The Minnesota Opera
Grapes of Wrath
page 279

14 Wednesday

Valentine's Day

15 Thursday

The Minnesota Opera
Grapes of Wrath

Minnesota Home and Patio Show

page 279

Cherokee Park

16 Friday	Dance Team Competition
	Minnesota Home and Patio Show
	page 279

17 Saturday	The Minnesota Opera
	Grapes of Wrath
	Dance Team Competition
	Minnesota Home and Patio Show
	page 279

18 Sunday	The Minnesota Opera
Tet	*Grapes of Wrath*
Chinese New Year	Minnesota Home and Patio Show
	page 279

The Dump

Ron Peterson

Mom occasionally referred to it as the Woods, to give it a bit of class, but me, Kenny, Harwood, the cousins, my sister, and most everyone else called it the Dump. To adult eyes—my eyes now—it isn't much, just a two-block by one-block rectangle with houses around the edge. The land is low, not suited for construction, so it only had a twenty-foot rise with a dirt road across the middle, where a street should have been, leading over to the scary two-story. Old people used to yell at you there if you got too close.

Before leaving for college I'd learned about more interesting spots: the walk through the Italian neighborhood; down through spooky, burnt-out Swede Hollow to confirmation class at First Lutheran; riding a bike up the steep hill past Saint Pat's out to Centerville and fishing; the climb up an ivy-covered wall to the Capitol Theater on Payne Avenue Saturday afternoons; not to mention really neat places like China, Europe, and California.

The Dump had stories oozing out from kids in the thirty houses surrounding it: about the wheelchair man on the corner, parents who were alcoholics, broken collar bones, school projects, girlfriends, sports, more sports, and stories that I've totally forgotten now.

In the winter—to junior-high eyes—the Dump was the place to slide after school. The rise in the middle became icy when the snow packed down. We'd run off the road, jumping on our sleds while still in the air, and plummet down the frozen hill, or even better, stand on the back boards of our American Flyers holding the cord like the rein on a horse. Getting to the bottom without crashing gave you bragging rights.

> . . . the place, the map of the Dump, virtually every tree,
> is stuck in my brain.

After supper we'd cut through the Dump quickly to get to Wilder Playground and its huge ice sheet and blazing lights. We lived for the ice—playing hockey, of course, but also a tag game where leaping into snow piles over your head made you safe. If our feet froze, we'd play basketball. Running home late along the edge of the Dump, sometimes—in the dark—the rats would chase you.

The Dump at Case and Bradley

To really young eyes—five, six, or seven years of age—the Dump was adventure. Mom finally let you go in there by yourself. Spring rains filled it up, so you could float on rafts left by big kids or climb out over water on fallen elms. Purple-pink weeds soon bloomed, and we caught bees in Skippy peanut butter jars with holes punched in the cover. And we'd see how many we could get in one jar, and later, how long it took them to die.

The Dump had dangers: like the deep caves that teenagers dug and covered with boards, the vine swings over drop-offs, and the places where people threw their junk. We dreamed of Davy Crockett, bank robbers, bogeymen or bogeywomen, and we sang pirate songs. A beautiful place—our Dump.

Unfortunately, the people stories are now too deep in my hippocampus to ever retrieve: who pushed whom, whose parents bickered about what, why Davy Crockett was shooting a dragon . . . but the place, the map of the Dump, virtually every tree, is stuck in my brain.

My sister's still around, but the cousins are out of state and I only see Harwood and Kenny every five or ten years at reunions. I suppose it would take a hypnotist, a psychiatrist, or God to dig our memories out now, especially the profound ones—the ones we learned with young, open eyes.

Four more generations of kids have grown up in the old neighborhood. I hope they've been as blessed. I'm only sure that, for us kids of the '50s, our East Side Dump was a patient, honest, and loving teacher.

The first mayor of Saint Paul, elected in April 1854, was David Olmsted. At the time he represented 4,000 residents.

FEBRUARY

S	M	T	W	T	F	S
				1	2	3
4	5	6	7	8	9	10
11	12	13	14	15	16	17
18	19	20	21	22	23	24
25	26	27	28			

19 Monday

Presidents' Day

20 Tuesday

Mardi Gras

21 Wednesday

Ash Wednesday

22 Thursday

Girls' Hockey Tournament

Saint Paul Chamber Orchestra

page 279

Schmidt Brewery. Soon a Condo near You?

23 Friday

Girls' Hockey Tournament

Girls' Gymnastics Tournament

Saint Paul Chamber Orchestra

page 279

24 Saturday

Girls' Hockey Tournament

Girls' Gymnastics Tournament

Saint Paul Chamber Orchestra

page 279

25 Sunday

Saint Paul: Home to the Greatest Tournament in the World

John Rosengren

The average teenage boy thinks about sex once every seven seconds; in Minnesota, he thinks about hockey the other six. From the day his parents first lace skates to his feet and lift him over the boards, the state pastime dominates a Minnesota boy's thoughts. Before puberty, those thoughts have escalated into dreams of playing in the Minnesota State Boys' Hockey Tournament, heralded by one Saint Paul sportswriter as "the greatest annual sporting event in Minnesota." To play in the tournament is the climax of the dream—the rest is foreplay. With the largest state high school tournament in the nation, Minnesota hockey is bigger than Texas football, and bigger than Indiana basketball. Over 100,000 fans attend the annual four-day tournament the second weekend of March. Another two million tune in on TV. Families argue over who gets to use the tickets each year. Bookies take bets on the games; scalpers include it on their schedules.

"Winning the state championship with my friends from the neighborhood topped the *Miracle on Ice* because we had talked about doing that since we were Peewees," Brooks said.

Just how big is the tournament? Howard was there. That's right, Howard Cosell, the mother of all sports announcers, provided color commentary in the '70s. The erudite sesquipedalian orator's presence elevated the tournament to the status of an Ali–Frazier title fight. No other high school tournament can claim that stature. The state dream looms larger than international miracles. Herb Brooks, who coached the '80 U.S. Olympic Hockey Team—half of them Minnesota boys—that upset the mighty Soviet juggernaut to capture gold, told *Sports Illustrated* that winning the state tournament was the bigger thrill. As a high school senior, Brooks scored two goals in the championship game to earn Saint Paul's Johnson High School the '55 title. "Winning the state championship with my friends from the neighborhood topped the *Miracle on Ice* because we had talked about doing that since we were Peewees," Brooks said. "When the smoke clears, your buddies

Xcel Energy Center

from high school are awfully important, probably more important than anything."

Thursday: 2001 Quarterfinals

The tournament returned to Saint Paul, "Tournament City, U.S.A." It had taken a two-year hiatus at the Target Center across the river in Minneapolis while the city of Saint Paul built the Xcel Energy Center on the site of the former Civic Center. The 130-million-dollar, state-of-the-art emerald with the 56,000 square-foot glass façade became Minnesota's hockey cathedral. Scattered throughout the concourses and Iron Range Grill were side altars to gold-medal men's and women's Olympic teams powered by homegrown talent and shrines dedicated to the likes of Frank Brimsek, John Mayasich, and Neal Broten. Adorning the pillars of the main concourse like the Stations of the Cross, the *Pioneer Press* front pages proclaimed news of the tournament dating back to its origins in the '40s. Hockey jerseys from Minnesota's high schools ringed the suite-level clerestory. Indeed, the home of the Wild was built upon the foundation of the state's devotion to high school hockey. Tournament City Mayor Norm Coleman, who had spearheaded the drive to return the National Hockey League to Minnesota and paraded through Saint Paul streets on a Zamboni when the league awarded the Wild franchise to his city, watched the first tournament at the Xcel from the press box. "The strength of hockey in Minnesota is in high school hockey," Coleman proclaimed. "I don't think the legislators would've gone for it without the high school tournament bringing people in from all over the state."

The Xcel sparkled in the shadow of the imposing Saint Paul Cathedral, hunkered on the city's summit. Modeled after the Vatican's Saint Peter, the Cathedral, with its massive copper dome, dominated the city's landscape and shaped its identity. Residents identified themselves by their parish affiliation. The Archbishop slept there.

Thursday morning, March 8, 2001, Saint Paul's finest, bundled in wool caps, directed traffic outside the Xcel. Yellow school buses and cars decorated for the occasion—"We love Greenway" painted across the rear window—circled the icy streets in search of elusive parking spots. For blocks, ramps flashed red "FULL" signs. From all directions, teenage fans—some wearing shorts and flip-flops—marched through light flurries toward hockey's mecca for the 12:05 p.m. start of the day's first game. Their numbers would've made Ferris Bueller proud. School? Today? You gotta be kidding. The tournament had officially begun on Wednesday with the Class A quarterfinal games, but for the vast majority of fans, it didn't really start until the Class AA opening-round games on Thursday. They likened the Class A quarterfinals yesterday, where Benilde won its game, to junior varsity playing before varsity games. Or to the bantamweight undercard to a heavyweight title bout. Bettors viewed it that way. They hardly took notice of the A tournament, but plunked down one hundred dollar or bigger bets on the AA tournament. The bookies' phones weren't as busy as they were during the NCAA Final Four, but they registered thousands of dollars from their customers. In one raid police found evidence of 163 wagers totaling $28,040 on the '91 tournament championship game between Hill-Murray and Duluth East.

Friday: Semifinals

On Friday morning the coldest place in the country was Embarrass, Minnesota. The Range town opposite Greenway reported dawn temps of –17°, while the day broke at a balmy 11° in Saint Paul. By 6 p.m., an hour before the first Class AA semifinal between Elk River and Hastings, the setting sun bathed the Xcel's glass façade in a yellow glow, the pot of gold at the end of the season's rainbow. The sun left trails of water running down the gutters it touched, but in the lengthening shadows, ice coated the sidewalks where fans streamed toward the golden arena. One young man with a goatee paced outside and shivered—his cotton sweater scant protection against the elements—complaining into his cell phone, "No way I'm going to spend thirty dollars apiece." He scrunched his face. "Relax, I'm looking."

**While a handful of the sets in Minnesota might be tuned
to XFL action or the Timberwolves playing the Magic
or even the movie *Dangerous Minds,* the Minnesota State High
School Boys' Hockey Tournament easily beat them
all in the ratings, claiming a 10-percent share.**

The scalpers worked the Xcel doors and the sidewalks for several blocks down West Seventh unmolested by the wool-capped cops directing traffic. One guy standing outside Tom Reid's Hockey City Pub bounced in the cold, a longshoreman's cap tugged low over his pock-marked face, and held high a scrap of cardboard scrawled with "TICKETS. Who's got 'em? Who needs 'em?" When someone stopped, he pulled a wad of tickets from his pocket. He had been out there all day. "You can make a living, if you work hard enough at it," he said.

He worked just the big events—Vikings, Twins, Wild, NCAA Final Four, and the boys' high school hockey tournament. He could get double the face value ($12 adults/$7 student), but that was way down from the tournament's glory days when not even the governor could find tickets. The split into two tiers, then two classes, had been hard on scalpers. Doubling the number of games had diluted interest and reduced demand—games no longer guaranteed sellouts. By Saturday night, when the losing schools had dumped their allotted tickets, standing out in the cold became a waste of time.

Inside Xcel's Gate 1, the crowd pressed several hundred thick in the lobby. Those not wanting to suffer the cold or pay the scalpers' markup took their chances in the box office lines, hopeful to snatch up one of the tickets the schools had returned. Towering over them, a lighthouse beacon waved across the ticket holders and ticket hopefuls waiting for the turnstiles to open at 6 p.m. It lit an Elk River kid with his shaved head painted completely red, even behind the ears. It lit a pair of Hastings girls in soccer shorts, knee-high socks, yellow Hastings tee shirts, and their cheeks painted with an H and an R. When the gates finally opened, the ticket holders pushed forward and released a loud cheer. Friday night, the stakes increased. Thursday, teams played the quarters to survive. Friday, they played for Saturday night. Each wanted to lick the pot of gold.

Saturday: Championship

Elsewhere that Saturday, Yoko Ono opened a forty-year retrospective at the Walker Art Center in Minneapolis. By executive order, President George W. Bush blocked the Northwest Airlines' mechanics union from striking, which initiated a sixty-day cooling off period. A minor low pressure system moved in from the northwest, though early morning clouds had cleared by late afternoon. But the main topic of conversation in Minnesota that day was Moorhead versus Elk River. The Spuds faced off against the Elks that night for the Class AA state title. At 6 p.m., an hour before the puck dropped, you couldn't find a seat at Tom Reid's Hockey City Pub on the corner of Walnut and West Seventh. Those who hadn't found a ticket had staked out their real estate to watch the Channel 9 broadcast. While a handful of the sets in Minnesota might be tuned to XFL action or the Timberwolves playing the Magic or even the movie *Dangerous Minds,* the Minnesota State High School Boys' Hockey Tournament easily beat them all in the ratings, claiming a 10-percent share. Over two million people statewide watched at least some part of the 2001 tournament. Countless others around the world watched the simultaneous cybercast. This was the Super Bowl of local sports.

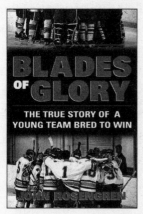

John Rosengren's Blades of Glory: The True Story of a Young Team Bred to Win *tells the story of high school hockey in Minnesota through a season spent with the Bloomington Jefferson Jaguars.* Sports Illustrated *praised the book's "impressive narrative" and Gordie Howe said, "Hockey fans everywhere will feel the chills of excitement and pangs of disappointment in a season spent with the Jaguars."*

March

Saint Paul Chamber Orchestra Mar. 2, 3, 17, 23, and 24

Saint Patrick's Day Parade Mar. 17

Irish Celebration Mar. 11—Dance, Mar. 17—Saint Patrick's Day
Celebration

**Saint Patrick's Day 33rd Annual Irish Dance at Randolph
Heights Elementary School** Mar. 17

Saint Patrick's Day Irish Ceili Dance at CSPS Mar. 17

Spring Flower Show Mar. 24–Apr. 29

The Minnesota Opera *Lakmé* Mar. 31

Minnesota State High School Leagues—

Boys' Wrestling Tournament Mar. 2–3

Boys' Hockey Tournament Mar. 7–10

See pages 279–280 for more information on March events.

In 1889 there were 40 millionaires living in Saint Paul.

MARCH

S	M	T	W	T	F	S
				1	2	3
4	5	6	7	8	9	10
11	12	13	14	15	16	17
18	19	20	21	22	23	24
25	26	27	28	29	30	31

26 Monday

27 Tuesday

28 Wednesday

1 Thursday

Selby Avenue

2 Friday

Boys' Wrestling Tournament
page 280

Saint Paul Chamber Orchestra
page 279

3 Saturday

Boys' Wrestling Tournament
page 280

Saint Paul Chamber Orchestra
page 279

4 Sunday

Saint Paul Politics for 2007

David Tilsen

This is guaranteed to be embarrassing. I am writing an article about the year 2007 in Saint Paul politics in January 2006, for an article in an almanac that will not appear until the following fall. Most of what I say will probably already be wrong by the time you read this, but hopefully you will only remember where I am right. The point here is not to be right, it is to be insightful or, barring that, entertaining.

The Mayor's Office

New Mayor Chris Coleman's honeymoon was shattered by the battle over the smoking ordinance. The Minnesota Legislature will not get involved (Saint Paul legislators are ducking under their desks whenever the issue of smoking is brought up). Mancini's on West Seventh has started refusing to have fundraising parties for politicians that support a smoking ban. Coleman has now joined Kelly in his pledge to veto any smoking ban that the city council passes. Restaurants and bars are benefiting from the Minneapolis smoking ban, and they want to keep it that way.

The Annes, Anne Hunt and Anne Mulholland, have fared differently in the mayor's office. Mulholland was a victim of the controversy and has "resigned" from office. Anne Hunt, on the other hand, is thriving and is now being talked about as a candidate for elected office.

Elections

Matt Entenza's race for attorney general will be successful. In the race for Entenza's 64A seat, there are over 200 candidates filing in the election. Candidate's forums consist of five-minute introductions from each candidate, and that's it. Because the audiences are leaving before the intros are half done, the advantage is going to those people whose names are at the beginning of the alphabet. This is credited for Don Arnosti's primary victory. The other primary winner is a real surprise: Green Party-endorsed candidate Jesse Mortenson. It appears that the Greens were the only party with a single candidate running, and their 4 percent was enough to give him second place in the primary. With two strong progressives in the race, the Republicans are talking about a write-in. Perhaps former Mayor Kelly?

The race between Finney and Fletcher for sheriff has become ugly and negative. Finney has tried to remain above it, but the attacks were just too personal, too mean, and too untrue (from his point of view) for him to ignore. As a result both candidates are spending a lot of money and time attacking each other. The voters are saying they don't like it, but it has replaced sports as the favorite water-cooler conversation in Saint Paul.

Superintendent of Schools

The new Superintendent started out with a lot of political support. She has used that support to mobilize community assistance to the schools. Although there has been some controversy surrounding some of her appointments, most reports are positive.

Sports

With the total collapse of the Wild, the Twins, the Vikings, and the Men's Gophers, Saint Paul is seeing a resurgence of interest in women's sports. Women's college basketball, golf, soccer, and now hockey are becoming revenue plusses rather than minuses for the U. They have not replaced men's sports, but they are drawing significant crowds. The Legislature once again refuses to build any of the three sports stadiums, and the Twins and the Vikings are daily issuing press releases about cities they might move to. Aside from Soucheray and Reusse, no one seems to notice.

Disclaimer

All prestidigitations, predictions, and statements here are totally the responsibility of the author, and not of the editors, publishers, spiritual guides, or internal demons of anyone else. Any similarities to actual events, persons, or tendencies are simply lucky guesses, or coincidences. If you want to complain, then go ahead, no one will be listening anyway. If you want to praise the author, however, you can read more of his drivel and comment on it on his blog at http://www.dtilsen.net/blog.

S	M	T	W	T	F	S
				1	2	3
4	5	6	7	8	9	10
11	12	13	14	15	16	17
18	19	20	21	22	23	24
25	26	27	28	29	30	31

James J. Hill came to Minnesota in 1855 when he was 17, from Ontario, Canada. At his death in 1916 he left behind his wife, Mary Theresa Mehegan, ten kids, and 63 million dollars.

5 Monday

6 Tuesday

7 Wednesday

Boys' Hockey Tournament
page 280

8 Thursday

International Women's Day

Boys' Hockey Tournament
page 280

Torre de San Miguel in District del Sol, Saint Paul's West Side

9 Friday   **Boys' Hockey Tournament**
                                              page 280

10 Saturday   **Boys' Hockey Tournament**
                                              page 280

11 Sunday   **Irish Celebration**
Daylight Saving Time Begins   *page 280*

Peaceful People in Saint Paul

Deborah McLaren

In a word,
Never let go on these three things:
Faith, hope, and love.
And know that the greatest of these
Will always be love.

Saint Paul in I Corinthians 13:1-13

Recovering from major surgery at Saint Joseph's hospital, I woke to see bombs going off on the television. For several days I was in pretty bad shape, lying in the hospital bed with tubes and monitors sticking out of me. In my haze I began to understand that the U.S. had gone to war with Iraq. In the middle of the night, I would wake from my drug-induced sleep only to see fiery images of Baghdad on the television screen. It was as if I'd slipped into another dimension and was stuck in some horrible video game. Where were the peacekeepers? Surely the whole world had not gone mad.

Shortly after being released from the hospital, I decided to join the peace activists on the Lake Street Bridge. I stood in the chilly winds over the Mississippi River with my family, waving anti-war posters and a Mother Earth flag. I felt a sense of assurance that there were, indeed, many other people in my community who shared my stance against the United States' invasion of another country. The profound act of neighbors coming together to advocate for peace was starting to spread through the city.

I wondered why Saint Paul had become such a visible place for peace activism. What made this city different? I needed to know. So I set out to try to learn who the folks were that were making this happen —and why Saint Paul?

I started by talking with people in my own neighborhood, Merriam Park. Krista Menzel, a web designer by trade who described herself as "very apolitical until the United States' invasion of Iraq," is one of the most visible peace organizers in our area. She explained how some neighbors met at an anti-war workshop led by Phil Steeger from Friends of a Non-Violent World (FNVW). In early 2003 these neighbors invited everyone in Merriam Park who had a peace sign on display at their home to a meeting at the local library. The turnout was so large the initial meeting had to move to Saint Mark's Church. That meeting spawned an active peace organization within the community as well as a growing network of other Neighbors for Peace organizations throughout the Twin Cities. The week after the bombing began, peace activists organized over 8,000 people marching to protest the war.

I tracked down Phil Steeger, who invited me to meet him at the Golden Thyme Coffeehouse on Selby Avenue—just down the street from his office. His organization, FNVW, has its roots in Quaker tradition and provides tools and training to help create community leadership in peace activism. A tall, lanky thirty-something with bright eyes and a warm smile for everyone, Phil talked about growing up in Minnesota and playing war games with his friends. The difference between then and now, he said, was that back then "we were actors playing games with our very real friends. Today children play technologically advanced video games that repeatedly de-humanize players and de-sensitize them to death and war."

I wondered why Saint Paul had become such a visible place for peace activism. What made this city different?

Phil thinks growing up with a strong Catholic background helped him understand that war simply stood against everything Jesus taught, especially love and peace. After working as an anti-war organizer around the country, he decided to move back home to Minnesota. Steeger feels that Saint Paul is like a bunch of small communities linked together and therefore much more manageable, and connected, than most large cities.

Saint Paulite Mel Duncan, an energetic fifty-three-year-old, has been an activist since his days at Macalester College. He is the founder of several nonprofit organizations, including the international Non-Violent Peace Force (NP). NP sends unarmed team members to areas like Sri Lanka and Palestine to protect human rights, deter violence, and help create space for local peacemakers to carry out their work. Duncan's work has grown from its rather dowdy first office on Front Avenue to an international federation of ninety member organizations from around the world with a presence at the United Nations.

Duncan doesn't see his work as peace activism alone. He sees peace, justice, and protecting the environment as part of the same

The Lake Street Bridge or "Peace Bridge"

cloth. As a father to several children, including some with disabilities, Duncan says he has seen how his work has created tangible results in real people's lives. He believes that getting a good education is a big part of our ability to advocate for ourselves and others. "Seeing the positive results of the work of so many people I know," Duncan says, "serves as a strong antidote to despair."

The long history of social activism in Saint Paul, according to Duncan, is due to a number of factors: from immigrants coming to escape oppression and military conscription, to a strong sense of community that was translated into the Farmer Labor Association, unions, and various other socialist movements. He also pointed out our lineage of strong progressive leadership in the area—Floyd Olson, Elmer Benson, Nellie Stone Johnson, Gene McCarthy, Katie McWatt, Roy Wilkins, Ric Cardenas, Bill Wilson, Paul Wellstone, Ellen Anderson, the Coleman family (Nick Sr., our current Mayor Chris), Elona Street Stewart, and Mee Moua, to name a few.

My pursuit of peace activists in Saint Paul has helped me move past that nightmarish vision of bombs over Baghdad. Instead, I'm seeing a dream shared by our neighbors and friends: to create a safe space for people to express their concerns as well as a belief and commitment in nonviolent conflict resolution and the right of all people to live in honor and dignity.

MoMs
IN REAL ESTATE
Intelligent Buying • Creative Selling

Seanne and Tasha

Moms in Real Estate are Tasha Merritt and Seanne Thomas. Both Tasha and Seanne are committed to and engaged in the Saint Paul community.

Before becoming a real estate agent nine years ago, Tasha was a case manager for the public housing sector. She teaches for the Home Stretch Program in Saint Paul and Burnsville and volunteers monthly to support Women Venture, Maxfield Elementary PTO, and Community Neighborhood Housing Service. Tasha Lives in the Hamline-Lexington neighborhood.

Seanne lives, works, and plays on the East Side of Saint Paul. She says a family that plays together stays together, and is actively involved as a volunteer board member at the local YMCA. She's also a volunteer board member of her local East Side Neighborhood Development Center.

Moms in Real Estate uses an innovative approach to real estate by creating an environment where parents, children, and real estate can find balance with each other. Moms in Real Estate is guided by three principles: real estate is a family affair, and Tasha and Seanne encourage their clients to include their family in the process; the definition of family is ever-changing and can range from a single person to an extended family and anything in between; access to decent, affordable housing is a right and not a privilege and so they empower their clients with knowledge of the process and advocate for their interests. Tasha and Seanne don't just want to sell you a house today—they want to build long-lasting relationships built on hard work, honesty, and integrity.

These philosophies lend themselves to the success of Moms in Real Estate—they consistently rank in the top 50 percent of real estate professionals in the Twin Cities Metro area.

Contact them at momsinrealestate.com or 651.224.4321.

The first paved street in Saint Paul was Third
Street (present-day Kellogg Blvd.). In 1873 it
was paved with pine blocks.

MARCH

S	M	T	W	T	F	S
				1	2	3
4	5	6	7	8	9	10
11	12	13	14	15	16	17
18	19	20	21	22	23	24
25	26	27	28	29	30	31

12 Monday

13 Tuesday

14 Wednesday

15 Thursday

Gingko—Come for Coffee and Sandwiches, Stay for Folk and Jazz Music

---

16 Friday

---

17 Saturday

Saint Patrick's Day

Saint Patrick's Day Parade

Irish Celebration

Saint Patrick's Day 33rd Annual Irish Ceili Dance
Randolph Heights Elementary School

Saint Patrick's Day Irish Ceili Dance
CSPS

pages 279–280

---

18 Sunday

The Houses are Still There

Tom Lewis

This is the street where
enigmatic Bill Lewis boarded,
must have worked alongside
one of Katie's brothers
at a metalworker's shop nearby.

She and her mother, the rest of the family,
lived on the same street, a block down.
All you see now: industrial sand
and clapboard, bricks and steel siding.
The houses are still there.

North up the bluff,
on the other side of the tracks,
another one of her brothers, Peter
Proetz, rolled cigars and packed
them in light wood boxes,
sold them out from the back
door porch; later, from a small
out-building behind—
his house is still there.

Do we feel some 1890s romance,
like a distant heat, coming off this information?
Some warmth out of old stoves lighting
another winter red amid Saint Paul's
working-class immigrant families,
a trolley-ride east, down Dayton's Bluff?
You would ride past the mansion
at the top of the hill, where
Katie was a domestic in 1893 and '94,
after she'd given up (or lost)
her job as a seamstress.

How much are these people,
their names, their addresses
and occupations, as present
as the smoke and dropped ash
from one of Peter's cigars now?
They are unreclaimable.
The red glowing end snuffed out.

As are Katie's thoughts the first time
she laid eyes on Harry or Clifford's workmate,
Bill Lewis, the orphan from Racine—
our records stop with him, we can't even say
how he wound up in Saint Paul,
let alone if he was English, Irish,
of unnamed Continental stock.
He starts from nothing.
First in Racine, then in the Twin Cities,
his name as blank as any old John Smith.

Did she wonder if her mother
and the family would approve
of her seeing a boy not a German?

The houses are still there.
The handwork's all gone or unlabelled.
Nothing left of how they all felt
some randomly chosen winter day
in the middle 1890s, around the corner
from East Seventh Street and down the road
from the meeting hall and a few of the saloons
a fellow could drench his workman's thirst in,
after laying burnt-red brick
or turning hot metal bars
into the frame of a gate or lattice,
an axle or the spokes of a wheel.

Saint Paulites fired the first and last shots of World War II for the U.S. The first shot was by Naval reservists from the destroyer *U.S.S. Ward*. The last shot was fired from the heavy naval cruiser *U.S.S. Saint Paul*.

MARCH

S	M	T	W	T	F	S
				1	2	3
4	5	6	7	8	9	10
11	12	13	14	15	16	17
18	19	20	21	22	23	24
25	26	27	28	29	30	31

19 Monday

20 Tuesday

21 Wednesday

Spring Equinox

22 Thursday

George's Shoe and Leather Repair on Grand Avenue

| **23 Friday** | Saint Paul Chamber Orchestra |
| | *page 279* |

24 Saturday	Saint Paul Chamber Orchestra
	Spring Flower Show Begins
	pages 279–280

25 Sunday

Watermelon Hill

Linda Back McKay

"Close the door and never look back.
This is finished for you now."
—Sister Marie Dolores

After she got herself in trouble, they sent her
away to Watermelon Hill, which was not really
its name, but what the boys yelled to the swollen girls
who were to come due at that home for unwed mothers.
A crucifix glared from the roof.
Laurel Taylor was not her real name.
What was real was absolved by Mother
Superior with a flap of her cloak.
Under the Immaculate Heart of Mary
was posted a litany of daily chores.
Miles of buffed linoleum, bars on the windows,
Dr. Crutchfield on Wednesdays, jelly jars
filled with vitamins. The tables were set for forty
or so depending on who was in labor.
The tuna casseroles smelled like bleach.
Girls back from the hospital sat on donut pillows.
Days passed and the moon sickened.

Laurel Taylor, on her horrible cot with the stars
burning inside her, tried to pray.
It was best to give up your baby, not see or hold it.
It was best to place your baby, make a plan for it.

Laurel Taylor tried to pray in the chapel,
her cardigan sweater open like a gate.
She fought to be good, to give her blood to some
nice family, to cleanse a child from her name.
Laurel Taylor tried to keep the monsters away
but under some god's baleful eye they rose

in a spine-cramping pain that was only the start
of the tearing off.

She lost her son in that war. Wading in water,
being able to see her feet again, she knew there would be
no anointing, no extreme unction.
After signing the surrender, she knew
the penance is fault and the loss is eternal.

River Woman and Her Dog Sculpture in District del Sol
Sculpture Designed by Amy Cordova, Mosaic Designed by Laura LaBlanc

S	M	T	W	T	F	S
				1	2	3
4	5	6	7	8	9	10
11	12	13	14	15	16	17
18	19	20	21	22	23	24
25	26	27	28	29	30	31

Saint Paul's population reached a maximum of 313,000 people in 1960.

26 Monday

27 Tuesday

28 Wednesday

29 Thursday

Sledding Fun near the Highland Water Towers

30 Friday

31 Saturday

Mawlid Al-Nabi

Cesar Chavez's Birthday

The Minnesota Opera
Lakmé
page 280

1 Sunday

April Fool's Day

Palm Sunday

The Minnesota Opera
Lakmé
page 280

Rondo Oral History

Oral History is the spoken word in print. Oral histories are personal memories shared from the perspective of the narrator. By means of recorded interviews, oral histories collect spoken memories and personal commentaries of historical significance. These interviews are transcribed verbatim and minimally edited for readability. The greatest appreciation is gained when one can read an oral history aloud.

Kate Cavett, oral historian,
HAND in HAND Productions

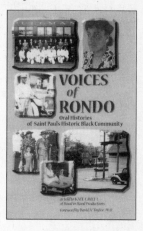

The following oral history is excerpted from Voices of Rondo: Oral Histories of Saint Paul's Historic Black Community *and is used by permission.* Voices of Rondo *won a 2006 Minnesota Book Award.*

Deborah Gilbreath Montgomery

My name is Debbie Gilbreath Montgomery. I grew up at 978 Saint Anthony, which is on the corner of Saint Anthony and Chatsworth. I was adopted by my grandparents, Isabella Gertrude Gilbreath, whom I called Mama, and Elbert Gilbreath, whom I called Dad.

Back then our neighborhood was a village. If you did something wrong or said something out of line or didn't respect your elders, you were going to be disciplined. You probably got lickings before you got home, and then when you got home you

Deb Montgomery

got another one. So it was a strong village environment, and everybody looked out for each other's family. If you needed something, you could holler across the street. If you needed a couple of eggs, or some milk, everybody kind of shared, Whites and Blacks together. It was a really close-knit community. It was a really loving community. People cared about you. They were concerned about your success.

Oxford Playground was a block away from our house. Back then it was a swamp. Bill Peterson was a twenty-one-year-old Marine who had just got out of the service. And he's got this playground that was a swamp. All it had on it was a little old warming house along with a merry-go-round and six swings. Here he's got all these little Black kids and a few White kids and he's sitting down there trying to teach us how to play ball. We learned how to play T-ball and softball and baseball.

I was a jock. I was very athletic and had a lot of energy. I was a little wiry thing. Down at Oxford, you had Dave Winfield and Paul Moliter. Bill Peterson was the baseball coach of the boys' Attucks Brooks–Legion All-State baseball team. Paul Moliter and Dave Winfield and all those guys, they all played on those teams, and they all came through Oxford.

Because it was a swamp and the field was not real good, nobody would come out and scrimmage our girls' team. A lot of the other rec centers wouldn't come and play us in our park because we didn't have a good field, so all of our games were away and a lot of our parents didn't have cars. The girls' softball team would scrimmage the boys' Attucks Brooks baseball team. Dave Winfield was the pitcher then and Paul was shortstop. We'd all be playing ball, and these guys were throwing that ball in there like they were throwing to guys! Anyway, I ended up being one heck of a softball player. I'd hit the ball Dave was pitching, and I'd just cream it! To this day, David'll say, "Boy, she just killed my pitches!" I was a good softball and basketball player and I ran track. I was a speed skater.

In the wintertime, Bill would get out there and flood this area for us to skate on. He just kept us engaged. Then he'd go out and beg, borrow, and steal skates so we all could skate. I must have had the biggest feet, because I ended up getting black speed skates. The other girls had white figure skates and the boys had hockey skates.

For the Winter Carnival, they would always have the races out at Como Park, and so he'd put all of us in his little red 1954 station wagon and drag us out to Como. We'd get out there, and I didn't know how to speed skate when I first started, so I literally outran people around the ice on these speed skates. Finally, they took an interest in me and saw that I had potential, and Bill got a couple of guys to work with me, to try to teach me how to stride and how to skate. I became really,

really good. I got all kinds of blue rib-
bon medals from skating at the Winter Carnival. I beat Mary Meyers, who
tied for the 1968 silver medal, two out
of three heats in the tryouts.

In High School

They had two speed skating clubs
that were close to us. The Blue Line
Speed Skating Club, which was kind
of a high-buck private speed skating
club on this side of town, and East
Side Shop Pond, over on the East
Side. Because the Blue Line Club was
over here, Bill took me over to try out
for the club, but they weren't letting
any Black kids in. The East Side Shop
Pond would take me in the club, but
we didn't have any transportation to get there. To this day, Peterson
says, "What could you have done if you had had any kind of training?"
I was obviously an athlete before my time.

There were so many things going on back then in the 1960s, that
skating wasn't an important deal. The sports part was secondary to
people getting the right to vote. You know, we didn't get the voting
rights bill in until 1965. We didn't get open housing in Saint Paul until
1960. So there were just tons of issues back then, and sports was an
outlet for me. It felt good to succeed, but I never dwelled very much on
"this is an opportunity missed."

When I was maybe thirteen, Allie May Hampton was a good friend
of mine, and when I say friend, she was an older woman that was real
active in the NAACP. She was just a gem. She saw I was a rabble-rouser
and intelligent and articulate, and she got me active in the NAACP.
She was getting us involved in the political process, getting us to understand the issues that were going on back then. This was in the late
'50s, early '60s. She took me to my first NAACP conference. After I
came back from the conference, they made me the president of the
youth group.

I got all the kids involved in the NAACP youth group. We had 650 kids
in it back then, because we had tons of kids and there were a lot of issues
going on. I got really involved with the civil rights movement after that

first conference and meeting all the kids from the South and the East and the West. Listening to what was going on down South, none of that was going on here like it was in the South. Our schools were integrated.

When the civil rights movement started they had buses going down to Mississippi and Alabama. In Minnesota, we were good for sending White activists down, and I was one of the Black youth that went down there.

Mama was scared to death because she was from Starkville, Kentucky, and Dad was from Lubbock, Texas, so they knew about the South. I didn't have a clue about what was going on, other than I knew I was fighting for a cause, and not realizing that people were killing people. I mean, I did realize it, but I didn't think it could happen to me.

I went on the bus with a lot of White kids and White adults and a few civil rights folks, and we got down there and we demonstrated and then got on a bus and came back. We were fighting for voting rights. I was probably about fifteen then. My parents were just scared to death, but I was just kind of a freewheeling kid. "I gotta go do the right thing for the right reason."

I became involved in the NAACP youth branch at the national level. We had to go down to Chicago, Atlanta, or Baltimore for conferences. Dad, he'd get me a pass and put me on the train. Dad and Mama never rode the train in their whole life, but because Dad worked with the railroad they could get passes. He'd take me down to the depot. He'd hook me up with a porter, one of his porter friends, and the porter would put me on the train. They'd usually put me in the food car because they could feed me there and make sure I was taken care of. Then when I got to Chicago and had to transfer, they'd take me by the hand and take me to another train and hand me over to another porter and say, "This is Gil's daughter. She's on her way to Baltimore, and she'll be comin' back at such-and-such a time. If you're on the train back, tell 'er where to meet you when you let 'er off. Let 'er know that you'll pick 'er up when she comes back."

When I was seventeen I was elected to the National Board of Directors for the NAACP. As I said, at fifteen and sixteen, I had gotten really active in national youth movement, so I made friends with the children of the national NAACP leaders. I was just a rabble-rouser. We were all active in the national youth movement, and so they're telling their dads, "Oh, man! She's neat, man. She's smart. She's articulate. She's from Minnesota." They thought Minnesota was off the world. So the kids got together at the national youth branch and said to me, "We're going to run you for the national board." They got together and they rallied all the kids together, and they got their parents together.

If you look at the NAACP history you'll see that at the age of seventeen, I ran nationally, at large. I got elected to the national board of directors, with Roy Wilkins. I mean, all of the people that you see in there, and here's this little seventeen-year-old girl out of Minnesota that's sitting at the board with all these big shots.

I was on a mission. I was fighting for civil rights. I was speaking up for people. Trying to get voting rights for the people. I mean, these Black folks, they were in the army, they were serving their country and yet they didn't have the right to vote? If you look at the history, Blacks were on the front lines and getting killed in larger numbers, and they didn't have the right to vote. They didn't have the right to own property. They had the poorest jobs.

On the national board it was interesting to listen to the discussions. I mean, you had lawyers, bankers, politicians. You had lawyers that were talking about legal issues. Thurgood Marshall, how he was going to deal with the legal issues taken to the Supreme Court. What's going on in Missouri? What's going on in Kansas? They had huge issues, and you're sitting there and you're listening to the discussion and listening to how they're going to handle it, who they were going to target. They were killing young people that were going down there in cars, similar to what I was doing.

I was kind of blessed. I marched from Selma to Montgomery with Dr. King, and I was in the March on Washington when he gave that "I Have a Dream" speech. There were just so many major issues going on back then, I didn't have time to think about little things. My mind was always out here. I'd come home and the adults here were always talking about how bright I was. I wasn't any brighter. I was just kind of active in everything, trying to figure out how you make things work.

I look at Mama and Dad and the folks on Rondo. They did not get high-paying jobs, but never once did I feel that we were poor. There was richness in our house. There was a strong faith in our house. My faith has been the stronghold in my life. I don't look at the downside. I just saw the up, and I wanted to help the next generation move up.

April

The Minnesota Opera *Lakmé* Apr. 1, 3, 5, and 7

American Craft Council Craft Show Apr. 13–15

Saint Paul Chamber Orchestra Apr. 14, 20, 21, 22, 27, 28

Saint Paul Art Crawl Apr. 20–22

25th Annual Minneapolis-Saint Paul International Film Festival Mid-Apr.

Minnesota Dance Festival Apr. 26–29

Downtown Saint Paul Farmers' Market Sat. and Sun., Apr. 28–Nov. 11

Spring Flower Show Through Apr. 29

See pages 280–281 for more information on April events.

Harriet Bishop became the first public school teacher in Minnesota in 1847 when she started a public Sunday school (a bit of an oxymoron).

APRIL

S	M	T	W	T	F	S
1	2	3	4	5	6	7
8	9	10	11	12	13	14
15	16	17	18	19	20	21
22	23	24	25	26	27	28
29	30					

2 Monday

3 Tuesday

First Day of Passover

The Minnesota Opera
Lakmé
page 280

4 Wednesday

5 Thursday

The Minnesota Opera
Lakmé
page 280

Marjorie McNeely Conservatory at Como Park, Open 365 Days a Year

6 Friday

Good Friday

7 Saturday

The Minnesota Opera
Lakmé
page 280

8 Sunday

Easter

City of Seasons

The Truth about Gardening in Saint Paul

Melissa Mierva

Saint Paul is positioned within our galaxy at precisely the perfect distance from the sun to have been blessed with more seasons than anywhere else in the universe.

Let us begin with the "mail-order/windowsill-vegetable-growing season" (Jan./Feb.). Saint Paul gardeners are fanatics. We pre-plan and pre-grow at subzero temperatures, thumbing through endless seed catalogs, planning the perfect border for our boulevard plot. We grow tomatoes from seed in our windowsills or under bright lights in our basements, eyeing the plants with delicious anticipation while transferring the laundry from washer to dryer. When we're not perusing the seed catalogs, you can find some of us at a nearby park digging in the snow for the Saint Paul Winter Carnival Medallion. As we dig furiously with our shovels, we are reminded yet again of the gardens we yearn to be in. Our shovels never really make it to the shed.

Next comes the "premature-uncoverers-of-straw-and-leaves-looking-for-that-first-sign-of-life season" (Mar./Apr.). We are the folks that have no patience. We are found sneaking out into the yard at odd hours dressed in snow boots and mittens, rake in hand, in search of that first miniscule green shoot sticking out about a quarter inch from the frozen ground. When we see that no one is watching, the hunt begins. At first, it is slow and clumsy but then rapidly builds into a frenzy of flying leaves and snow. Once we've found that first shoot, it is difficult to stop there and before we know it, we have uncovered the entire length of the garden. Embarrassed and completely satisfied, we replace the leaves as best we can, hoping to cover up any tell tale signs of tampering, and retreat back into the great indoors.

Then we have the "quick-get-it-into-the-ground-there's-only-three-months-before-it-snows-again season" (May/June). There's something about the smell of unfrozen earth that drives us wild. We flock in hoards to the nearest garden center to spend most of our tax return on flowers, vegetables, trellises, manure, and so on. Before you know it, Saint Paul has been transformed into a garden paradise. Geraniums and impatiens abound. You can see stacks of pot-shaped clumps of dirt held together by the roots of last years' arrangements piled up next to the

homemade compost bin in the back yard. It's finally here, the chance to make all kinds of extra work for ourselves.

And so this is quickly followed by the "where-did-all-these-weeds-come-from/did-I-really-plant-all-these-green-beans? season" (July/Aug.). Here we have gardens where most of the flowers have completely disappeared under lush stalks of nettle, motherwort, tall native grasses, and beautiful ground covers that you swear you never planted. You can thank the birds that you have attracted to your bird feeders for many of these. I especially like the wild poppies that have come up all over my vegetable garden. They go well with the chamomile that have sprung up everywhere. And what about all those green beans? Last year I had to climb a ladder and reach up with the grilling tongs to get them down. I swear each bean can grow to maturity in less than five minutes.

Now comes "the-State-Fair-is-over/bring-in-the-grill-and-cover-up-the-plants-we're-heading-inside season" (Sept./Oct.). Some folks actually do this. But for us die-hard gardeners this is the best time to be outside. Everything looks great. Even the marigold plants are big, bushy, and full of flowers. And if you had a heart to leave the nettle and motherwort plants to thrive in the hot sun, you can get a bountiful harvest for medicinal purposes or use the chamomile for some great wintertime tea. And by the way, the folks who started their tomato plants in the kitchen windowsill, well, they've been back in the kitchen now for the past two weeks making their umpteenth batch of tomato sauce.

Finally, we arrive at the "okay-I'm-pooped-let's-just-rake-the-leaves-into-the-garden-and-take-care-of-it-next-year season" (Nov./Dec.). This is when we accept the fact that there are already three inches of snow out there and we can't get into the ground anyway. We must put it and ourselves to rest for a while. The holidays come and go and before you know it, we're back to the seed catalogs and arranging our pots on the windowsill, carefully tending our tomato seedlings. We dream of a boulevard full of color or the biggest tomato on the block. Are we passionate? You betcha!

Central Library, completed in 1917, is located across the street from Rice Park and today holds approximately 350,000 books.

APRIL

S	M	T	W	T	F	S
1	2	3	4	5	6	7
8	9	10	11	12	13	14
15	16	17	18	19	20	21
22	23	24	25	26	27	28
29	30					

9 Monday

10 Tuesday

Last Day of Passover

11 Wednesday

12 Thursday

The Grand Ole Creamery Makes its Own Ice Cream

13 Friday

American Craft Council Craft Show
page 280

14 Saturday

American Craft Council Craft Show
page 280

Saint Paul Chamber Orchestra
page 281

15 Sunday

American Craft Council Craft Show
page 280

Taxes—Part of the American Dream

Wa Yang Thao Sees Life in America as Chance at Success

Sao Sue Jurewitsch

When he first arrived in the U.S., Wa Yang Thao had planned to come to America to just visit his oldest daughter and her husband. That was in 2001. He and his wife, Xai Moua Thao, have not left since; they became permanent residents in October of 2004. It was not an easy decision for Wa Yang and Xai Moua, mainly because their younger children are still living in Laos. At first, the couple wanted to return, but relatives in the Twin Cities did not want them to go. Finally, Ma Yang's daughter's family was able to sponsor them. Now they dream of a better future in Minnesota. While a chore for most people, filing their first income tax return has the couple excited. It helped that Cheu Lee, owner of Lee's Tax and Payroll Services, processed their return for free. An immigrant himself, Mr. Lee was impressed by the couple's positive outlook.

> **"I worked very hard in Laos, but I never could make any money. In America, if I will work as hard as in Laos—and I will—I am sure I can own my own home."**

At almost fifty years old, Mr. Thao is not a young man anymore. Still, he is full of optimism about his family's future. He is used to hard work. In Laos, he grew vegetables for sale at the local market. Often, he had to work fourteen-hour days, only to earn less than a dollar. Since October, when he got his work permit, he has been employed in an assembly plant putting CD covers together. He earns nine dollars per hour. His wife works at the same plant, making a little less than that. While this may not seem like much to most people, to Wa Yang Thao and his wife it represents hope: hope to one day bring their children to this country, hope to buy a home for themselves. Already, they were able to move out of their daughter's house and find their own place to live. Mr. Thao was also able to save enough money to buy a car.

Coming from a poor country, the Thaos find America not only a land of opportunity; they see life here filled with luxuries only the wealthy

Wa Yang and Xai Moua Thao with Their Tax Preparer

enjoy in Laos. Where they lived, people had no running water and no sewer system. Here they enjoy having their own bathroom, where they can just open the faucet to get water. Wa Yang is still amazed by how he can just turn on the heat and the apartment gets warm. These may be everyday conveniences for most Americans, but to him they are luxuries to be enjoyed and shared with the rest of his family.

Wa Yang Thao hopes that he will be able to bring his remaining five children to Minnesota in the coming year. After that, he plans to work as hard as he can to build a better life. "I feel strong enough to work, and I will work as long as I can," he says. Then he added, "I worked very hard in Laos, but I never could make any money. In America, if I will work as hard as in Laos—and I will—I am sure I can own my own home. I will work as long as I am able to do that."

Those who have gone through it know it is not easy to leave one's home country. Still, generations of immigrants have come to America through the centuries to do exactly what the Thao family is doing—working hard to build a new life in a new world.

The first professional baseball team in Saint Paul, the Saint Paul Saints, started their first season in 1884.

APRIL

S	M	T	W	T	F	S
1	2	3	4	5	6	7
8	9	10	11	12	13	14
15	16	17	18	19	20	21
22	23	24	25	26	27	28
29	30					

16 Monday

17 Tuesday

18 Wednesday

19 Thursday

Jonathan Padelford Moored at Harriet Island on the Mississippi

20 Friday

Saint Paul Art Crawl

Saint Paul Chamber Orchestra

page 281

21 Saturday

Saint Paul Art Crawl

Saint Paul Chamber Orchestra

page 281

22 Sunday

Earth Day

Saint Paul Art Crawl

Saint Paul Chamber Orchestra

page 281

Crossing the River

Jami Leigh

I was born and raised in Saint Paul by two Saint Paul natives (my mom and dad) in a comfortable home between Como Park and the State Fairgrounds. So you might say I grew up between a park and a fair place. A fresh-faced Saint Paulite girl with all the joys of Saint Paul before me, I grew up (more stories on that part some other time), ran off to college (even more stories on that!), then returned to Saint Paul for a two-year stint as a new graduate in an old apartment on Western Avenue by the railroad tracks (yes, yes, stories by the trainload . . .). But then, in a wild moment of reckless abandon, I moved away. Well, okay, a few thousand moments . . . actually, it took about a day and a half to move. And not just anywhere, no, I moved to . . . Minneapolis. Yes, me a "Saint Pauly" girl in the land of "all the way over there?"

Several years after that I continued my westward ho movement into Bloomington, where I am now fairly firmly planted while raising two children of my own. But the thing about growing up in Saint Paul is that you never forget it or the hold it has on you. So I return every once in awhile to remember, I return to see what has changed, and I return to experience those unique joys that only Saint Paul can provide—which brings me to my list. Here are some of those joys that will get me to cross back over the river, some of the many reasons to return to Saint Paul:

1. **Cafe Latté on Grand Avenue.** Yes, this place serves delectable desserts with which even many Minneapolitans are familiar, but I make special journeys to Cafe Latté for the absolutely *best* vegetarian chili. Anywhere. Ever. Try it sometime and see what you think. Just leave some for me . . .

2. **Grand Ole Creamery—this is really part two of one, because it's the perfect place to go after Cafe Latté, and it's just down the street.** My kids and I have spent several years now trying all the assorted ice cream shops available in the Twin Cities and this is still our/my hands up holding-that-freshly-made-waffle-cone favorite! They have so many wonderful flavors of ice cream that they can't make them all every day. But they will offer to take your name, number, and favorite flavor and call you when yours is available.

3. **Circus Juventas.** If you haven't yet seen one of their shows, you have been missing some of the most spellbinding and inspiring theatrical/acrobatic performances. These circus-school performers, children from ages four to eighteen, put on such spectacular shows you just have to experience them to believe them. Thanks, Circus Juventas, for "Swash" and "Drynwych!"

4. **The Winter Carnival and those ice palaces.** I know, I know, you don't create and build palaces, ice block by ice block every year, but when you do, you bring such extra delight and magic to winter on top of the already joyful and "looking on the bright side of cold" attitude that the Winter Carnival encourages. That last palace was especially impressive: lights, music, and ice glowing, making spirits bright. Brilliant! Just waiting with icy breath to see what you come up with next.

5. **Como Park.** Saint Paul, I am so proud of you for injecting all the wonderful improvements into this accessible-to-all treasure in the heart of Saint Paul. The conservatory, the Japanese gardens, the zoo, the lake and trails, the pavilion, the carousel, and the golf course (which, when my dad's not on it golfing, doubles as a skiing/sledding recreation area—you kids *do* still sled down some of those gigantic hills, don't you?)

6. **The State Fair.** All right, there's always this bit of debate about the State Fair actually residing in Falcon Heights, not Saint Paul. But the way I see it, I could walk a few blocks west from my childhood home in Saint Paul and I would be standing in the fairgrounds. I went to high school in Saint Paul—the other side of the fairgrounds from where I lived—and to get home to Saint Paul from there, I walked through the fairgrounds. So I'm counting it as Saint Paul's own. This is one of the biggest reasons we Westerners cross the river. More fun, food, frivolity, and "free" things packed in days than pretty much anywhere else in the country—hey, maybe even the world . . . I know there are about a million of you out there that agree. See you there in August!

7. **Grand Avenue.** Grand Old Day or any old day, the shops are unique, the walking is pleasant, the food and drink choices tantalizing. I won't be able to name all of the attractions, of course. You'll just have to stroll down the avenue and find your favorites.

Grand Avenue near Red Balloon Bookstore

8. **Museums.** The Children's, Science, and History Center museums are all worthy of an all-day trip. I'm a bit past the Children's Museum stage with my kids now, but I really appreciated this place where they could freely explore through touch when they were younger. The Science Museum is fascinating for all ages—I even spent the night there once with my daughter! (No, we didn't lose track of time and get locked in . . . it was a special sleepover event.) I've enjoyed many family days at the History Center appreciating the hands-on activities as well as the exhibits and actors portraying "living" characters from the past.

9. **Music.** The Ordway and the Fitzgerald are beautiful venues for music lovers like me. And sorry, Minneapolis, but it is no contest which arena makes me sing. I think the Xcel Center is acoustically superior with staging and seating that is much more concert goer-friendly than the Target Center.

I suppose it's time for number 10, since most lists are all about the top 10, aren't they? But number 10 is hard to say because there are so many more reasons than ten to cross the river and return to Saint Paul. If I had to pick just one more, though, it would be family. And not just my own, some of whom are still strongly rooted there, but the family that is Saint Paul. For Saint Paul is a community that continues to change, but somehow stays the same, with deep convictions and time-tested traditions, with so much to offer, and a spirit that always seems to speak softly with a smile, "Welcome home, we're glad you're here."

Love Letter

Karin Simoneau

I hadn't spent much time in the city before the day I walked into the character-filled apartment in the red-brick fourplex on Grand Avenue. It was spring. Moving to Saint Paul from Uptown seemed a drastic change for me, yet I was ready for change, ready to be away from the claustrophobic setting that was driving me mad, driving me away. It was happenstance. A friend had a friend who needed a roommate. I had always thought Saint Paul was beautiful, but also uneventful and dry and family oriented—not exactly what I was looking for at the time.

So with a deep breath and slight hesitation, I made the move, not knowing if or when I would grow to like the city. As the late spring snow melted away and the brown ever so slowly turned to green, and the sun began to warm and light my way, I started to venture out. I walked. I walked down Summit, admiring the homes and the architecture and the foliage; walked down Grand, appreciating the quaint shops and not-so-quaint shops, grabbing my morning coffee from any number of places along the way; and I walked along the winding roads and leafy streets and neighborhoods that encompassed my street. The college students from Saint Thomas and Macalester lit up the streets and made me reminisce about my college days, filling me with a sweet sadness and longing, and yet a kind of hopefulness and maturity. It didn't take long. It happened that spring. I fell in love with Saint Paul and knew I would not be leaving anytime soon. Like an old, comfortable sweater or a scent that sends you, I felt a sense of security. I had found my home.

The score of the first professional baseball game in Saint Paul between the Saint Paul Saints and the Minneapolis Millers was 11 to 3, the win going to Saint Paul.

APRIL

S	M	T	W	T	F	S
1	2	3	4	5	6	7
8	9	10	11	12	13	14
15	16	17	18	19	20	21
22	23	24	25	26	27	28
29	30					

23 Monday

24 Tuesday

25 Wednesday

26 Thursday

Minnesota Dance Festival
page 281

27 Friday

Minnesota Dance Festival

Saint Paul Chamber Orchestra

page 281

28 Saturday

Minnesota Dance Festival

Saint Paul Chamber Orchestra

Downtown Saint Paul Farmers' Market

page 281

29 Sunday

Minnesota Dance Festival

Downtown Saint Paul Farmers' Market

Spring Flower Show ends

pages 280–281

The Best Park in All Saint Paul

Judith Niemi

We've got many great parks here for picnics, birding, or hunting for Winter Carnival Medallions, but there's only one in which a dog can race around off-leash (legally), and be welcomed. It's Arlington/Arkwright Off-Leash Dog Area, completely fenced, and run by the Saint Paul Parks and Recreation with help from a great bunch called ROMP, Responsible Owners of Mannerly Pets, who've made our region tops for urban dog parks. I'm writing this on behalf of my friend Bailey. She's a German short-haired pointer, and she has strong feelings about Arkwright, but lacking opposable thumbs, hasn't a chance of writing about it. (We call it just "ARKwright," to fit with, "Do you want to Bark in Park? At Arkwright?") So I'm telling you why she loves this park passionately, and I also think it's a hoot.

We go in one of the north gates (latching the gate carefully behind us) to a big, open field covered with wood chips, so it isn't as muddy as you'd think. There are always at least a dozen dogs romping around. The big game here in The Commons is dog tennis, and there are always two or three green tennis balls lying around. Finding them is another good game for hunting dogs—and leaving your own dog toys home means no private property issues. We just bring along the Chucker—with my lousy throwing arm I need this faux-atlatl to keep up my end of the game with an athlete like Bailey.

There are usually other pointers and Labs and golden retrievers playing tennis, too, and Bailey particularly likes horning in on their games. With her lanky Marlene Dietrich legs (way longer than breed standard), she can beat out any golden retriever. We are teaching her "Take it to your new friend" so she brings the ball to the golden's person, who is flattered and pleased, and allows her into the game. Goldens are so easygoing that they never really mind. I have never seen dogs fight over the ball, even when they steal it from each other on the run—apparently a sort of dog hockey they all understand. Sometimes a border collie lurks and stares, and tries to round up the ballplayers, but they pay no attention.

Past the field there's an open bowl with a really steep hill. People don't race up and down it much, but the dogs do. In summer, the people sit on the hilltop in the lawn chairs and chat with strangers, pretending to admire each others' dogs, and beaming at their own. The dogs slurp the fresh water provided, and dance around, and meet each other more intimately. Smart owners move on soon, avoiding territoriality. There's a nice wooded area, with a wide wood-chip trail, and a lot of other paths that dogs have made for their own purposes. Here there are squirrels, or at least the idea of squirrels, so the hunting breeds have a lot of important and absorbing work to do.

Okay, dog parks aren't for everyone. Some people—including some dog trainers—dislike off-leash parks, worrying about dog fights, and it is true that really little dogs or fearful ones should not come.

Dogs simply have different play styles. Bailey doesn't like rough play, and the rambunctious ones leave her alone. Except—well, once, in winter; she wore her blaze-orange warm-up suit, looking very spiffy, and two bully-type dogs got quite growly with her. As soon as we took off the vest, they lost interest. We keep an eye out. Our policy is that when we see a rowdy gang of dogs, we move off to some other part of the park. If a really tough looking dog turns up—an intact male pit bull having a bad day, or any dog we mistrust—well, we just go home. The rules say if a dog can't play well with others, and gets aggressive, it has to leave, but we wouldn't count on that or take risks.

A dog park is a great thing, and not just for exercise, though even a little park like Arkwright (4.5 acres) sure provides that. It is just so interesting to the dogs. It gives them lots of new experiences, which dogs need for self-confidence. Temple Grandin, who uses her autism to understand animals' thinking and feeling, has said that in the past when everybody's dogs ran around loose, there were fewer neurotic

Arkwright Dog Park

and aggressive dogs, because they had a chance to work out their so-cial relationships and learn to handle conflict. Adolescent dogs can learn from their elders all the ways to defuse tense situations.

At Arkwright you can watch dogs enjoying each others' company, making judgments, working things out, and forming their own affinity groups—racers, wrestlers, hunters, herders, and those who just stick with their people. Bailey has met a white German shepherd of im-peccable manners, genial slow Newfies and Bernese mountain dogs, alarmingly nutty puppies, and lots of interesting blends. She likes wei-maraners and other pointers best. We've visited a few other parks in the Twin Cities Metro area; in one she thought the people and dogs a bit yuppy-ish and standoffish, but at Arkwright, the regulars, canine and human, are a nice, mostly gemütlich crowd.

At Arkwright you can watch dogs enjoying each others' company, making judgments, working things out . . .

Arkwright is just a few minutes' drive from downtown (at the corner of Arkwright and Arlington—near the Maryland exit on 35E). There are no parking or admission fees. The rules for dogs: be licensed and vaccinated; be controllable and come when called. We like Arkwright because it's such a good place to practice recall—Bailey, a bit of a rambler, has learned to leave even the most fascinating parts of the park because "Come" means getting bits of hot dogs (when no other dogs are near to get jealous). The basic rule for people: be responsible for your dog's behavior—and pick up the poop. To be good citizens of Arkwright—and Bailey is very much a rule-following, good-citizen sort of dog—you bring old plastic bags to replenish the several poop bag stations, and plastic jugs of water to share.

I think that's what Bailey would want to pass on. It's not that she wants to encourage lots of playmates; really, other dogs are never nearly as interesting as tennis balls and squirrels. Still, she loves their company, in a detached way—or maybe loves the audience—and she's better behaved around other dogs everywhere after becoming a regu-lar at Arkwright. It's a park that's mad fun for almost all dogs; it makes people smile, picking up this contagious joie de vivre—and it's educa-tional, for all of us.

May

Como Memorial Japanese Garden May 1–Sept. 30

Festival of Nations May 3–6

Cinco de Mayo May 5–6

The Minnesota Opera *The Marriage of Figaro* May 5, 6, 8, 10, and 12

Saint Paul Chamber Orchestra May 5, 10, 11, 13, 17, 18, 19, 25, and 26

Minnesota Bonsai Society Show May 12–13

Living Green Expo May 5–6

Summer Flower Show May 5–Sept. 30

Downtown Saint Paul Farmers' Market Saturdays and Sundays, Through Nov. 11

See pages 281–282 for more information on May events.

Some items invented in Saint Paul: the plastic drinking cup, Scotch tape, lithium-powered pacemaker, and the shopping bag.

MAY

S	M	T	W	T	F	S
		1	2	3	4	5
6	7	8	9	10	11	12
13	14	15	16	17	18	19
20	21	22	23	24	25	26
27	28	29	30	31		

30 Monday

1 Tuesday

2 Wednesday

3 Thursday

Festival of Nations
page 281

Blair Arcade Building on Selby Avenue

4 Friday

Festival of Nations
page 281

5 Saturday

Cinco de Mayo

Minnesota Bonsai Society Show
Living Green Expo
Saint Paul Chamber Orchestra
Downtown Saint Paul Farmers' Market

Festival of Nations
Summer Flower Show begins
Cinco de Mayo Festival
The Minnesota Opera
The Marriage of Figaro

pages 281–282

6 Sunday

Living Green Expo

Festival of Nations
Cinco de Mayo Festival
The Minnesota Opera
The Marriage of Figaro
Downtown Saint Paul Farmers' Market

pages 281–282

Cinco de Mayo . . .
What do We Celebrate?

Eva Palma

"Cinco de Mayo? . . . Well, I don't know what we celebrate on Cinco de Mayo." Answers like this one were given by most of the people I interviewed when I asked if they knew what the holiday was about. The American people I asked had no idea about the meaning of this big event, which is understandable, but the big surprise was that many Mexican people didn't know what Cinco de Mayo was about either.

Every year thousands of people from different cultures participate in this celebration. Just as the Latino community celebrates Thanksgiving here in the U.S., Americans also go to Cinco de Mayo parades in Minneapolis and Saint Paul, eat Mexican food, dance to tropical Latin music, and drink Mexican beer. So, right, given all of that, no wonder nobody cares about the historical meaning of this celebration.

We met María at a Mexican bakery and she gave us a closer answer: Cinco de Mayo is related to a big historical event." She was not really sure what happened on that date, May 5, but she made a good point, tellin me that Cinco de Mayo is celebrated mostly by Americans and Mexicans living in the U.S., and not by Mexicans living in Mexico. "The most important date for us in Mexico is Independence Day, which is on September 16," she said.

María is exactly right. Many Mexicans consider Cinco de Mayo a Chicano festivity, and in fact, they don't quite understand why the community celebrates this date with more enthusiasm than the actual Mexican independence day itself.

Guadalupe, another Mexican immigrant to Minnesota, gave us a much better answer: "Cinco de Mayo celebrates the battle of Puebla." Finally, someone not really lost in history! Yes, on May 5 of the year 1862, the Mexican Army defeated French forces in one of the many battles in the three-year war, which started when Mexico found itself struggling under the weight of an enormous budget deficit. In order to meet the basic needs of the country, in 1861 the government of Benito Juárez cancelled the payments of Mexico's foreign debt.

Try to be early so you don't miss the popular and delicious corn from El Burrito Mercado.

Spain, England, and France formed an alliance and invaded Mexico. Later on, this alliance was dissolved and the French Army, headed by Count Laurencez, was the only army that kept fighting. On May 5, 1862, the Mexican Army defeated the French in the town of Puebla, giving the entire country a renewed sense of pride.

Okay, now that we know a little bit more about the historical background of this celebration, we can just enjoy the great food, the contagious live music, and the whole party that will take place on Friday, May 5, and Saturday, May 6, in District del Sol on Saint Paul's West Side. There is plenty of fun for everyone but try to be early so you don't miss the popular and delicious corn from El Burrito Mercado.

For more information, visit www.districtdelsol.com/cinco.html.

Cinco de Mayo on Cesar Chavez Street on Saint Paul's West Side

Many famous people have visited Saint Paul over the years, including Sitting Bull in 1884, Susan B. Anthony, Mark Twain in 1882, Winston Churchill in 1901, and Fred Astaire—who danced at the Orpheum Theater when he was ten years old.

MAY

S	M	T	W	T	F	S
		1	2	3	4	5
6	7	8	9	10	11	12
13	14	15	16	17	18	19
20	21	22	23	24	25	26
27	28	29	30	31		

7 Monday

8 Tuesday

The Minnesota Opera
The Marriage of Figaro
page 282

9 Wednesday

10 Thursday

The Minnesota Opera
The Marriage of Figaro

Saint Paul Chamber Orchestra

page 282

Highland Movie Theater

11 Friday	**Saint Paul Chamber Orchestra** *page 282*

12 Saturday	**The Minnesota Opera** *The Marriage of Figaro* **Minnesota Bonsai Society Show** **Downtown Saint Paul Farmers' Market** *pages 281–282*

13 Sunday Mother's Day	**Saint Paul Chamber Orchestra** **Minnesota Bonsai Society Show** **Downtown Saint Paul Farmers' Market** *pages 281–282*

Como Lake and Lake Phalen

Teri J. Dwyer

Here in the Land of 10,000 Lakes, the most storied urban waters are probably Saint Paul's Como Lake, in the North End, and Lake Phalen, on the East Side. Both played important parts in the city's early growth and remain popular today.

The City of Saint Paul first became interested in Lake Phalen in 1869, when it began using the lake for the city's water supply. Legal rights to Phalen's waters were acquired in 1882; the lake continued to be the primary source of the city's water until 1913. In 1873, the city acquired 300 acres of land for $100,000 for the future Como Park. In 1899, it paid $22,000 for the acreage that would become Phalen Regional Park. Frederick Nussbaumer, superintendent of parks from 1891 to 1922, then hired landscape genius H. W. S. Cleveland to create the two parks. In designing Lake Phalen, Cleveland fashioned a landscape that provides links to the greater region through the city's streams and lakes. Today, Lake Phalen's trails connect on its southeast end to the Gateway Trail and the Bruce Vento Trail. At the north end of the lake, trails lead to Ramsey County's Round Lake and the Keller chain of lakes.

Como Pavilion

Initially, both parks were on the fringe of the city and were used by city residents chiefly as summer holiday and weekend destinations. In winter, Lake Phalen's ice was cut and delivered by ice vendors to Saint Paul residents' homes and fashioned into the Saint Paul Winter Carnival's impressive ice palaces and Rice Park ice sculptures. Vince Gillespie, who has worked as special services for the Parks and Recreation Department since 1972, says that the recent revival in ice palaces began with a castle built adjacent to Lake Phalen in 1986.

Gillespie has watched both parks grow and change. "Como Park is the second most visited destination in the state of Minnesota," he says, after the Mall of America. Como's amenities are distinctly urban: conservatory, zoo, golf course, picnic grounds. The park's old bandshell was renovated in the early 1990s and now boasts a deli, restaurant, and coffee shop. Phalen, in contrast, has shaggy upland woods, rolling hills, and a larger lake, which offers more shoreside amenities and superior fishing.

Both lakes can be fished from piers and boats. Their fishing reflects the difference in the parks' profiles: at Como, the fishing is urban and modest—"perch, that sort of thing"—while at Phalen, Gillespie says, anglers have a good chance of catching tiger muskies, northerns, walleyes,

Como Lake

Lake Phalen

crappies, as well as perch and catfish. Both lakes offer canoes and water bikes for rent.

Although neither Como nor Phalen suffers from the shoreline residential development that challenges other urban lakes, both "catch a lot of storm runoff," says Gillespie. The city is currently replacing shoreline plantings and rock with native plants to improve water quality: "With deep-rooted plants, there's a better opportunity to filter out and clean water."

The city's parks and recreation planners have specific goals for each lake as part of citywide and regional development. Lake Phalen will become the more active lake, Gillespie explains. "It's got a good layout for rowing. We're going to be working with the Minnesota Boat Club to establish a learn-to-row program. It's probably safer to learn on Lake Phalen than it is on the Mississippi River. We've got a Red Cross sailing program at the boathouse."

Surrounded as they now are by Saint Paul, Como Lake and Lake Phalen are even more treasured as public respites from city pressures. "Citizens of Saint Paul really have a sense of ownership of both these lakes. People who grew up on the East Side talk about walking the lake, skating on the lake. And it's the same with Como.

"If you grew up in one of the neighborhoods near the lakes, you've got childhood experiences at the lake. My wife and I walked the lakes, both lakes, with our kids when they were young. And now I've got grandkids, and my kids are walking my grandkids around the lakes. It's been going on that way for generations."

The Saint Paul Parks and Recreation website is a great source of information about the amenities available at Como Lake, Lake Phalen, and the city's other parks: www.stpaul.gov/depts/parks.

Lake Phalen Beach

The cable car system began running in 1888, and for ten years dominated public transportation in Saint Paul. The Selby Avenue line was the steepest cable car line in the Midwest with a maximum grade of 16 percent, just below San Francisco's 22-percent grade.

S	M	T	W	T	F	S
		1	2	3	4	5
6	7	8	9	10	11	12
13	14	15	16	17	18	19
20	21	22	23	24	25	26
27	28	29	30	31		

14 Monday

15 Tuesday

16 Wednesday

17 Thursday

Saint Paul Chamber Orchestra
page 282

Harriet Island Pavilion on the Mississippi River

18 Friday	Saint Paul Chamber Orchestra
	page 282

19 Saturday	Saint Paul Chamber Orchestra
	Downtown Saint Paul Farmers' Market
	pages 281–282

20 Sunday	Downtown Saint Paul Farmers' Market
	page 281

The Girl

(an excerpt)

Meridel Le Sueur

That spring was a cold spring. It rained and turned into sleet and still snowed in May. Clara lay in bed all day quite still. They moved Belle out of her place after Hoinck was buried and Ack was sentenced to life. It's life in this state if you are mixed up in a bank robbery, even if you don't kill anyone, if you are even just driving a car you get life, because they want to show how important banks are. Clara and Belle and Butch's mother were on relief, and they all moved into a tenement on Seventh where they were nearly all women on relief. There was only one old man lived downstairs back on the alley and he was very old, but most of them were women and children, each living in one room, with a stove and the relief gave you wood, and only one toilet to a floor and running water in the hall.

> **You could hear footsteps all day and all night, it was like a husk, every footstep resounded like a drum. Someone walks downstairs and you can hear them walking all around you, even after they've stopped doing it.**

I stayed with Belle and hid when the relief came. You went in the front door and there were initials on the wall heart-shaped, and dust and crumbs and battered mail boxes and the steps were in an oval shape. It was an old building and had been condemned but now the relief paid the people on the hill a good price for it. Amelia told me a woman who owns the building went to Mexico every year just on what she got from it. The halls were dark and full of rubbish, apple cores, papers, cigarette butts, crusts of bread, old shoes, and once I saw some pancakes that had fallen out of somebody's garbage. There were long pieces of string hanging from the bare light bulbs in the hall so the kids could pull them because in the daytime it was as dark in there as a closet. Some of the windows were boarded up.

You could hear footsteps all day and all night, it was like a husk, every footstep resounded like a drum. Someone walks downstairs and you can hear them walking all around you, even after they've stopped doing it. As long as it is day some sound keeps up but when night comes the halls are dark and damp like grief, and the floors sag down, and the bed bugs walk on the walls.

When you go to sleep you dream people are shooting craps and you can hear a woman next door say, for Christ's sake shut up. I never had a good sleep in that house. In the back, little porches are fastened up with wire onto the wall and you can sit there if summer ever comes. The fire escape stairways go back to the alley where there are heaps of ashes, garbage in cans and muddy water thawing from the black sooty snow heaps.

From the porch you can see the spires of the cathedral and the capital. I like to see it. I like this part of it. In winter you can see the river and the houseboats.

It beats all how you can hear everything though like the house was a drum and every whisper made a sound, children talking. Quick steps of driven women, a baby falling down. Women cry a lot and you can even hear them when they are still, rocking. Women rock a lot at night.

I was trying to get on relief and I went to the clinic and they told me that to have a good baby you got have one quart of milk per day and oranges. . . . Well, oranges don't grow in the fine tropical climate of Minnesota.

The Girl *is published by West End Press and is available at The Valley Bookseller at 217 North Main St. in Stillwater. There is a new edition with an introduction by Linda Ray Pratt. If you send a check for $13.95, West End Press will send you the book, postage free. West End Press, P.O. Box 27334, Albuquerque, NM 87125.*

S	M	T	W	T	F	S
		1	2	3	4	5
6	7	8	9	10	11	12
13	14	15	16	17	18	19
20	21	22	23	24	25	26
27	28	29	30	31		

In 1915 there were 17 theaters in downtown Saint Paul.

21 Monday

22 Tuesday

23 Wednesday

24 Thursday

Highland Water Tower, Designed by Cap Wingington

25 Friday	Saint Paul Chamber Orchestra *page 282*
26 Saturday	Saint Paul Chamber Orchestra Downtown Saint Paul Farmers' Market *pages 281–282*
27 Sunday	Downtown Saint Paul Farmers' Market *page 281*

The First Car in Saint Paul

Dr. Ivar E. Siqveland

Written in 1942

I must digress a little from my dental life and reflect on a few experiences I had with my first car.

Shortly after I began my practice, my mother, sister, brother, and I moved to White Bear Lake. Within two years we bought a home at Bald Eagle Lake and settled down there. I began to tire of commuting by train and bicycle after a few years. Believe me, pedaling a bike over sand roads to Saint Paul and back each day was tiresome. I guess it was natural to be intrigued when I read that a horseless carriage was being introduced by the Winton Company. It was a one-cylinder beauty, guaranteed to reach the fabulous speed of fifteen miles per hour. It sold for $1,400, which in 1899 was big money. It was then I threw fortune to the winds and bought the "Winton" instead of Henry Ford's stock.

> "I thought I may have trouble with people like you, and the government has given me special permission to carry this Gatling gun. Now you get those wagons off the road or I'll blow them off."

The most useful and trouble-free part of the car was the crank. It was a long nickel-plated affair with a ratchet that made a very loud click when turned backward. When not in use for cranking the engine, which incidentally was seldom, it rested in a velvet case under the dash. This crank was instrumental in saving the car, and maybe me, soon after I made my purchase. Being the very first gasoline car in Saint Paul, horses were constantly being frightened by its loud exhaust. One day when loudly making my way home from a busy day at the office, I was stopped by a road block made up of a large group of indignant farmers armed with pitchforks and shovels. The part of the road where they stopped me was bordered on each side by a swamp. With a roar, the leader hollered, "Get out of that so-and-so contraption and we will throw it in the swamp. We are tired of having you scare our horses every day."

They were only too serious, and I wondered what to do. Glancing down, I saw that beautiful crank and it gave me an idea. I picked it up

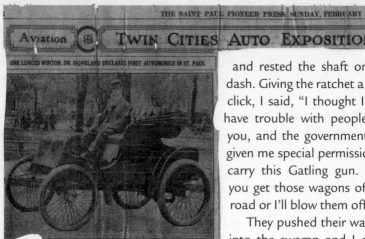

Aviation TWIN CITIES AUTO EXPOSITION

ONE LUNGED WINTON, DR. SIQVELAND DECLARES FIRST AUTOMOBILE IN ST. PAUL

Dr. Siqveland Driving the
First Car in Saint Paul

and rested the shaft on the dash. Giving the ratchet a loud click, I said, "I thought I may have trouble with people like you, and the government has given me special permission to carry this Gatling gun. Now you get those wagons off the road or I'll blow them off."

They pushed their wagons into the swamp and I drove by. Needless to say, I changed my route after that experience.

Another funny experience was had while commuting to Saint Paul. One morning a farmer with his wagonload of eggs was traveling to the market in Saint Paul. As I passed him, his horse reared and backed into the ditch. The wagon rolled over and twelve crates of eggs exploded on the farmer who was pinned underneath. He looked like an omelet when I dragged him out. The horse was on his side nibbling grass and was in much better humor than the driver. After dragging the man out and cleaning him off, I said, "If you hadn't gotten so excited and hacked up the reins, you would have been all right, but I am willing to pay damages. What do I owe you?"

Accompanied by much vile profanity, the old boy said, "Twelve crates of eggs, a broke shaft on my wagon, and my clothes ruined will cost you three dollars, by gun."

How things have changed.

My last car story is as follows: one day after pulling into town, a big Schmidt's Brewery dray was lumbering up the Tenth Street hill. It was loaded with several kegs of beer and pulled by two teams of those beautiful horses they used on their drays. When they saw my car, the horses reared and the dray got out of control. The barrels started to roll off one by one and downhill they went from side to side, as barrels do. People were jumping over and around them and having a hilarious time. Fortunately, no one was hurt and no serious damage was done.

On April 1, 1934, John Dillinger shot his way out of an apartment building on Lexington Parkway after being confronted by the police.

MAY

S	M	T	W	T	F	S
		1	2	3	4	5
6	7	8	9	10	11	12
13	14	15	16	17	18	19
20	21	22	23	24	25	26
27	28	29	30	31		

28 Monday

Memorial Day observed

29 Tuesday

30 Wednesday

31 Thursday

The State Capitol, Designed by Cass Gilbert

1 Friday	
2 Saturday	Capital City Classic Cruisers *page 282* Flint Hills International Children's Festival *page 283* Downtown Saint Paul Farmers' Market *page 281*
3 Sunday	Grand Old Day Flint Hills International Children's Festival Downtown Saint Paul Farmers' Market *pages 281–283*

Rondo Oral History

Oral History is the spoken word in print. Oral histories are personal memories shared from the perspective of the narrator. By means of recorded interviews, oral histories collect spoken memories and personal commentaries of historical significance. These interviews are transcribed verbatim and minimally edited for readability. The greatest appreciation is gained when one can read an oral history aloud.

Kate Cavett, oral historian,
HAND in HAND Productions

The following oral history is excerpted from Voices of Rondo: Oral Histories of Saint Paul's Historic Black Community *and is used by permission.* Voices of Rondo *won a 2006 Minnesota Book Award.*

Anisah Hanifah Dawan

Grew up in the Rondo neighborhood as Elizabeth Payne Combs

I'm Anisah Hanifah Dawan and I've lived in Saint Paul since 1922. I was born in North Dakota. I was transferred to a home for orphan children because my mother had died. That was in Owatonna, Minnesota. And I remember being in an orphanage or hospital where there were cribs in the room, and there was another little boy. He was a Black boy. He had a big, red truck in his crib, and I think that's when I fell in love with the color red, because I wanted that so bad. And there were two White nurses, and they were laughing and making fun of me. They called me a little pickaninny. I remember it so plain, and I wondered why we were there.

Anisah Hanifah Dawan

The next thing I remember is being on Rondo, at 250 Rondo in a flat. We were upstairs and the lady's name was Mrs. Holiday. She was showing me off to my adopted mother. I was brought here to be adopted by a family that lived on Carroll, 403 Carroll—Martha and Albert Payne. He was a railroad man. I believe it was Northern Railroad that he worked for. He was a waiter. I was in a crib down there on Rondo, because I remember the little dog would jump up and look at me, and I'd look at him. And people were standing around looking at me like, "Here she is."

So that was the day that Momma brought me home to 403 Carroll. I must've been two or three, something like that, because I can remember it so plain. We lived between Western and Arundel. It was an integrated neighborhood, and all the children would play together. There were Italians, Irish, and Polish. There was another Black family, who lived on the right side of us, and their last name was Green. The mother was Anna Green, and the son was Douglas Green. She seemed to be sickly all the time, because when we would play outside on the lawn, we'd be making a lot of noise, and she would get someone to tell us to cut it down a little. And Catholics lived next door to us on the other side.

I remember our street. There was a grocery store on the corner of Mackubin and Rondo. Chief Finney's mother had a beauty parlor. I used to get my hair done there at Arundel and Rondo. And across the street from her was a barbecue place, Ed Warren's Restaurant. They had the best barbeque. Let's see now, going way back, there was the Rondo Police Station at Western and Rondo—it was closed and we used to go and look through the keyhole.

There was a big playground, between Virginia and Saint Anthony, and Rondo and Western. They had swings there. And we crossed the playground to go to the Welcome Hall. It was like a community center—right next door to the Zion Presbyterian Church that I went to. Reverend George W. Camp, his family lived on Saint Anthony and he was the minister of the Presbyterian Church there. We used to have music down at the Welcome Hall, but it would be somebody playing the piano or something like that. Miss Camp would say, "Now, children, you have to dance because you're going home at eight or ten o'clock." Whatever it was. And she'd make us dance. Oh, dear, it was fun. They had a lot of projects over there.

We could leave our doors open. We could go around town, go anywhere, go shopping and come home, and nothing would be moved.

Can you imagine that? I got two locks on that door now. But it was just beautiful. I think now how well we got along in the neighborhood. All the kids played together, all would roller skate together in the street, and parents would be mingling and talking. And the kids would be out there having a ball. It was just wonderful, all these different families, different hues of people. We all got along.

The kids all played together out in the street. Jews, Italians, Blacks, Swedes. The boys mostly played ball. Momma had fixed up the back shed. It was like a little playhouse for us, and I had my dolls out there and everything. A White girl friend would come over and play in my back yard.

We were all friendly. We got along. They weren't prejudiced, that's for sure. And we weren't prejudiced, so we all got along good. Everybody just looked out for the kids, and it didn't make any difference what color they were. Their mothers would look out for me. I don't remember all the kids' names, but I could remember their faces, and we used to have so much fun.

My dad, he brought me a little car, a little roadster—and, oh, was I popular! The kids would ride on it. I was looking at some old pictures. They used to come around and photograph kids, you know. I was in my car and they took a photograph of me in my little car. When I would take it out on the sidewalk, all the kids would get on that could get on. Mama didn't like that too much because they can't be all on the car.

My father was making good money and he'd always come home and teach me how to count with silver dollars and all that stuff. I think he only went through the fourth grade. But he got hired onto the train.

Anisah in Her Roadster

You know, if you could do the work, there was no problem. And he would go up to Seattle and Winnipeg.

Then the Depression came and Daddy lost his job. He had a brother out in Seattle and his mother lived out there, too. The next thing I know, he was packing up to go out there, maybe to a better life or whatever. And that was one day that I cried so hard, because he was trying to explain to me that he was going. I didn't understand what was going on, but I knew that Daddy was leaving. He only came back to visit us. In fact, when he passed, we didn't even have money to go out there to the funeral and that hurt pretty bad. I must've been about seventeen. The Depression lasted a long time.

When the Depression came, I remember we had a six-room house with hardwood floors, a furnace, a stove. I'll never forget that. A gas stove. It was really nice. Our furniture was all leather, and we had an old console radio, and Momma had a piano because she liked to play. And our house was really nice. In fact, I would say that we lived like middle-class people.

My mom didn't have to work until then. Then she took in wash. I don't know how she knew these people, their name was Love. Well, Mom had to wash the clothes. We were pretty broke. We lived in that house one winter. I don't think we made it through the winter, but Mama would get bricks from the basement or out in the backyard. She'd put them on the gas stove to heat them up, so we wouldn't freeze. She'd wrap them up in blankets and put them up in bed, during the Depression. We had been buying our home, but we lost it. We were homeless, you might say.

Since we couldn't pay for our house at 403 Carroll, we rented it out to some poorer White people. They had gotten off the farm. They couldn't make it out there so we rented the house out for nine dollars a month! And they would come over to pay it in pennies! I mean, it must've been a pretty hard Depression. And because I was adopted, or because I was dependent, the welfare started giving us surplus food.

Some neighbor that lived on Fuller, her name was Miss Arvilla McGregor. I never will forget her. She used to visit. They'd visit, back and forth. Well, she died, and I remember when Mr. McGregor let us live at his house. We moved. Mama pulled me in a sled, took me over to McGregor's house at 494 Fuller. Boy, that was the first time I'd ever seen a stove. And it was a big thing! It was way up like that, and it was silver, and it had isinglass or something all around, like it was plastic. But it wasn't plastic. It was the prettiest thing I'd ever seen.

Mr. McGregor was a redcap, worked on the depot. I remember they used to give tips down there, and we ate off of the tips. He had had two sons, but they died when they were young. And his wife died, so he started renting the upstairs out. And we had the upstairs.

I went to Mechanic Arts High School and when I was sixteen, I went down to the Public Safety Building, in the basement. They had a tailor shop down there and I worked for this lady tailoring. I worked for two dollars a week. Forty hours. Walked to work and walked back. And you talk about proud! I'm thinking, "I'm makin' money!" Two dollars a week! Oh my goodness! So that was about 1935. I did that in the summertime. Yeah, I bought my fall shoes. I never will forget. A pair of black suedes. I used to work in the summer, but I thought, "Oh boy, this is my first job," and I used to go down and get chow mein somewhere down on Robert Street or something. The young women that worked there, they'd bring their skirts and I'd press them.

I was going to the Hallie Q. Brown like it was my second home, which it was, at Aurora and Kent. I was in a girls' group. We would be selling cookies and different things like that. Whenever money we made, we wanted to have a dance. So we did. I can't remember now what our music was, but it was good, because we danced! We were all teenagers, and Lola Finney used to come in and teach us about cosmetology. She was working out of that business. She had to go to Chicago and get some studying. She was really good.

We would have carnivals. After the carnival, we'd have a party with the money we made. All the young men had to wear white coats, and I made my dress, because I was always tall and store-bought dresses were too short for me. So Mom started buying material, and she brought material home and patterns. She said, "You're on your own."

I'd stay up all night and make a formal. You could get material for about ten cents a yard. Five yards would do it. We made formals all the time because we had parties from our club. And I started sewing by hand. Yeah! I made my first formal. Oh, it was pretty purple flowers on a white background. It was flared out. And then a jacket, too. It was pretty.

Those years were hard, but I have very good memories. At Hallie they taught you how to get along with people in the workplace and everywhere else. You had to be prepared and many of my successes have come from that early training.

June

Capital City Classic Cruisers Every Saturday night, June 2–Sept. 29

Flint Hills International Children's Festival June 2–3

Grand Old Day June 3

Saint Paul Sommerfest June 8–10

Twin Cities Hot Summer Jazz Festival June 15–16

Saint Paul Blues Festival Dates to be announced

Solstice Film Festival June 20–24

Minnesota Crafts Festival June 22–24

Back to the '50s Car Show June 23–24

Taste of Minnesota June 29–July 4

Downtown Saint Paul Farmers' Market Sat. and Sun., Through Nov. 11

See pages 282–284 for more information on June events.

In 1957 the City Council bought "Little Italy" and relocated its residents. Soon after, the area became a scrap yard and only now are developments bringing Saint Paulites back to the Mississippi River. The area is now called Upper Landing.

JUNE

S	M	T	W	T	F	S
					1	2
3	4	5	6	7	8	9
10	11	12	13	14	15	16
17	18	19	20	21	22	23
24	25	26	27	28	29	30

4 Monday

5 Tuesday

6 Wednesday

7 Thursday

8 Friday	Saint Paul Sommerfest *pages 283–284*

9 Saturday	Saint Paul Sommerfest *pages 283–284* Capital City Classic Cruisers *page 282* Downtown Saint Paul Farmers' Market *page 281*

10 Sunday	Saint Paul Sommerfest *Concours d'Elégance* *pages 283–284* Downtown Saint Paul Farmers' Market *page 281*

Saint Paul Street Machines

Drew Tilsen

Hot-rodding and car shows have come a long way. It all started in the 1920s and 1930s in the southern U.S. with the whiskey-runner bootleg cars. They needed to go faster to outrun law enforcement in the Prohibition days. They started the aftermarket performance parts market. Then the zoot suiters of southern California (Mexican Americans) pioneered the street machines of the '30s and '40s. They lowered their cars and used two-tone paint to show stature in society. We can thank the wealthy in America for creating a market for the high-end cars—Cadillacs and Lincolns that pioneered car technology.

In the 1950s Porky's drive-in restaurant was built at 1890 University Avenue in Saint Paul and started what is now a premier hot rod hang-out. The cars here were different. They were new! Saint Paulites had taken ideas from the zoot suiters, the bootleggers, and the high-end cars to build real street machines. Saint Paul was soon on the car crafters' map.

After the car crafters had cruised up and down University Avenue and eaten at Porky's, the competition for whose car was faster would soon come after nightfall. They would cruise to Red Rock Raceway—not actually a raceway but a secluded dead-end road in Saint Paul. Because of the dividing river, the police had to inconveniently enter two different cities to access Red Rock. Since police could not get there easily, it was a prime location for illegal drag racing. Cars

Porky's Restaurant on University Avenue

Drew in front of His Garage

raced here on and off for over forty years until, tragically, somebody got hurt in this wicked unorganized racing. Now there are concrete barriers blocking the road.

Today you can still cruise on University Avenue every weekend evening with street machines all around you. Go to Porky's and have an all-American burger, onion rings, and a side of fresh coleslaw. Check out the machines opened up with windows down so you can look at the stylish interior, hoods propped to see the beautiful power plant, and the owner nearby, usually eager to answer questions. Also, there are tons of people, some motorcycles, and every now and again a monster truck.

Saint Paul is now home to some of the most elite car shows and swap meets in the country, including Car Craft Summer Nationals, where they have thousands of cars of all kinds, a Dyno Challenge, a burnout contest, and, of course, the Bikini contest; and Minnesota Street Rod Association's Back to the '50s event, which is the second-largest car show of its kind in the world. Both events are held at the Minnesota State Fairgrounds in Saint Paul.

Saint Paul continues to set the standard for the rest of the world in what a true street machine is by having some of the most featured cars in popular magazines. Some say trends start in the West and make their way East. Not in street machines. It all starts here. With its many strong car clubs and creative people, hot-rodding and innovation will remain in Saint Paul.

Drew Tilsen is a full-time, certified mechanic. Visit Magic's Automotive Repair and Towing at 237 Richmond St., Saint Paul, or call his office at 651.292.1286 or cell 651.402.9899.

The Saint Paul City Hall/Ramsey County Court House was added to the National Register of Historic Places in 1983 due to its elaborate American art deco design.

JUNE

S	M	T	W	T	F	S
					1	2
3	4	5	6	7	8	9
10	11	12	13	14	15	16
17	18	19	20	21	22	23
24	25	26	27	28	29	30

11 Monday

12 Tuesday

13 Wednesday

14 Thursday

Fishing Pier at Como Lake

15 Friday	**Twin Cities Hot Summer Jazz Festival** *page 284*
16 Saturday	**Twin Cities Hot Summer Jazz Festival** *page 284* **Capital City Classic Cruisers** *page 282* **Downtown Saint Paul Farmers' Market** *page 281*
17 Sunday Father's Day	**Downtown Saint Paul Farmers' Market** *page 281*

Our River

Beadrin Youngdahl

No small portion of the world's geography, this Mississippi River of ours.

It lacks the waltz qualities of the Danube. Had Cleopatra decided to grace it with a royal cruise, she might have been reduced to barge operator.

Ours is a hardworking, murky passage of serious water.

Learning to spell M-I-S-S-I-S-S-I-P-P-I at an early age perhaps sets us up to respect rhythm, sound, and satisfaction in rugged achievement.

It is our river. From that little jump-across pond at Itasca it slips along, gaining power and vitality on its southward journey, with little pause for playful rest.

Lake Pepin is a coffee break. "Think I'll spread out a bit, watch the eagles nest.

"Okay, back to work."

Mark Twain, it is no surprise, did not write of kisses under or over bridges on the Seine, marvelous as those may be. He was a Mississippi River fellow. He wrote of things rugged and sometimes difficult. Don't we look at the same water?

It was for him, and remains for us, a pragmatic body of water. On its shores, for sure here at its tender beginning, live pragmatic and solid life forms. That would be us, the hearty souls who inhabit the

Boat Slips in Saint Paul

The Lake Street Bridge across the Mississippi

upper Midwest and love those deep and certain waters of the Mississippi, even if we just grumble passing over its bridges on our drives to work every day, barely pausing to look. We know every ripple; we know the ice breakup in the spring; we know its rise and fall through the seasons; we know those catfish on the bottom are ugly and astoundingly large; we know Harriet Island holds summer events, and we know Nicollet Island actually holds a community of historical homes. We know there is an elaborate system of locks and dams arranged for navigation of vessels, large and small. We have insider knowledge of the bridges—"Come across the High Bridge" or "Over there by the Ford Bridge."

It is our river to crisscross time and again while the world learns how to spell its name.

Learning to spell M-I-S-S-I-S-S-I-P-P-I at an early age perhaps sets us up to respect rhythm, sound, and satisfaction in rugged achievement.

Memorial Hall in the Saint Paul City Hall/Ramsey County Court House is three stories high, measuring 85 feet by 21 feet. On the walls in black Belgian marble are all the names of Ramsey County soldiers who died in wars from World War I to the Grenada Conflict.

JUNE

S	M	T	W	T	F	S
					1	2
3	4	5	6	7	8	9
10	11	12	13	14	15	16
17	18	19	20	21	22	23
24	25	26	27	28	29	30

18 Monday

19 Tuesday

Juneteenth

20 Wednesday

Solstice Film Festival
page 284

21 Thursday

Summer Solstice

Solstice Film Festival
page 284

James J. Hill House

22 Friday	Solstice Film Festival
	Minnesota Crafts Festival
	Back to the '50s Car Show
	page 284

23 Saturday	Solstice Film Festival
	Minnesota Crafts Festival
	Back to the '50s Car Show
	Capital City Classic Cruisers
	Downtown Saint Paul Farmers' Market
	pages 281, 282, and 284

24 Sunday	Solstice Film Festival
	Minnesota Crafts Festival
	Downtown Saint Paul Farmers' Market
	pages 281 and 284

Hometown Baseball

Mark Connor

The Saint Paul Saints rang in the return of professional baseball to Minnesota's capital city in 1993, winning the Northern League championship in their first season. Being a minor league team in a metropolitan area that a two-time World Series champion calls home, the Saints have thrived through a combination of great baseball, creative extracurricular entertainment, and the overall atmosphere of Saint Paul's charm. Playing home games at Midway Stadium, just west of Snelling Avenue on Energy Park Drive, amounts to great fun for baseball purists as well as the less-than-passionate sports fan.

"It's so much more entertaining than other ballparks," says Andy Crowley, the team organist since the 2003 season. Leading much of the ritual celebration that Saints games are, Crowley keeps a steady beat going with his organ each inning, coordinates all pre-taped music, and maintains the PA system for the announcer. In the meantime, a vast array of antics go on, entertaining fans beyond the game itself while simultaneously accentuating what happens on the field.

> . . . every game has a theme attached to it, like
> the '70s disco night. "People seem to have a good time,"
> Crowley explains. "They like to dance and have fun,
> wear crazy clothes. It really seems to work."

For starters, the fans are continuously directed by "ushertainers," a group of ushers doubling as cheerleaders. Many of them are well-known actors in the thriving local theater community, and they're always dressed thematically for the occasion. "They'll wear some silly costume that ties into a baseball reference," says Crowley. "They do a fair amount of messing around with the crowd, cheerleading, and entertainment between innings."

Also, every game has a theme attached to it, like the '70s disco night. "People seem to have a good time," Crowley explains. "They like to dance and have fun, wear crazy clothes. It really seems to work."

There are also theme nights designed to highlight specific sponsors, sometimes even involving the players. "There was one promotion for a company that makes clothes for medical work, so players came onto

Midway Stadium—Home of the Saint Paul Saints

the field wearing medical clothes with numbers on them instead of Jerseys," Crowley remembers.

Since the first season, Midway Stadium has expanded from 3,100 to 6,069 seats, placing fans down both foul lines. There is a hot tub over the left field fence, and picnic areas are located behind the third-base bleachers. Also, an area down the first baseline is the Buca Table, sponsored by the popular restaurant, serving groups a full course Italian meal during games. The expansions are largely credited to the vision of Mike Veeck, co-owner and team president, who got his education in the baseball business from his father, who owned the Chicago Cubs. Marv GoldKlang is also a co-owner and the chairman of the board, and another Chicago connection is co-owner and team psychologist Bill Murray, the famous actor who also was an original cast member of the "Not Ready for Prime Time Players" on TV's *Saturday Night Live*. Murray has substituted as both first-and third-base coach on occasions, including the greatest comeback victory in Saints history, when they tackled a 9 to 2 deficit to defeat the Sioux Falls Canaries on August 10, 1997. This and other stories can be found on the Saints website at www.saintsbaseball.com.

Whether you're a die-hard baseball fan, a passively interested fair-weather spectator, or a tourist from another country who doesn't know the rules of the sport, you'll enjoy yourself at a Saints game. It's one of the Saint Paul summer experiences that will keep our city in a soft spot of your heart forever.

The state soccer teams call Saint Paul home, both the men's Minnesota Thunder and the newly created women's Minnesota Lightning. Our pro-soccer teams play at James Griffin Stadium, home to the Minutemen of Saint Paul Central High School.

JUNE

S	M	T	W	T	F	S
					1	2
3	4	5	6	7	8	9
10	11	12	13	14	15	16
17	18	19	20	21	22	23
24	25	26	27	28	29	30

25 Monday

26 Tuesday

27 Wednesday

28 Thursday

Como Park Pond

29 Friday	Taste of Minnesota *page 284*

30 Saturday	Taste of Minnesota *page 284*
	Capital City Classic Cruisers *page 282*
	Downtown Saint Paul Farmers' Market *page 281*

1 Sunday	Taste of Minnesota *page 284*
	Downtown Saint Paul Farmers' Market *page 281*

I always Sang for My Father
Or Anyone Who Would Listen

(an excerpt)

Vic Tedesco

The Shoe Leather Meets the Streets

I had been in never-never land my first six years on the council. I thought the prestige and fun of being commissioner of Parks and Rec would go on forever. Now I was merely a council member.

But there were still surprises to keep life interesting.

One evening I saw a TV news clip showing U.S. Sen. William Proxmire, D-Wis., working in a factory. Bingo, I say to myself, what a great idea. I announced I would spend one of my weeks of vacation each year doing city employees' jobs. I had my first chance at a week's work in July 1974.

On Monday, I went to work on the garbage truck. And I did work. I didn't want anyone to say I was loafing on the job.

Susan Spencer covered the event for WCCO-TV. It was her first assignment at the station; she went on to CBS in Washington, D.C. All the other TV stations covered the garbage-truck event as well. It really wasn't bad work, not as tough as Tuesday, that hot summer day when I worked with a street-patching crew spreading asphalt. I think my legs and back were hurting for days.

"Garbage hauler was one of the many city jobs I worked to show support for Saint Paul city workers"

In a nursing home, I gave baths to Alzheimer's patients who called me every name in the book, and I tended bar and drove a cab.

Wednesday I helped bathe an elephant at my old stomping ground, Como Zoo. In the rest of the week, I walked along with a water-meter reader and traveled with cops and firefighters.

My police job was to patrol in the Selby-Dale area with two black police officers, Corky Benner and Bill Finney. Finney later became the chief of the Saint Paul Police Department. Most of the day was boring. I still remember Bill Finney's words—"Hours of boredom, minutes of sheer fright. On one call." His words came true when we were called to an apartment complex on a domestic. A woman came running out of the building, screaming, and she was bleeding profusely. Her boyfriend had cut her up with a razor.

My firefighting day was spent at the fire house on Payne Avenue just up from Seventh Street. It was a little like the police experience—boring until we got a call. Then it became downright dangerous for the real firefighters.

The fire was downtown in the Lowry Building. I was in full attire for the situation—helmet, boots, rubber coat with flannel lining. The firefighters didn't let me get near the fire while they were pouring water on it from their hoses. My job was to sweep away the water that was making the floors slippery.

Speaking of firemen, they are the most powerful political group in Saint Paul. The Democratic-Farmer-Labor Party, and I suppose the Republican Party, mostly give lip service to their candidates. But the firemen campaign door to door, in uniform, for or against you. You don't want to get them teed off. I had their support in nine of eleven elections. I guess a couple of times I did not support their causes. Apparently they weren't too angry with me as they didn't work too hard against me.

I must say they eat good, and if you're invited for lunch or dinner at a station house, don't pass it up.

When I got back to council work, I suggested that the city find cooler summer wear for that job. Those flannel-lined rubber coats were awful in the heat.

I did about forty different city jobs over the eight years that I took my "vacation work week." I operated an elevator at City Hall, and swept

"Firefighting wasn't the only hot summertime job.
Street repairmen had to work with steaming asphalt"

the sidewalks too. I worked as a librarian at the Sun Ray branch on Saint Paul's East Side.

And I spent a day with the health inspector. We went to a house on Stewart Street on the West End. The place was filthy. Dog dung all over the house—you had to walk in an aisle because there was so much debris. I just can't see how people can live like that. The tenants were given a citation to clean up the feces and the junk in a hurry. I actually went home ill. It was a short day for me.

I also did jobs that weren't on the city payroll but were related to places that were licensed by the city, since I was chairman of that committee. In a nursing home, I gave baths to Alzheimer's patients who called me every name in the book, and I tended bar and drove a cab.

And I stayed overnight in the city morgue. The morgue had various-size jars sitting around with body parts in them. I understand they were kept as evidence in court cases. There were no calls while I was there, and about 4 a.m. I begged off and went home. What a boring job!

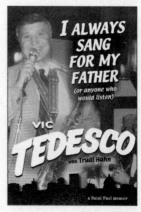

I Always Sang for My Father or Anyone Who Would Listen *is Vic Tedesco's new memoir about his life in Saint Paul. Available at Syren Book Company* 1.800.901.3480

July

Taste of Minnesota June 29–July 4

Hmong Sports Festival July 7–July 8 (tentative)

Dragon Festival and Dragon Boat Races Dates to be announced

Rondo Day July 21

Highland Fest July 20–July 22

Car Craft Summer Nationals July 20–July 22

Circus Juventas July 27, 28, and 29

Sixteenth Annual Rib America Festival July 26–July 29

Downtown Saint Paul Farmers' Market Through Nov. 11

See pages 284–286 for more information on July events.

JULY

S	M	T	W	T	F	S
1	2	3	4	5	6	7
8	9	10	11	12	13	14
15	16	17	18	19	20	21
22	23	24	25	26	27	28
29	30	31				

The City of Saint Paul is 6.07 percent water.

2 Monday

Taste of Minnesota
page 284

3 Tuesday

Taste of Minnesota
page 284

4 Wednesday

Independence Day

Taste of Minnesota
page 284

5 Thursday

6 Friday	
7 Saturday	**Capital City Classic Cruisers** *page 282* **Hmong Sports Festival** *page 285* **Downtown Saint Paul Farmers' Market** *page 281*
8 Sunday	**Hmong Sports Festival** *page 285* **Downtown Saint Paul Farmers' Market** *page 281*

A Taste of Minnesota

Evelyn Klein

Saint Paul built into wooded bluffs
of the Mississippi River
lies lulled in clouds
the pulsing river at its feet
steadfast

layers of a social order
of people converge
form Fourth of July parade
at the foot of the capitol
the cultural mix
streams past roses
to taste hot dogs and corn on the cob
staples of their celebration
pulsing

My daughter and I drift
past vendors and food booths
through 224 years of independence
at the pinnacle of a new age
to revisit the bygone and move forward
with ice cream cones
talk and laughter of our freedom
carrying the water of our friendship
we try on sundresses
that tie the mother-daughter bond
anew

Happy Birthday America
we'll watch the fireworks
of expansion and growth
the right to seek refuge
in wide-open spaces
to come and go in a crowd

or to retreat
behind the third-story club window
near the Mississippi River bluff
in celebration of all Fourth of Julys
a country's tradition
a family's tradition

rhythm
set to music
of a warm summer night
this river in darkness below
pulsing
in continuity

JULY

S	M	T	W	T	F	S
1	2	3	4	5	6	7
8	9	10	11	12	13	14
15	16	17	18	19	20	21
22	23	24	25	26	27	28
29	30	31				

The City of Saint Paul has 290 bridges, but only eight are major river crossings.

9 Monday

10 Tuesday

11 Wednesday

12 Thursday

Minnesota Women's Press on Raymond

13 Friday	
14 Saturday	**Capital City Classic Cruisers** *page 282* **Downtown Saint Paul Farmers' Market** *page 281*
15 Sunday	**Downtown Saint Paul Farmers' Market** *page 281*

Coasting

Vernon Holmberg

On a summer Saturday morning in 1937, Nils Ohmstead brought the new car home; a 1935 Ford V8 Tudor Sedan. It was two years old and had only 10,000 miles on it. The body was a light tan and it had dark brown wheels.

Nils had driven the new car in off the alley into the yard alongside the garage to wash it. Ernest's job was to wash the wheels. Nils gave him an old paint brush that had been stiffened by neglect and a small bucket of soapy water. Ernest scrubbed away at the short stiff spokes, the hub. He scrubbed the hubcap with its circle in the middle broken by the V8 symbol and the blue background around the V8. He scrubbed the spare wheel too. The spare, mounted on a horn-like brace on the trunk above the bumper, was all covered with metal. Nils had to unlock the spare tire cover, snap off the disk, and then unsnap and remove the metal tread cover.

"How come that tire is all covered up, Dad?" asked Ernest.

"To keep it out of the sun. If you drive around with it out, the sun and weather dries it out, and it gets hard and cracks."

After washing, Nils put Simonize wax on it in small patches and rubbed it until it reflected. He put some Simonize on the wheels and gave Ernest a strip of cloth to polish the wheels. Ernest slipped the cloth around a spoke and pulled the cloth back and forth and up and down until he could see his face all squeezed and stretched reflecting back at him from the spoke. When Nils finished Simonizing the body and Ernest was through with the wheels, Nils got some chrome polish to polish the grille, bumpers, door handles, and hubcaps.

"Careful not to get that stuff on the paint. We don't want to ruin our wax job," he said.

Ernest's part of chrome polishing was the hubcaps and the bumpers. He polished the hubcaps until he could see his distorted, reflected face broken by the V8 symbol and then he polished the heavy metal bumpers. When the bumpers were polished he stood back and watched his reflection get all squatty and then he moved down to the end of the bumper where it curved and he saw himself get all skinny. The car gleamed. "Let's take her for a spin to see if she's fit to travel," said Nils.

"Hope for GO," yelled Nils, as they neared the stop-and-go sign in the middle of the street at Cleveland.

Ernest perched on the front edge of the passenger seat, grasping the dashboard with his hands so he could stretch to see out the windshield.

Nils started the car and said, "Ooh, she's quiet. These Ford V8s are really smooth," as he pushed the long, curved shift lever between them way forward into reverse and the car moved backward. After turning out of the alley onto the street, he moved the lever forward again, and, after a short while, pulled it back again and they were going on Forty-sixth Street toward Saint Paul. They followed the curve over a little bridge and drove around another curve toward the Ford Bridge over the Mississippi River, just above Lock and Dam No. 1. They continued across the bridge, past the Ford Motor Company's Twin Cities Assembly Plant, and on up the hill on Ford Parkway until they got to Snelling Avenue. Nils stopped at the stop sign and went across the street to the Highland Water Tower. There he turned around in the little parking lot, re-crossed Snelling Avenue and accelerated, starting back down the hill.

"Now, we're going to see if we can coast all the way home," said Nils, moving the lever forward and leaning back in his seat. The car was absolutely quiet. Ernest could hear the sound of the tire tread squishing on the road and the wind coming in over the top of his side window. The car went faster and faster down the steep eight-block road before the road flattened out after Fairview Avenue, then the car picked up more speed as it streaked down another incline to Cleveland Avenue.

"Hope for GO," yelled Nils, as they neared the stop-and-go sign in the middle of the street at Cleveland. The semaphore was shining its green GO as they skimmed by it. "Boy! We were hitting sixty-five when we went across. Hope we have enough steam to make the bridge."

The car started to slow down but picked up speed again as they went down toward the river. "We're going fifty!" Nils shouted as they started up the arch of the bridge. The car slowed rapidly but then picked up a little speed on the crest of the arc at the center of the bridge and down around the curve to Forty-sixth Avenue. They bumped across the streetcar tracks at Forty-sixth Street and Forty-sixth Avenue and rolled on past Forty-fifth Avenue. Slower and slower they rolled until they just reached their alley after Forty-fourth Avenue, where they nearly stopped and Nils said, "Damn, not quite enough steam," as he pulled the lever down and drove into the alley.

Only in Saint Paul will you find more miles of sidewalk than street, 1,250 miles to 855 miles respectively.

JULY

S	M	T	W	T	F	S
1	2	3	4	5	6	7
8	9	10	11	12	13	14
15	16	17	18	19	20	21
22	23	24	25	26	27	28
29	30	31				

16 Monday

17 Tuesday

18 Wednesday

19 Thursday

20 Friday

Highland Fest

Car Craft Summer Nationals

page 285

21 Saturday

Rondo Day

Highland Fest

Car Craft Summer Nationals

Capital City Classic Cruisers

Downtown Saint Paul Farmers' Market

pages 281, 282, and 285

22 Sunday

Highland Fest

Car Craft Summer Nationals

Downtown Saint Paul Farmers' Market

pages 281 and 285

The Grotto Under SuperAmerica

Susan Larson and Tom Lewis

When American cities like Saint Paul grow, space gets tight and land prices go up. If we're not careful, historical buildings and green spaces from the early days become targets of demolition, to be replaced by more financially viable developments. Real estate economics work against unique places if people don't stand up for them. Typically, some distinctive spot in our peripheral vision disappears, and the first we know of it is when we're treated to the grand opening of one more strip mall, high-density apartment house, or just another gas station.

A painter and stonemason by trade, Gabriel Pizzuti started building his grotto in 1934 as a memorial for his daughter Dorothy, who died as a child.

In the late 1980s this is exactly what happened to a unique visionary environment, once home to a rare urban grotto complex as big as a city block. A visitor to the SuperAmerica gas station at the corner of Rose and Arkwright on the East Side would never guess that it stands over Gabriel Pizzuti's Apostolic Grotto of Saint Michael—probably the most impressive urban grotto of the twentieth century.

Now buried under gas pumps, cheap fluorescent lighting, and asphalt, it was built as a grand visionary grotto environment and chapel during the Depression. Pizzuti maintained the place over the years, until his death in 1981.

A painter and stonemason by trade, Gabriel Pizzuti started building his grotto in 1934 as a memorial for his daughter Dorothy, who died as a child. The chapel was a small interior space hollowed out of an artificial hill the size of a house that he had heaped up with his sons' help.

Pizzuti made or salvaged most of his building materials, having bought up scraps of the first Ramsey County courthouse for the chapel's side panels, altar, and pews. He also served as chaplain, conducting regular services in the chapel or on the grounds outside. The Pizzuti children regularly took part in services at the chapel, helping their father in his chaplain duties and playing the organ.

As the site grew, the landscape elements evolved. Visitors from the street encountered two large concrete pillars at the entrance, dedicated

Pizzuti's Grotto

to Saint Gabriel and Saint Mary. The grounds were covered with a well-maintained lawn, broken by winding concrete paths that led the visitor around several river stone and concrete pillars almost five feet high. A birdbath, also built out of concrete and stone, stood in one corner of the site.

A shrine to Jesus was built into the south side of the artificial hill in its own man-made cave. Outside, the chapel was crowned with a tall Mission-style steeple topped by a large cross and an open arch with a single, hand-wrung bell. In photos of the interior, we see details of the altar and other ornamentation at one end of a cramped room.

Although the grotto was a popular stop for tourists and gawkers, interviews with neighbors and friends of Pizzuti reveal that he was wary of exploitation. Not that he was a recluse: Pizzuti and his family often set up long tables in the garden for everyone in the neighborhood to enjoy holiday celebrations.

After Pizzuti's death, the cost of repairing the plumbing and bringing the site up to code kept any would-be preservers of the site from doing much beyond fending off vandals. By spring of 1988, the chapel's roof had collapsed. In May of that year, the entire block was bulldozed, echoing words written many years earlier by a Saint Paul columnist: "Already [Pizzuti] can see the ridicule on the faces of men who would bulldoze so odd a sketch of city life into the dust from whence it and the builder came."

Some fragments of the original structure—the interesting birdbath and some of the religious features—were preserved by the family before the bulldozers did their work. The rest has disappeared in all but a set of photographs held at the Minnesota Historical Society.

Saint Paul may only have 342 traffic signal intersections, but this adds up to 14,234 light bulbs.

JULY

S	M	T	W	T	F	S
1	2	3	4	5	6	7
8	9	10	11	12	13	14
15	16	17	18	19	20	21
22	23	24	25	26	27	28
29	30	31				

23 Monday

24 Tuesday

25 Wednesday

26 Thursday   Sixteenth Annual Rib America Festival
page 285

Highland Fest

27 Friday	Circus Juventas
	Sixteenth Annual Rib America Festival
	page 285

28 Saturday	Capital City Classic Cruisers
	Circus Juventas
	Sixteenth Annual Rib America Festival
	Downtown Saint Paul Farmers' Market
	pages 281, 282, and 285

29 Sunday	Circus Juventas
	Sixteenth Annual Rib America Festival
	Downtown Saint Paul Farmers' Market
	pages 281 and 285

Canoeing the Wilds
of Saint Paul

Judith Niemi

The heron was sneaking around in the shadowy backwaters.

"Hey," said my canoe partner. "An egret!"

Yeah, there was one. Right behind the heron on the brushy shore. Bits of late sunlight filtered through the trees to light it up. We'd passed five beavers, starting their evening of nibbling willows in that little channel by Pike Island. That made us alert, so next we spotted the woodchuck rambling along the bank, and now, because we were woodchuck-watching—floating still and silent—we paid attention to the pointed stumps in the weeds. Not a stump, a bittern! Bitterns aren't rare, but you just don't see them right next to you like this. Great camouflage! Its beak pointed rigidly skyward, its beady eye on us.

I started to laugh. "This is like one of those puzzle pictures in the books you bring to kids with chickenpox! 'Can you find one rooster, two shoes, three wading birds?'"

A deer stepped out of the woods then, right behind the egret. A nice buck; not a Boone and Crockett type, but he had a lot of nice points on his shiny antlers, and a midsummer red-gold coat. He looked like Bambi's dad—that elusive Golden Stag—with his big shoulders and big attitude.

"I don't believe this!" said my friend. She was visiting from Detroit, and I guess they don't have that many deer and beavers right in town. "This is more wildlife than I saw on my two-week trip in Quetico."

Her voice was drowned out by a 747 taking off from Minneapolis-Saint Paul Airport. Maybe it was a 757 or 767—one of those big numbers, anyway, the kind that jiggles the water under your canoe, vibrates your bones, and just about deafens a canoeist under the flight path. The birds and beasts seemed to ignore it.

We were paddling where the Minnesota and Mississippi rivers join, the very center of the earth according to the Dakota who lived there. You can slide a canoe down the bank in Mendota, near the fur traders' houses, or put in at the Hidden Falls beach or landing. You can putter around the backwaters, or go down to Lilydale or Harriet Island. At low-water levels, you can paddle back up the sluggish current to Hidden Falls, or go up the Minnesota.

For paddling or walking in this area, maps are available from the Department of Natural Resources for Fort Snelling State Park, the Minnesota River, and the Mississippi River. Information about the Saint Paul parks bordering the river (Hidden Falls, Crosby, Lilydale, and Harriet Island) is online at www.stpaul.gov/depts/parks. The Parks and Recreation Department number is 651.266.6400.

Once I paddled there with a friend's visiting mother as a passenger; she was definitely not your outdoors type, but enthusiastic about her canoe adventure. "How pristine!" she cooed, clutching the gunwales. "How . . ." Two 757s roared right overhead, so when they'd passed, she was shouting. "How peaceful! How desolate!"

"Desolate" isn't quite what comes to mind for a place under the flight path, with townhouses and high rises up on the river bluffs, but it's true that much of this area is ungroomed, undecorated, and that's the weedy charm of it. Parks with lawns and tidy shores are fine, but what's really valuable are the leftover places with a hint of wild. If you're a canoeist, you don't want to be limited to the Boundary Waters—you need home places to paddle. If you teach canoeing, as I do, you really like a back yard area for a nice afternoon or evening—and a hundred times better when your river has a certain scrappy look to it, including tall swamp grasses and sandy banks torn up by spring floods.

A few canoeists and fishermen hang out down there with the wild-life. Year round. Two guys I know try to paddle Hidden Falls on New Year's Day on any ice-free year. The earliest I've canoed at the conflu-ence was on spring equinox, one unusually warm year. That time, we put in far up the Minnesota River to float home. The day started with way too much organizing, a dozen high-octane people all focusing their urban skills—their managing, their efficiency—on the simple task of getting boats on muddy water. Within half an hour, though, the river had mellowed us all out—we pulled ashore on a marshy bank, spread tarps on the mud, opened our Urban Canoe Lunch: Belgian chocolate, calamata olives, hummus in three flavors, and Chilean grapes. Then we turned our Crazy Creek chairs to the sun, and leaned back for the real point of the trip—the first outdoor nap of spring.

Late that afternoon, down toward Fort Snelling State Park, we heard a motor, and met the only other party on the river that March day. A waterskier in head-to-foot black neoprene, towed by an aluminum fishing boat. He waved and cruised by twice—not in that arrogant, show-off style of summer skiers, kicking up a wake, to the irritation of canoeists. No, just friendly—a performance artist, doing a nutty thing, surprised and happy to find an audience.

A warning note here! Early spring can be a really bad time to canoe in Minnesota, what with potential flooding or even moderately high water. The lousiest day of canoeing I've ever had was an April day at the confluence. I think I was tricked into it. A nice middle-aged woman in one of my canoe classes got me to agree to a private lesson for the German exchange student living with them—a young woman whose dream was to paddle on the Mississippi. In May or June, I figured, but—oh, no—it turned out the kid was going home to Germany. It was now or never. Mid-April—and Helen and sixteen-year-old Grete showed up without raincoats. I dug up some old ratty ones, and stowed a pile of extra wool jackets with our lunch in waterproof packs. We left a car at Harriet Island, and launched my biggest, most barge-like canoe at Hidden Falls. The rain started. The wind picked up. After Pike Island, where the river gets wider, things got quite nasty. A stiff upriver wind meeting a fast downriver current produces steep, peaky waves. I'd started out paddling stern, and stayed there—to hell with teaching, I was staying in control. In the bow Grete paddled on, steady as a metronome, her head ducked into her raincoat. Helen in the "duffer" post in the middle wiggled, trying to stay warm, and handed us damp sandwiches, which we stuffed down between paddle strokes. The rain turned to sleet.

Mississippi River

. . . if you catch it on the right day, you may see muskrats
sunning themselves on the ice and diving right
through the slush for snacks. My best count was eighty.

Another warning: Come to think of it, unless you've got good canoe skills and really good judgment, you might want to think twice about paddling here at any season. If you go upstream from Hidden Falls, there's the Ford Dam. The backwash below a dam can pull the unwary canoeist or power boater upstream, capsizing them in the dangerous backcurlers and foam. On warm summer days you'll see skilled whitewater paddlers practicing—below that backwash, down in the run-out—but a noted local paddler confessed (after a beer or two) that he once rode those waves totally out of control. His pointy-ended solo boat was caught by waves from behind and picked up. Surfing the waves may seem like a hell of an exhilarating ride, but it's less fun when you're being carried at top speed right toward a concrete embankment.

And then there are the towboats. They kick up quite a disturbance in the river when pushing a half-dozen barges, and at any time the prop wash is something to stay well away from. Towboat waves are most impressive in the narrow stretches, or where concrete walls edge the river. The Mississippi doesn't like being hemmed in, and those waves come slamming back, ricocheting from the shore, and get you coming and going.

You don't actually need to get on the water to enjoy the undeveloped river edge. Wander around in Crosby Farms Park, where weedy little floodplain lakes are full of waterfowl. Get off the trails, so you can track deer and beaver in the sand left over from the last flood.

Or if you really want to be canoeing, but would rather stay out of the river currents, there's always Pickerel Lake, a floodplain lake in Lilydale Regional Park. A few years ago fifty-five-gallon drums with paint or dubious chemicals turned up in the park. Beater trucks with massive tires went mud-racing up the steep hillside. The park's been cleaned up these days, and you hardly ever find a ratty sofa dumped in the lake anymore, just the odd tires.

In spring, the ice of the lake turns to mush—if you catch it on the right day, you may see muskrats sunning themselves on the ice and diving right through the slush for snacks. My best count was eighty. There's plenty of evidence of beaver work, and when the ice leaves, the Canada geese and ducks cruise in. Songbirds, too, and there are a few glorious weeks of fine canoeing and birdwatching, until the lake gets too weed-choked for easy paddling. There's no official landing, just a small, cleared mud-gravel slope used by a few fisherpeople and a canoeist or two. Come to think of it—do I want more people there? I'll warn you, the parking area is a mud hole; most years it requires a high-clearance vehicle. There are all those old tires around, and piles of cardboard. You wouldn't like it. Pickerel Lake—it was a scuzzy place to take Sunny, a nice middle-aged woman wearing neat pink and white clothes. She was planning a Boundary Waters trip, and wanted a solo canoe lesson. We could have gone to some nice lake with a sand beach, but Pickerel was closer. And there was the privacy factor. Who wants to try their first solo paddling or capsizing with an audience of picnickers? Pickerel offered solitude and a chorus of warblers. Our two tiny boats glided silently as she practiced turns and got some confidence. Then, at the far end of the lake, where the weeds were thick, we looked over the treetops at thunderheads that had sneaked in. Big slaty ones. "Head for shore right here, Sunny," I called. "Wind's going to happen!" Wind arrived instantly, and the squall capsized her. But at the end of Pickerel Lake, up there where the muskrat houses are, was just four feet of water over a foot or two of goose shit. Up to her armpits in water, she started to laugh. "Don't even try to get back in," I yelled over the wind. I paddled, she waded; just as we hit shore, the wind whirled by with a last hurrah. One of those huge old hollow cottonwoods slammed down into the water, right between us.

We settled for discretion then. We dragged our boats through the wet, stubbly cattail field to the road. Sunny was beaming. "You've got mud on your nose," I said. (Everywhere else too.) "I know!" she said, with pride, and didn't rub it off. I hope her Boundary Waters trip wasn't an anticlimax.

Judith Niemi has been operating Women in the Wilderness *from an office on Saint Paul's West Side since 1986. It's one of the oldest women's adventure programs in the country. Specific programs (many for women, some for men and women) vary from year to year, but they have usually included international travel, particularly in the Arctic; canoe travel and instruction; northern Minnesota retreats for cancer survivors and others; and writers' workshops.*

2007 plans include the Amazon rainforest and Machu Picchu, Feb. 17–March 1, winter and summer programs in northern Minnesota, and, in Saint Paul, private canoe instruction, classes in reconnecting with the natural world, tracking, and writing workshops, some for credit from Hamline University. For a calendar of Women in the Wilderness *trips and classes, call 651.227.2284 or email judith@womeninthewilderness.com.*

August

Circus Juventas Aug. 2, 3, 4, 5, 9, 10, 11, and 12

Irish Fair Aug. 10–12

Japanese Lantern Lighting Festival Aug. 19

Twin Cities Black Film Festival Aug. 17–19

Minnesota State Fair Aug. 23–Sept. 3

Downtown Saint Paul Farmers' Market Through Nov. 11

See page 286 for more information on August events.

Saint Paul isn't really known for its floods, but as recently as April 13, 1997, the Mississippi River crested at 22.35 feet, 8.35 feet above the flood stage. The highest flood was recorded on April 16, 1965, with a crest of 26 feet.

AUGUST

S	M	T	W	T	F	S
			1	2	3	4
5	6	7	8	9	10	11
12	13	14	15	16	17	18
19	20	21	22	23	24	25
26	27	28	29	30	31	

30 Monday

31 Tuesday

1 Wednesday

2 Thursday

Circus Juventas
page 286

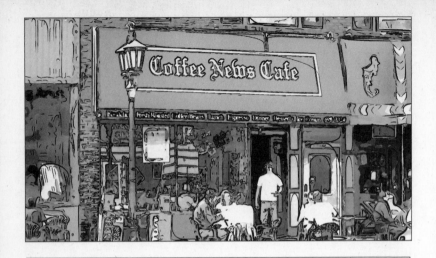

3 Friday	Circus Juventas *page 286*

4 Saturday	Circus Juventas *page 286*
	Capital City Classic Cruisers *page 282*
	Downtown Saint Paul Farmers' Market *page 281*

5 Sunday	Circus Juventas *page 282*
	Downtown Saint Paul Farmers' Market *page 281*

Minnesota Waffles

3 eggs (separated)

1 tbsp. sugar

1 pinch salt

½ cup melted butter

1 pint milk

2½ cups flour

2 tsp. (rounded) baking powder

Beat yolks, add sugar, salt, milk, butter, and flour. Beat whites until stiff, and fold in last with baking powder.

from *The Bride's Book of Recipes and Household Hints,* published and copyrighted by Carleton J. West, 902 Lindeke Building, Saint Paul, Minnesota, 1939 (from Lore Tilsen's beautiful collection of recipe books).

Hampden Park Co-op at 928 Raymond

Slanted

May Lee

Maybe this time I won't italicize them
Foreign words
Hmoob words
My words
They aren't foreign to me
But the MLA Handbook says
I must differentiate them from the others
Isolate them
Slant them next to all the straight letters
Show they are not as solid with their squiggly lines

But they will think I am dumb
Too dumb to even know how to break the rules
They will wonder how kuv, in its lower case-ness,
could ever compare to the mighty, capital I
or how hlub, light and airy in sound,
could actually have as much depth as love
or how koj, its sound harsh to the ears,
could merely mean you

They will wonder at all these things
And never see a world beyond their own
So then I think I must create it
A world in which I exist
In which kuv is the norm
Not the alien
I will leave the letters alone
I will leave them upright,
standing tall
and, in my eyes,
natural

The Better Business Bureau was created right here in Saint Paul in 1911. Finally consumers were able to protect themselves against fraudulent businesses.

AUGUST

S	M	T	W	T	F	S
			1	2	3	4
5	6	7	8	9	10	11
12	13	14	15	16	17	18
19	20	21	22	23	24	25
26	27	28	29	30	31	

6 Monday

7 Tuesday

8 Wednesday

9 Thursday

Circus Juventas
page 286

Gates Ajar Flower Display at Como Park

10 Friday	Circus Juventas
	Irish Fair
	page 286

11 Saturday	Circus Juventas
	Irish Fair
	Capital City Classic Cruisers
	Downtown Saint Paul Farmers' Market
	pages 281, 282, and 286

12 Sunday	Circus Juventas
	Irish Fair
	Downtown Saint Paul Farmers' Market
	pages 281 and 286

The Ford Bridge

Vernon Holmberg

As a forbidden summer activity, we enjoyed swimming at the Ford Bridge over the Mississippi River between Minneapolis and Saint Paul. We would leave our clothes at the base of one of the columns on the Minneapolis side, crawl up on the concrete arches until we were over the deep water, and then dive or jump into the river. We didn't know it was illegal or prohibited because there were no signs. We did know, however, that it was not proper to run around outside naked. One afternoon in July we were diving from the arches into the river. When we were all up on the arches, a police car pulled up under the bridge.

"Hey, you guys, come here," yelled a policeman as he got out of the police car. He probably wanted to tell us something that we didn't want to hear, so we started up the arch toward the Saint Paul side of the river. The other policeman got out and they both got up on the bridge arches.

"Hey, you guys, get back here."

The police, knowing the third bridge column stood in the water on the Saint Paul side, thought they had us trapped. We, knowing that there was a rope to swing to shore with, kept running over the arches. All ten of us, without a stitch of clothes on, swung on the rope one by one, reached the bank, tied the rope to a pipe, scrambled up the bank to the bridge roadway, sprinted across the 1,500-foot bridge, ran down the hill on the Minneapolis side, got to the police car, and then let the air out of two tires. Then we put on our clothes and strolled home.

The Artists' Quarter

Bradley Wakefield

Jazz. Jazz is cool, and they play it at the AQ. If you're lucky trendy enough, you might get to see Happy Apple play. I'm not—they're always sold out. So you can settle for Fat Kid Wednesdays or Green instead. Green sometimes is accompanied by Envy—who also goes by Intersept when they aren't following up Envy . . . and they have the hottest bari sax player this side of the river, Jake Wylie. And even though Billy Holloman is gone, the organ night still remains. So jazz is cool 'n all, and they play it at the AQ about every day.

Except Mondays. That day they open up/branch out from the usual jazz scene and move into murkier territories. The open mike night. Dun DUN DUN! It's a two-drink minimum to get in, but it's more of a heavy recommendation rather than an order.

You can sit down and watch others embarrass themselves as they trip over their crappy poetry. Lament! Woe! Not to be so closed minded, however, there is the occasional talent that graces the stage for the allotted five-to-seven minutes and will keep you from talking, make you feel, and possibly make you laugh (with them). But it's open, so it's not just poetry. You also get guitar players who think playing DMB will get themselves some chicks. I still applaud the bravery it takes to go onstage. You also get the comedian who's funny, the singer who's hot, and the writer who's beautiful—which is why I go.

The Artists' Quarter

S	M	T	W	T	F	S
			1	2	3	4
5	6	7	8	9	10	11
12	13	14	15	16	17	18
19	20	21	22	23	24	25
26	27	28	29	30	31	

Saint Paul has over 160 parks, 41 recreation centers, eight 18-hole golf courses, and over 100 miles of trails on 24 paths.

13 Monday

14 Tuesday

15 Wednesday

16 Thursday

University Avenue at Fry Street

17 Friday	**Twin Cities Black Film Festival** *page 286*

18 Saturday	**Twin Cities Black Film Festival** *page 286*
	Capital City Classic Cruisers *page 282*
	Downtown Saint Paul Farmers' Market *page 281*

19 Sunday	**Twin Cities Black Film Festival**
	Japanese Lantern Lighting Festival
	Downtown Saint Paul Farmers' Market
	pages 281 and 286

Twins

GeGe Youngdahl Anderson

I grew up in Minneapolis. For me, Saint Paul was a mysterious city mentioned on the dinnertime news, but rarely visited. There were exceptions—the State Fair in August and the occasional trip to Como Park Zoo. When my oldest brother ventured off to the University of Minnesota, I would hear him mention the Saint Paul campus and I'd think it wondrous that he could travel to that mysterious land for some of his classes. It was a faraway kingdom to me.

I am not sure why Saint Paul was such a mystery. I do remember meeting teenagers at the annual State Fair. There was always good-hearted teasing that the biggest advantage that Saint Paul (or Minneapolis) had was the beautiful city across the river.

So why the confusion about the unidentical twins?

I was born in 1945 at the end of the Big War. Returning soldiers were eager to establish the good life in good communities where no one goose-stepped or dropped bombs. They wanted safe neighborhoods for the soon-to-be-born baby boomers. They would carry their lunch pails to work daily and take their wives shopping in the one-family car on Friday nights. After homework and chores were completed, the children had city park programs, YMCA, scouting programs, and, of course, the church. These organizations were within walking distance and used to entertain, educate, and guide these shiny-faced boomers. There was no need to leave the immediate community. It was self-contained.

Saint Paul residents and Minneapolitans stayed with their own. It was not intentional. The world was just a much larger place in the 1950s—no need to venture to the other side of the river.

Minneapolis and Saint Paul have been called the unidentical twins, but it's like twins raised in different households. I look at Saint Paul as the classy twin and Minneapolis as the hip twin. Minneapolis is progressive and Saint Paul conservative. Saint Paul is Sophia Loren to Minneapolis' Goldie Hawn. Both have charms.

The Twins are like any siblings. They complain about each other, they resent the advantages of the other, and yet, let an outsider criticize them and there is trouble. Years ago (but not nearly enough years—I can still remember it), our former governor, who loved the glamour of the entertainment industry, was on a late-night talk show. He made a remark about the streets of Saint Paul having been designed by a drunken Irishman. I have been lost in Saint Paul on many occasions and I've complained about my lack of understanding the street-grid logic, but that suburbanite-turned-governor crossed the line when he ridiculed my twin to the entire nation. He was out of line. I wanted to meet him and question his mother's footwear or his legitimacy. I was angry. Saint Paul is a sibling.

That faraway kingdom is closer than it once was. I still get lost on my journeys there, but I have matured enough to genuinely embrace my city's twin. I am proud of her and her style and grace. I know she respects my let's-go-forth-and-be-cool style. We bicker, we roll our eyes at each other's policies, but we're sisters, and we believe the sum of our parts is fabulous!

First National Bank Building from Raspberry Island

Saint Paul received three deer as a gift in 1897. So the Como Zoo was created; the deer were put in a fenced-in pasture.

AUGUST

S	M	T	W	T	F	S
			1	2	3	4
5	6	7	8	9	10	11
12	13	14	15	16	17	18
19	20	21	22	23	24	25
26	27	28	29	30	31	

20 Monday

21 Tuesday

22 Wednesday

23 Thursday

Minnesota State Fair
page 286

Sweeney's Saloon on Dale Street. A Writing Place for August Wilson.

24 Friday	**Minnesota State Fair** *page 286*

25 Saturday	**Minnesota State Fair** *page 286* **Capital City Classic Cruisers** *page 282* **Downtown Saint Paul Farmers' Market** *page 281*

26 Sunday	**Minnesota State Fair** *page 286* **Downtown Saint Paul Farmers' Market** *page 281*

Food on a Stick

Minnesota State Fair

Russ Ringsak

It is the largest state fair in the country and it features most of the things that any of the other fairs feature, including hogs the size of full-grown steers, steers up there at a ton, heavy as bison, and pumpkins the size of easy chairs. The puke-inducing rides, the sling-shot launching folks up into the goose flyways, the ring-the-bell mallets, darts and balloons, floating ducks, and all the rest. National rock and country acts in the grandstand, stages all up and down the midway, people carrying huge stuffed animals.

What really separates this fair from a lot of others, however, is that, for ten days at the end of summer, it is likely the world's largest market for boiling oil and sharp sticks. There is an incredible array of food offered on a stick here, thirty-seven varieties at last count, including Deep Fried Candy Bars, Cheese on a Stick, Chocolate Covered Cheese, Chocolate Covered Bananas, five kinds of Pickles on Sticks, the Field and Stream (walleye and prime rib), Pizza on a Stick, Scotch Eggs, Teriyaki Ostrich, and Alligator—either breaded or as Naked Alligator on a Stick. And to cleanse the palate for some stick-mounted Fudge Puppies and Taffy Pops, try Watermelon on a Stick.

Probably a good thing for all of us that the fair only comes once a year; and that, at least so far, we have no chains of boiled-in-oil food-on-a-stick restaurants either.

The Minnesota State Fair runs for the last ten days of summer, including Labor Day. The fairgrounds are located on Snelling Avenue and Como Avenue north of Interstate 94 in Saint Paul.

"Food on a Stick" is an excerpt from Minnesota Curiosities, *a guidebook to things quirky, odd, and outrageous in Minnesota—a fun, short read. The new edition came out in December 2006. Find it at your local bookstore or order it at www.globepequot.com.*

Friend on a Stick

Kelsey Bour-Schilla

Back in seventh grade, whenever one of my friends was sick and away from school, we would make them "a page." A page was a notebook piece of paper with their picture drawn on it—we would tape it to their desk in every class. It would be "the Marin page," "the Sam page," et cetera. This was something we kept up through high school.

My best friend Steph spent her senior year of college in Chile as an exchange student. We always went to the State Fair on a special day—just the two of us—so instead of moping about her being gone, I used the computer to print out an 8 × 10 photo of her head on thick paper and I taped it to a stick and brought her to the fair, just me and her. We ate corn dogs and saw the animals and the horse shows. We had a blast. I even had our pics taken in an old black-and-white booth to send to her in Chile.

Another Year Together
at the State Fair
Photo Booth

Steph on a Stick

The Saint Paul City High School Conference was born on Friday, October 28, 1898. That night Central High School played Mechanic Arts High School in a football game. Central won 25–0.

AUGUST

S	M	T	W	T	F	S
			1	2	3	4
5	6	7	8	9	10	11
12	13	14	15	16	17	18
19	20	21	22	23	24	25
26	27	28	29	30	31	

27 Monday

Minnesota State Fair
page 286

28 Tuesday

Minnesota State Fair
page 286

29 Wednesday

Minnesota State Fair
page 286

30 Thursday

Minnesota State Fair
page 286

31 Friday   Minnesota State Fair
                                       page 286

1 Saturday   Minnesota State Fair
                                       page 286

                              Capital City Classic Cruisers
                                       page 282

                          Downtown Saint Paul Farmers' Market
                                       page 281

2 Sunday   Minnesota State Fair
                                       page 286

                          Downtown Saint Paul Farmers' Market
                                       page 281

Rondo Oral History

Oral History is the spoken word in print. Oral histories are personal memories shared from the perspective of the narrator. By means of recorded interviews, oral history documents collect spoken memories and personal commentaries of historical significance. These interviews are transcribed verbatim and minimally edited for readability. The greatest appreciation is gained when one can read an oral history aloud.

Kate Cavett, oral historian,
HAND in HAND Productions

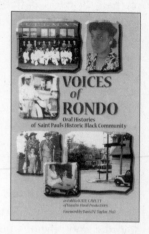

The following oral history is excerpted from Voices of Rondo: Oral Histories of Saint Paul's Historic Black Community *and is used by permission.* Voices of Rondo *won a 2006 Minnesota Book Award.*

Nathaniel Abdul Khaliq

I am Nathaniel Abdul Khaliq, formerly Nathaniel Raymond Davis, also known as Nick Davis. I was born and raised at 304 Rondo, and I remember our house was probably a quarter of a way off of the cross street of Farrington. Growing up, I didn't have any brothers or sisters. I was raised by my grandparents, and so my cousins, the Ransoms, who lived down the street from us, were just like brothers and sisters to me. We had a ton of fun. You know, no drama.

I remember my grandfather, Reverend George Davis, who was a wonderful man and he was a minister, and he would be out

Nathaniel Abdul Khaliq

in the yard and these people would come by with liquor and cussing and raising hell. And they would see him and hide the liquor, and the cussing would cease. And they would greet him, "Howya doin', Reverend Davis?" and go on about their business and continue on with their unacceptable behavior.

Another fond memory I have of Rondo was the respect that people had for my grandfather. He was a reverend but he didn't have a church. The house had a sign on it: Union Gospel Mission. And so he would have little church services and maybe one or two neighbors would come besides the family. And he lived by very strong principles. I didn't find out until later that he used to be a drunkard. And I found out later about his history that he was the son of a former slave master, that he spoke Spanish fluently and spoke other languages, and he was from Texas. He was a child of the slave master, but he was one of the few slaves that was able to go to school and stuff. He was a tremendous individual. I remember his station wagon, his bib overalls, and every now and then he would put on a suit and a derby hat and go on about his business.

My grandmother, Bertha Miller Davis, was blind and was the most spiritual and religious person I've ever met in my life. She never ever complained about anything. Every day all she talked about was God. At that young age I just couldn't figure it out. She's blind and she doesn't get to hardly do anything, just around the house doing all these things. But she never complained. So I had a very strong spiritual upbringing and foundation. My grandfather and grandmother were outstanding role models for me as far as being rooted in spirituality.

He would talk about other Blacks during that time, about they're so smart and everything, but they still can't get the same respect as White men get because segregation in the South was running rampant, and even up here we had de facto segregation. In Saint Paul our de facto segregation was that certain places you just knew you didn't go—Rice Street, even Grand Avenue.

The story goes his real name wasn't Davis. I believe it was Stewart. He was raised on a plantation and was the child of a Black woman and a White man, and he was mixed with all kinds of different things. Beautiful man—golden brown skin, white hair, and a beautiful mustache and everything. And so he came up here. He had had a conflict down there and supposedly killed a White man, and they got him out of town and he ended up here in Saint Paul. When he first came here he was in a boardinghouse a little while. Then he met my grandmother, who came up here with a couple of her brothers and sisters from Memphis, Tennessee. So she got hooked up with that no good scoundrel, as he was at that time, and he evolved and turned himself around and they stayed here. They had, I believe, eleven or twelve kids.

Well, one of the things that stands out in my mind is he was a man of enormous courage, and I think it's difficult to have courage unless you have faith. And I would just watch him interact with some of these mean people on the streets, and he demanded respect, from the police and everyone. I didn't just grab it at a young age and say I'm going to get here and get involved. I didn't really come to my senses until later in life. But as I would reflect on how courageous he was and how he had a sense of justice and demanding justice and respect, it's just something that sort of stuck with me later in life.

He felt very passionately that with the freeway coming in he should not lose his home. For some reason I wasn't aware that we were really the last house on Rondo. People were moving out and I knew they wanted to do the freeway and everything, but I wasn't really aware of the deep controversy, even though I watched his demeanor and attitude change, and he got a little more embittered. Something I noticed later on when this whole thing about them taking the house—he expressed a bitterness towards White people that I had never heard him express before, because he was part White himself. He kept saying over and over again how he wasn't giving up his house. He couldn't understand why all these other people that were a lot smarter and had money to get attorneys and do all this other stuff, why they would just give up without a fight. He wasn't going to do that.

And my grandmother, she would just sit there and listen. And he made it clear that he would draw the line in the sand, and I knew he had a shotgun, but he wasn't going anywhere. If they came in there to take him out of his home someone was going to get hurt, and he was willing to give his life because he felt that was his, that he was old and he'd probably never own any land, and land was important to him.

So one day I went to school, and when I came home, these White dudes were tearing the house up with sledgehammers and axes. Not knocking it down, but later I realized they were just making it unlivable. I'm walking around looking, no Grandma, no Grandpa or anything, and I'm wondering, "What's going on?" And I started crying, and I don't know if it was a highway patrolman or a police officer, but someone came up and I told them who I was and stuff, and they said, "We'll take you to your grandma and your grandpa."

As they started one by one knocking down these houses, this cocoon that many of us had been blessed to be a part of started falling apart.

What they had done, they threw all this stuff in the back of the truck and moved us from 304 Rondo off to a house up on the hill on East University past Regions Hospital, it's where Valley Apartments is now. It had to be thirty or forty steps from street level to get up to the house. And they dumped all her stuff in there.

So when they dropped me off and I walked in there my grandpa was just—they just beat him down. I mean not physically of course, but he just didn't have it. He just lost it. I mean not screaming and hollering, but he was just a shell of a man after that. My grandparents stayed there awhile and then I eventually moved in with my mom and they ended up moving onto Central Avenue. Shortly after that, I'd say maybe a year or two after that, he passed.

It just tore him up. I don't know if he lost faith. I know my grandmother didn't, but I don't know if he lost faith or what. He was never the same. Our interactions and stuff, when I would go by and visit him—he just never got over it, how they could do that to him. Nobody—I mean no organizations, nobody—did anything about anything, about his situation and how they treated him.

I was so young back then, but I just think that somehow the way they presented that thing, it sort of caught people off guard and people didn't get a chance to react and respond to it. As they started one by one knocking down these houses, this cocoon that many of us had been blessed to be a part of started falling apart. One minute we're living in this community where there's Black businesses and people getting along and everything is just wonderful, you can sleep on the porch. All these insulators were there to protect us, by the grace of God, and then all of a sudden, you're losing this family, and you're losing that family. And people wonder what is going to happen, where are these people going to go? There wasn't any comprehensive plan to say, "Well, we're going to bring a freeway through here, and then we're going to relocate people if they want to relocate in this particular area or that particular area." It was like they dropped a bomb and pieces of the cocoon went scattering all over, never to be put back together.

Some of those older folks. I don't think their heart ever mended from that. You know, a lot of relationships that people had established, "How ya doin', Mr. So-and-So?" over the years, talking to people over the fence, on the sidewalk. That was gone. And being transplanted somewhere else where you pretty much had to start all over.

My grandmother's faith carried her through the day. I never heard her complain until the time she passed—she probably passed some fifteen, twenty years later—she never spoke a bitter word about it. She got through it. She managed.

My grandparents' faith was always an inspiration to me. I think first of all, we are all children of Adam and Eve, and of Abraham. My new faith, Islam, is just an extension of my earlier experience with my grandmother and grandfather, even though they were Christians. We're trying to reach the same destination. I'm trying to get the same moral strength that they gathered from faith—without putting a title on it—and for whatever reason, God has decided to give me a little different understanding. I may not say the Father and the Son and the Holy Ghost. I say Allah, but it's just a different name. It's the same entity. And so as I got older, I began to appreciate and understand why he and my grandma was so strong. Because if you're out here in this mad world and don't, as we say, hold on to the rope of God and have some faith, you're going to get into a little bit of trouble. You will end up succumbing to all the different things out here.

That's not to say that I've led a perfect life. I can't even come close to that. But because of that spiritualness, and that foundation from my grandparents, it set some limits in my madness. That early experience with my grandfolks would bring me back to reality. I've said I'm sorry a lot of times in my sixty years, and have pleaded and begged for forgiveness. I'm sure I would have my grandfather's blessings. Even though it's not of the same faith, it's the same road, and we're just using different means to get to our destination.

So now, God willing, when I go on this Hajj, one of the first things we will do is discard all our garments, and we all put on the same two-piece wardrobe, covering your top part and your bottom, so when you look around you don't see a king, you don't see someone with diamonds. You don't know who you're standing next to. That's that transformation, and I'm just thankful and blessed that God has chosen me to be a part of this.

September

Minnesota State Fair Aug. 23–Sept. 3

Minnesota American Indian Festival Dates to be
announced

Selby Avenue JazzFest Sept. 8

Saint Paul Classic Bike Tour Sept. 9

Wild River Music, Comedy, and Film Festival Dates to be
announced

Ramsey Hill House Tour Sept. 16

Downtown Saint Paul Farmers' Market Through Nov. 11

See pages 286–287 and 294 for more information on September events.

In 1955 Saint Paul became a sister city with Nagasaki, Japan. This was the first sister city relationship between the U.S. and Asia.

SEPTEMBER

S	M	T	W	T	F	S
						1
2	3	4	5	6	7	8
9	10	11	12	13	14	15
16	17	18	19	20	21	22
23/30	24	25	26	27	28	29

3 Monday

Labor Day

Minnesota State Fair
page 287

4 Tuesday

5 Wednesday

6 Thursday

7 Friday

8 Saturday

Selby Avenue JazzFest
page 287

Capital City Classic Cruisers
page 282

Downtown Saint Paul Farmers' Market
page 281

9 Sunday

Saint Paul Classic Bike Tour
page 294

Downtown Saint Paul Farmers' Market
page 281

Saint Paul Classic Bike Tour

Heidi Annexstad

When we pedaled our bikes down East River Road for the Saint Paul Classic Bicycle Tour last fall, I was sleepy (it was early Sunday morning), grumpy (I ran out of time to make coffee at home), and a little bit bored. I didn't need to pay attention—the route was numbingly familiar to me from countless rides and walks. I was there for the exercise, not the views.

Only my seven-year-old, Simon, kept me alert. I took sag duty with him while my husband and the older boys zoomed ahead to the first rest stop at Hidden Falls Park. I was anxious about the distance; this was Simon's first fifteen-mile trip under his own power, and I didn't relish the thought of pushing him if he wore out. Mostly, however, I feared he would ride like a second-grader, with more enthusiasm than judgment. I warned Simon against performing his latest feat of bravery—riding with his hands off the handlebars—and took up my position directly behind his rear tire.

I needn't have worried. After a couple of near misses and a stern lecture about passing etiquette, he became a model bicyclist. By the Ford Motor Plant, he was sprinting madly, just for the pleasure of yelling "On your left" to the unsuspecting riders ahead. He would have raced past Hidden Falls if I hadn't finally gotten close enough to him to utter the magic words, "Snacks on your right!"

There was plenty of food, coffee, and music at the rest stop. We were both well fortified as we wheeled off down Shepard Road. We had just rounded the bend of the river when Simon stopped so suddenly I nearly ran him over. I hustled him out of the peloton and asked what was wrong.

"Nothing is wrong, Mom," he said. "Look! From here I can see everything in the world." Behind us, Fort Snelling loomed over the junction of the Minnesota and the Mississippi; ahead of us, Saint Paul rose up into the bluffs; and all around in the September sunshine, bicycles flowed with the river to downtown. Perhaps it wasn't the whole world, but it was an excellent slice of the cosmic pie.

The ride kept getting better. Simon gamely pedaled four-fifths of the way up Ramsey Hill before he slid off his seat and walked the remaining yards to Summit Avenue. As we puffed to the top, he said, "Mom, I just

Saint Paul Classic Bike Tour

can't wait to see what's up there." I knew exactly what lay ahead—impressive houses, colleges, and the river. But Simon believed there was magic just over the crest of the hill, and who was I to argue? Let Summit Avenue be the yellow brick road to Oz!

We flew down Summit, eager to find the rest of our family and swap road stories. Simon kept up a nonstop monologue, pointing out every cool house, pretty church, and school we passed. We rode through the triumphal balloon arch by Saint Thomas convinced that this was the best bike ride in the most beautiful city on Earth.

Until the Classic last fall, I thought I knew all about Saint Paul. I had figured out what to do with the car in a snow emergency, which restaurants have the best pho noodles, and where to sit at a Saint Paul Saints game. I knew exactly what I needed to know to function in the city. I knew exactly enough to be bored.

It would be both mawkish and untrue to say that I saw the city with a child's eyes when I rode with Simon. I saw the view from Shepard Road with the same myopic eyes I've been peering through for forty-two years. What I found as I trailed along in Simon's wake wasn't insight but blessed ignorance. Maybe there's something about Saint Paul I don't know. I'd like to find out.

The Saint Paul Classic includes thirty-mile and fifteen-mile routes almost completely free of car traffic. Rides begin at Saint Thomas. Early registration cost of twenty-five dollars benefits Neighborhood Energy Consortium (NEC). Check out the website at www.spnec.org or call 952.882.3180.

Saint Paul is home to 13 higher education institutions, the second highest concentration in the U.S.

			SEPTEMBER			
S	M	T	W	T	F	S
						1
2	3	4	5	6	7	8
9	10	11	12	13	14	15
16	17	18	19	20	21	22
23/30	24	25	26	27	28	29

10 Monday

11 Tuesday

12 Wednesday

13 Thursday

Rosh Hashanah
Ramadan

14 Friday	

15 Saturday	Capital City Classic Cruisers *page 282* Downtown Saint Paul Farmers' Market *page 281*

16 Sunday	Ramsey Hill House Tour *page 287* Downtown Saint Paul Farmers' Market *page 281*

Boyd Park

Virginia L. Martin

If the two men had been alive, there is little question who would have won the competition. Despite their deaths decades earlier, it was still surprising that a Black union organizer beat out a wealthy entrepreneur who had amassed a fortune, including owning a railroad with James J. Hill.

Both Frank Boyd and Norman Kittson were in transportation and both men helped mold Saint Paul, but any resemblance stops there. They were, by proxy, competitors in a park-naming competition in the Summit-University neighborhood in the 1970s. The park, on Selby between Farrington and Virginia, is pretty and lively with cool shade trees, tended grass, flower-lined walks and plots, picnic tables, grills, and vividly colored playground equipment. It is usually busy. On a summer day, a couple of Black men play chess, another fires up a bar-beque grill and pushes picnic tables together, getting ready for a large gathering. Children play boisterously on slides, swings, and gym bars. People stroll meditatively along the paths; couples hold hands; and many use the park as a shortcut from Dayton or Marshall Avenues to the bus that runs on Selby—or to Nina's Coffee Shop on the corner of Selby and Western that local resident and writer Garrison Keillor made famous in his book *Homegrown Democrat*.

In 1973 the Ramsey Hill Association unanimously decided to name the park for Norman Kittson. The association had been formed a few years earlier in the midst of urban renewal, partly to rescue as many of the historic and beautiful old houses as possible and to help people restore them to their former glory in very practical ways. Kittson, one of Minnesota's most important pioneers, was an early fur trader in the American Fur Company. His Red River Transportation Company, formed to transport furs, included a line of steamboats on the Red River and the two-wheeled ox-drawn Red River Carts, famous for their picturesqueness (at least from a distance) and loud squealing from their ungreased axles. Early residents of Summit-University could hear them from miles away as the oxcarts crossed Marshall and Saint Anthony Avenue before heading south and east to downtown Saint Paul.

Kittson moved from the fur trade settlement of Pembina (now in North Dakota) to Saint Paul in 1855, where he was elected mayor.

Already wealthy, he joined James J. Hill in acquiring the Saint Paul and Pacific Railroad, which eventually became the Great Northern Railway. He bought land from Jeremiah Selby's widow up on the bluff above the city called Saint Anthony Hill, where in 1884 he built a beautiful lavish Second Empire mansion. After his death in 1888, the Kittson family broke up, and the mansion was neglected and eventually it became a rooming house. Kittson's neighbor, James J. Hill, was offended by the flophouse nearly next door, and in 1904 the site was turned over to the Archdiocese of Saint Paul, which tore down the old-fashioned mansion and built the Saint Paul Cathedral, a massive, commanding presence that looms over the city.

Porters were expected to work 400 hours a month or travel 11,000 miles with almost no provisions for their rest. They were summarily fired for the slightest transgressions— such as falling asleep after several contiguous shifts.

The Ramsey Hill Association wanted to name the park for the old fur trader, saying (inaccurately) that Kittson was "the oldest settler in this region," and that "Saint Paul will always remember Norman Kittson as one of its most substantial and enterprising citizens." The Saint Paul City Council agreed.

Not so fast, responded the Selby-Dale Freedom Brigade, whose opinion of Kittson was radically different from that of the Ramsey Hill Association. The brigade was part of a group of people, mostly young, who had moved into Summit-U in the late 1960s and 1970s when they could find cheap rooms and apartments in these chopped-up big old houses. Most were students and dropouts from the nearby colleges and universities, and many of them had embraced the counterculture in these turbulent years of the Vietnam War protests and the violence and upheaval of the civil rights movement. A range of ideologies was represented, from liberals and left-wingers to a handful of communists and Maoists, but all of them tried to ally themselves with the African Americans and with the poor in Summit–U as the neighborhood confronted urban renewal (which the Blacks called "Negro removal"). A major issue was that the people in the community had very little voice about what was happening and that housing units were being torn down faster than new ones could be built.

The Selby-Dale Freedom Brigade, which emerged out of this melange of ideologies, objected to using Kittson's name for the park on the grounds that this nineteenth-and early twentieth-century entrepreneur was not a fit man to memorialize. Not only had he had at least two and as many as four Native American "wives" before marrying European Mary Kittson, he sold liquor to the Indians and bought their fur pelts for a pittance and sold them for exorbitant amounts. One brigade member said Kittson "personifies the destructive, imperialistic aspect of American history," and he urged that parks and public buildings be named "for people who have contributed to the struggles faced by those exploited."

Frank Boyd was their candidate. He had moved in 1912 to Saint Paul, which had become a major railroad center, and got a job as a sleeping car porter for the Pullman Company in 1919. It was considered a good job, more desirable than fieldwork, as historian Arthur McWatt, a lifelong resident of Summit-U, and a retired teacher, writes. But the jobs came "at a high price." Porters were expected to work 400 hours a month or travel 11,000 miles with almost no provisions for their rest. They were summarily fired for the slightest transgressions—such as falling asleep after several contiguous shifts. "The Pullman Palace Car Company became the largest private employer of African Americans by the 1920s," writes McWatt. Many of the men employed as porters were well educated—engineers, lawyers, science and business majors. One resident estimated that 50 percent of the Black men in Summit-U were porters.

Boyd Park

Frank Boyd's Bust and Plaque

Attempts to form unions started in the early years of the twentieth century. By 1919, said Boyd, "Every thinking porter was talking organization." In 1925, A. Philip Randolph accepted the leadership of the newly formed Brotherhood of Sleeping Car Porters (BSCP), though it would be another twelve years before the Pullman Company was forced to recognize it.

In that same year, 1925, Boyd organized his first group of porters and in January 1926, the newly organized local #3 of BSCP held its first meetings at the Welcome Hall on Farrington and Saint Anthony streets in Saint Paul's Rondo neighborhood. During the meeting, Boyd was notified he should not report for his run the next day.

McWatt wrote that although Boyd had been fired for his "troublemaking," he went on to lead "one of the most extraordinary movements in American labor history." For forty years, he worked to advance the pay and conditions of sleeping car porters. One writer called Boyd "perhaps the most effective labor leader in Saint Paul history."

Although Boyd was (and is) almost unknown to most people, perhaps naming the park for him is a fitting tribute in a fitting park in the neighborhood that is still home to most of the African Americans in Saint Paul, many of whom owed their own beginnings to the onerous jobs as porters that their fathers and grandfathers held. Near the entrance on Selby Avenue, a small area is set aside for a small bronze bust of Frank Boyd on a pedestal, surrounded by a brightly colored flower garden. The plaque underneath reads, "A fighter for his union, his people, and his class." It looks a little like a contemplative place, a sacred place, and maybe it is.

S	M	T	W	T	F	S
						1
2	3	4	5	6	7	8
9	10	11	12	13	14	15
16	17	18	19	20	21	22
23/30	24	25	26	27	28	29

Saint Paul has 1,813 parking meters along with 24,701 streetlights lining the streets.

17 Monday

18 Tuesday

19 Wednesday

20 Thursday

The Old Beauty Hut on the Corner of Clifton and Jefferson

21 Friday

UN International Day of Peace

22 Saturday

Yom Kippur

Capital City Classic Cruisers
page 282

Downtown Saint Paul Farmers' Market
page 281

23 Sunday

Fall Equinox

Downtown Saint Paul Farmers' Market
page 281

What's a Booya?

Patrick Kahnke

So you're browsing the City of Saint Paul's website, and you come upon this fact about the Highland Park Pavilion: "It has two kitchens and a booya building that can be reserved separately. Groups holding booyas will be required to rent both pavilion kitchens and the booya building for two days."

Like an itch at the back of the brain, a memory emerges of that fire station with a sign out front that said, "Booya this Saturday." You remember the bar down the street with the marquee, all year long, that reads, "Booya October 3rd." Then one after another, images you've seen all over town come flooding back, "Booya tomorrow—everyone invited," "Booya July 15th, Rain or Shine." You can't stand it any longer, so you turn to your dog and shout, "What's a booya, for crying out loud?"

The dog smiles and wanders off into the living room, but you can't shake the curiosity. You have to know. Then you realize, "It's Saturday! I'm going to the Fire Department Booya, and I'm getting some answers."

At the fire station you see people everywhere—laughing, talking, kids falling off the fire truck—and you learn your first fact: a booya is a social event.

Preparing Booya at the Booya Building at Highland Park

Highland Park Booya

But you quickly notice a large group huddled around what turns out to be a thirty-gallon cooking pot—and a couple of older gentlemen are stirring the pot with . . . canoe paddles? An image comes to mind of the "booya paddle" spending 364 days a year gathering "seasoning" dust in the garage with the snowshoes and the fly rod, but you banish the thought and note your second fact: a booya is a food.

But it's a food like no other—or more accurately, like all others. If you look closely enough, you swear you can see some of every food known to humankind floating in the pot. It seems that everyone here has brought some kind of meat or vegetable and dumped it in. So you note your third fact—a combination of the previous two: booya is a social food.

You start asking around, and everything else you learn about booya is contradictory, from the preferred ingredients to the origin of the word. Most don't know where the word came from, but some who hazard a guess say it's a form of the French word *bouillabaisse*—a fish stew. This sounds convincing, until others insist it's derived from the Walloon word *bouyu*, which means "to boil." A student in a Macalester College sweatshirt says it's derived from the Klingon *ghaw'* meaning "igvah liver soup," but you're almost certain that's not correct.

In the end you down your third Styrofoam cupful of the concoction and write your own definition: "Booya: a social food of questionable origin and uncertain ingredients endemic to the Saint Paul, Minnesota, region; enjoyed in vast quantities by a cross-section of the populace in a variety of settings. See also: Luau (Hawaii), Clam Bake (New England), Cheese Eat (Green Bay)."

In 1995 the Friends of the Parks and Trails of Saint Paul and Ramsey County began the Yellow Bike Coalition. A committee fixed up hundreds of bikes, painted them yellow, and made them available for public use.

SEPTEMBER

S	M	T	W	T	F	S
						1
2	3	4	5	6	7	8
9	10	11	12	13	14	15
16	17	18	19	20	21	22
23/30	24	25	26	27	28	29

24 Monday

25 Tuesday

26 Wednesday

27 Thursday

View of the River from Mississippi Boulevard

28 Friday	

29 Saturday	Capital City Classic Cruisers *page 282* Downtown Saint Paul Farmers' Market *page 281*

30 Sunday	Downtown Saint Paul Farmers' Market *page 281*

Caves and Crooks
Saint Paul's Seedier Side

Liz Pasch

It's a typical autumn day in downtown Saint Paul. The sun is bright, the air is crisp, and the sugar maples are aflame with gold and crimson hues—a sure sign that it won't be long until the temps drop below freezing.

The view of the downtown riverfront is stunning. Elegantly restored paddle wheelers are docked near the Saint Paul Yacht Club. The opposite bank is landscaped with a walking and biking trail. Antique-looking street lamps remind me of days when the city was home to such prominent residents as novelist F. Scott Fitzgerald and railroad mogul James J. Hill. The downtown skyline juxtaposes renovated historical landmarks with twenty-first-century financial centers, museums, and concert halls.

If I were visiting here for the first time, the view would make me think that only the most dignified of ladies and gentlemen had ever called this capital city home. But being a local, I know better: this beautiful city spent much of the 1920s and '30s as a haven for gangsters. Even better, many of the gangster hangouts are in the downtown area or within easy walking distance of it.

Criminals, Caves, and Clubs

The era of Prohibition saw sandstone caves along the Mississippi River bluffs—originally formed from mining silica used in glass production—transformed into speakeasies, gambling halls, and nightclubs. One of the more famous clubs is still being used today and from downtown, it's just a ten-minute walk south on Wabasha Street.

I soon find myself standing in the parking lot of a nightclub formerly known as Castle Royal (now called the Wabasha Street Caves), and I realize it looks much the same as in photographs from seventy years ago. It has a brick, castle-like façade that appears to guard the entrance to something dark and sinister.

Okay, maybe my imagination is getting a little carried away. I'm early for the forty-five-minute walking tour, so after opening the squeaky, heavy front door, I have a few minutes to look at the old photos hanging in the entry room. In the 1930s gangsters came to the Castle Royal on the weekends—and the wealthy of Minneapolis and Saint Paul came to see the gangsters. The lavishly decorated caves featured performers including Cab Calloway, the Dorsey Brothers, and Harry James.

> Many residents and most visitors never know
> they're in a former haven for the likes of
> Bugsy Siegel, John Dillinger, and the Ma Barker gang

Nowadays, the caves are used for wedding receptions, business meetings, and live big-band shows. While the guide talks of how a young woman unknowingly danced here one night with John Dillinger, I can almost hear the music and smell the cigars. The room is cozy with warm lighting, updated carpeting, and painted stucco walls and ceilings. I almost forget we're sixty feet underground.

We move into another room, where illicit gambling once raged. Our guide points to bullet markings on the fireplace and talks of a card game turned deadly. I follow the guide deeper into the caves and feel my neck hairs rising. Unlike the outer caves, these rooms are dimly lit, cold and damp, with unfinished ceilings. They're used for storage, as they were in the gangster era, though the goods being stored nowadays are legal. The guide chooses this creepy cave to mention a recent wedding reception that included a gangster-ghost sighting, later verified by psychics.

Wabasha Street Caves

Landmark Center

A few minutes later, I'm at Grumpy Steve's Coffee Shop next door, sipping a latte to warm the chill in my spine, when I notice a motor coach getting ready for a two-hour tour of gangster sites too far for walking. This guide is dressed as "Baby Face Nelson" in a pinstriped suit. He's toting a Tommy gun and is well into character as I climb aboard and spot a front-row seat.

"Who is you?" he demands, scanning his list for my name. "Okay, den. Sad-down and shadd-app!"

He explains how Saint Paul Police Chief John J. "The Big Fellow" O'Connor rolled out the welcome mat for gangsters before World War II with his "layover agreement," which guaranteed safe harbor on three conditions: commit no crimes within city limits, check in upon arrival, and make a "contribution" to the police retirement fund. Then, the bus takes us to the actual hideouts where Bugsy Siegel and Ma Barker took shelter from the fuzz, where John Dillinger was shot, and where others were kidnapped or murdered.

Funny, but the "hideouts" include a regular office building and nondescript white house. I've driven past both countless times, never the wiser.

To the Museum, Madam

The apple I ate earlier wore off at some point between where John Dillinger was shot and where the grandson of the Hamm's Brewery founder was kidnapped. After a stop at a pizza shop, I made my way across the river to downtown Saint Paul, then headed west a couple of blocks on Kellogg Street, where I ran smack into my next gangster site—though it doesn't look like one now.

The Science Museum of Minnesota stands at the former location of the home of Nina Clifford, the area's most prominent gangster-era businesswoman. Her brothel was conveniently located across the street from a gentlemen's club, from which an underground tunnel is rumored to have led to Clifford's back door.

The Minnesota Club, still standing at 317 Washington Street, doesn't deny its association with Clifford and in fact appears to be quite proud of it, given the portrait of the legendary madam hanging on the wall above the main bar. Years after the brothel was demolished and the building site excavated, more than 14,000 artifacts were found, some described as "Victorian love devices."

I spent several hours in the Science Museum, and although some of those "devices" were intriguing, I was eager to walk onward.

Movers and Shakers

A couple of blocks from the Science Museum is the Landmark Center. Built in 1902, it originally served as Saint Paul's federal courts building and housed the office of Minnesota Congressman Andrew Volstead, author of the national Prohibition Law—which many people say actually

The Saint Paul Hotel

Minnesota Club

spurred the growth of organized crime in America. Ironically, the former office of the city's most prominent bootlegger, Leon Gleckman (aka the "Al Capone of Saint Paul"), is just across the street in the Saint Paul Hotel.

I walk toward the hotel and recall what the bus tour guide had said earlier, that gangsters used its circular driveway to transfer illegal alcohol. I find myself standing on the red brick, maybe on the very spot where they once stood, and wonder if any of today's hotel guests know they're staying where gangsters once conducted clandestine "business affairs."

Before my imagination gets too carried away, I treat myself to a late-afternoon cocktail at the lobby bar, watching men dressed in power suits check in at the front desk. They're the movers and shakers of the business world, much like gangsters were in their day, using the hotel as a temporary base. Today, I think, the goods being moved are legal and the shaking isn't deadly. Nevertheless, I skip the second drink, leave a big tip, and take my overactive imagination out the side door.

My car is parked only a fifteen-minute walk across the river, but I read somewhere that the bridge is yet another chapter in gangster history, and an unpleasant one at that.

On that thought, I quicken my step while it's still light. I'd like to get one last look at the colorful landscape before the cold settles over Saint Paul again.

October

Fall Flower Show Oct. 6–Nov. 25

26th Annual Twin Cities Marathon Oct. 7

Saint Paul Art Crawl Oct. 12–14

Sur Seine Music Festival Oct. 12–21

"La Familia" Latino Family Festival & Expo Dates to be announced

Zoo Boo Oct. 20, 21, 26, 27, 28

Great Pumpkin Festival Oct. 28

Day of the Dead Family Fiesta Oct. 28

Downtown Saint Paul Farmers' Market Through Nov. 11

See pages 287–288 for more information on October events.

Built in 1891, the James J. Hill House at 240 Summit Avenue covers 36,000 square feet, took three years to build, and cost $931,275.01. The house had central heating, gas and electric lighting, 13 indoor bathrooms, telephones, and a security system.

OCTOBER

S	M	T	W	T	F	S
	1	2	3	4	5	6
7	8	9	10	11	12	13
14	15	16	17	18	19	20
21	22	23	24	25	26	27
28	29	30	31			

1 Monday

2 Tuesday

3 Wednesday

4 Thursday

Black Dog Cafe and Wine Bar in Lowertown

5 Friday	
6 Saturday	**Fall Flower Show begins** *page 287* **Downtown Saint Paul Farmers' Market** *page 281*
7 Sunday	**26th Annual Twin Cities Marathon** *page 294* **Downtown Saint Paul Farmers' Market** *page 281*

That Old Nash Rambler

Linda Back McKay

Even though there was no reason to expect anything,
he planted his arm of land in Saint Paul, Minnesota,
a magnet of hope, peppered with blackbirds.
He wore his greasy cap until it was the same
Wildroot Cream oil smell as his sweaty head.
I hung by my knees on the jungle gym
not knowing it would be for the last time.
I loved that old Nash Rambler station wagon.

All of the geese are flying south, save the ones
who are already south. None of the fences
have done their jobs. The last of the unkempt
stalks stagger the field, overcome
by pigweed and nettle. Worms
trail brownly through emaciated fruit.

Lilacs cower in their unpreserved utopias,
just sticks with pods of cargo.
I loved it when we went fishing.
See how the vulnerable lake turns circles in the wind,
its invisible song detailed by finches.
The ground exhales the final scent of summer.
All things are made to be given away.

Hmmm . . .

Larry Schilla

Maxfield Elementary School—Land Where the Circus Giraffes Stayed

I was born in 1956 on the upper flats off Shepard Road and James. Our house had no indoor plumbing.

Grandmother was born in a house on Victoria and Saint Anthony in 1906. When she was a little girl, the Shrine Circus came to town and put their animals up across the street—right where Maxfield Elementary School is today. She woke up in the morning and there was a giraffe eating the leaves off the trees outside her window.

Granddad lived on Victoria and Rondo. He ran a store and butcher shop. The nuns from Saint Luke's would come and buy meat. He would take 10 percent off for them. But when weighing it, he would put his thumb on the scale to make up the difference.

In 1962, when I was six years old, they started to make way for 35E through Saint Paul—demolishing homes and building roads and bridges. Part of the project was a bridge that goes over Victoria near Jefferson Avenue. They built it in 1966. When the freeway was finally finished in 1985, they had to resurface that bridge, which had never carried traffic.

When I was eleven or twelve (1967 or '68), I was at the Saint Clair playground and Vic Tedesco was having an ice cream social. Vic asked me to help out, and I did, and it was fun. About a week later, he came to my house and personally thanked me and gave me some tickets for rides at Como Park. He had my vote from then on.

S	M	T	W	T	F	S
	1	2	3	4	5	6
7	8	9	10	11	12	13
14	15	16	17	18	19	20
21	22	23	24	25	26	27
28	29	30	31			

In the 1880s and 1890s there was a bowling alley by the name of Felsenkeller in the bluffs behind Plato Boulevard on the West Side.

8 Monday

9 Tuesday

Lailat-ul-Qadr

Indigenous People's Day

10 Wednesday

11 Thursday

James J. Hill Reading Room at Central Library

12 Friday	Saint Paul Art Crawl
	Sur Seine Music Festival
	page 287

13 Saturday	Saint Paul Art Crawl
Eid-al-Fitr	Sur Seine Music Festival
	Downtown Saint Paul Farmers' Market
	pages 281 and 287

14 Sunday	Saint Paul Art Crawl
	Sur Seine Music Festival
	Downtown Saint Paul Farmers' Market
	pages 281 and 287

You Bring Out the Vietnamese In Me

Bao Phi

After Sandra Cisneros, "You Bring Out the Mexican in Me"

Toi la mot ngoi Vietnamese
Bilingual
Poetry
MC
You want to thank me well
Khong co chi
Let me take you for a ride
Of my refugeography
If your mama could cook
You know she'd make a batch of me
Nasty catastrophes
Oi trio oi
Fatality
See
Bao Phi
La mot nguoi bat lich su
Well, excuse me
I say one for Asian
Two for American
And three for love
You may say hot like whoa
But I say hot like pho
Pho sheezy
Pho life
Pho real
Pho king pho nominal
Because
You
bring out the Vietnamese in me

The waiting fireball.
The suntanned angel on a rice terrace.
The black haired miracle.

You
bring out the Vietnamese in me,
the salted yellow boat child and military brat on airplane in me,
the tracer-bullet eyed Buddhist who gets presents on Christmas in me,

the nuoc mam, ca phe sua da, mangoes and mang cut,
mit and coconut, sugar dried strawberries in Da Lat
and sweet sa sui stains Asian American in me,

the dry-season-heat hearted and black-eyebrow-as-floodgate
for monsoon eyes in me,

the three stripes of song huong blood
under yellow flag skin and song mekong spine in me,

the phillips to cedar square projects to frogtown
in a powderblue used Datsun blaring Depeche Mode in me,
the whole can of aquanet in my hair, switchblade in my right pocket,
razor boxcutter in left pocket
baseball bat in the backseat
gun in the glove compartment
in case you want to f--k
with the refugee in me,

You,
yes you,
whiplash of black hair
and your heart a rose of flame,

You bring out the Vietnamese in me,

The agent orange kool aid drinker and burner of government cheese in me,
The sharpener and painter of fingernails
sipping ginger ale in plastic snap champagne glasses
at Prom center while twisting tornado tango fandangoes
in mango colored suits and white ruffled shirts in me,

the I'm not gonna talk about love
I'm gonna be it in me,

You bring out
the college degree prodigy thug in me,
the communist/republican/I wish there were more
Vietnamese progressives around
in me,
the I'll change the oil filter my goddamn self and
blow the money I saved on lottery tickets in me,
the incense and cigarettes and white clothes at the funeral in me,

You bring out the Vietnamese in me,
circling on the Le Loi boulevard loop
with a thousand other young Saigon Viets,
blinking tail lights of Honda Dream II mopeds like flicked
cigarette butts and laughter
like wind in our faces,

You bring out the Vietnamese in me,
The mua thu la bei
And Saigon dep lam Saigon oi Saigon oi
the firefly in a lee kum kee jar,
the terraced voice,
the sugarcane chunks in plastic bags,
the weak beer and strong cigarettes,
the fanta cola toothpick slinger,
the yogurt-based soft drinks,
the sudden death syndrome,

You bring out
The leaky boat that won't sink
The family photo clutched tight to a chest
When all the rest of the world burns

You
bring out the Vietnamese
in me

tell my life by reading my palm
and you'll find callouses

that's why love is at home
in my tired muscles

and burns under my eyelids
while I sleep,

men, women, soldiers of every color
have walked into my life,
left burning flag shaped scars,
left ghosts shaped like my family,
left me
for dead,

I was the one who survived to love you.
Even if you save me, I won't thank you.

I love to save myself from myself,
I love so these things become me without ruling me,
I love you
because you bring out the Vietnamese in me,

You

Yes, you

Yes, you.

The Marjorie McNeely Conservatory at Como Park, founded in 1915, hosts nearly 400,000 vistors annually.

OCTOBER

S	M	T	W	T	F	S
	1	2	3	4	5	6
7	8	9	10	11	12	13
14	15	16	17	18	19	20
21	22	23	24	25	26	27
28	29	30	31			

15 Monday

Sur Seine Music Festival
page 287

16 Tuesday

Sur Seine Music Festival
page 287

17 Wednesday

Sur Seine Music Festival
page 287

18 Thursday

Sur Seine Music Festival
page 287

19 Friday

Sur Seine Music Festival
page 287

20 Saturday

Sur Seine Music Festival
page 287

Zoo Boo
page 288

Downtown Saint Paul Farmers' Market
page 281

21 Sunday

Sur Seine Music Festival
page 287

Zoo Boo
page 288

Downtown Saint Paul Farmers' Market
page 281

Trick or Treat

Patrick Kahnke

I've got issues about this topic—I'll admit it. Truth be told, I vaguely remember trick-or-treating one time when I was about three years old. I'm pretty sure I went, because I have a memory of holding my mom's hand as I crossed a street, and a kid in a pillowcase with eyeholes was stumbling along on the other side of me (probably one of my many siblings). I remember a scene of a small pile of candy spread out on the living-room floor, and of my hands counting the pieces. I doubt I got to eat most of it (the siblings, again).

I remember one other time I went trick-or-treating—I got to go because our church kids were going around with small milk cartons from UNICEF. I watched the other kids yelling "Trick or Treat!" and getting bags of peanuts, rice crispy bars, and malted milk balls. Then I would say, "Trick or Treat for UNICEF" and wait while the person at the door confusedly fumbled in his pockets for loose change. I found out later that the more socially adept church kids asked for candy as well as money for UNICEF, but I missed

this detail. So my one true childhood experience of trick-or-treating netted me about $1.29 for some other kid. I tried to feel good about the whole thing, with mixed success.

So this year I went on my first extended trick-or-treating safari, escorting my kids, of course. We went with some other families. We had a chili party first, then unleashed our tots on the neighborhood.

I think I really like trick-or-treating. Here were a bunch of people getting to know their neighbors a little better, spending time out in the neighborhood on a beautiful night, sharing things with one another, laughing . . . building community, in other words. As a pastor I've shied away from making a big deal about Halloween, but this was a special night.

The Current and the Temptations

Pat Kahnke

"Papa was a rolling stone, my son
Wherever he laid his hat was his home
(And when he died) All he left us was alone"

How did I get to be almost forty and never hear this song?

I was listening to 89.3 The Current the other day as I was driving, and this song (from 1973, by the Temptations) came on. It lasted seven minutes, and I wanted it to keep going and going. I listened to a few different versions afterward on the 'net, and I've decided that it's one of the top twenty songs of all time—any genre. You've got your Beethoven's *Ninth Symphony,* your *Brandenburg Concertos* by Bach, your "Visions of Johanna" (and a bunch of others) by Bob Dylan, your "Amazing Grace" by John Newton, your "Star Spangled Banner" by Francis Scott Key, and your "Papa Was a Rolling Stone" by the Temptations.

It's such a good song I don't think it's possible to do a bad recording of it, but I think I like Lee Ritenour's version slightly better than the Temptations'. But hey, they're both outstanding.

Sort of dysfunctional subject matter, I suppose, but not as dysfunctional as the country classic "You're the Reason Our Kids Are Ugly."

Anyway—I love The Current. I would have gotten to be eighty years old and never heard this song if it weren't for 89.3.

Saint Paulites need a permit to own these animals: badgers, bees, bison, chickens, chimpanzees, chinchillas, deer, ducks, ferrets, geese, hoofed animals, lizards, miniature pot-bellied pigs, mink, monkeys, pheasants, pigeons, raptors, snakes, turkeys, weasels.

OCTOBER

S	M	T	W	T	F	S
	1	2	3	4	5	6
7	8	9	10	11	12	13
14	15	16	17	18	19	20
21	22	23	24	25	26	27
28	29	30	31			

22 Monday

23 Tuesday

24 Wednesday

United Nations Day

25 Thursday

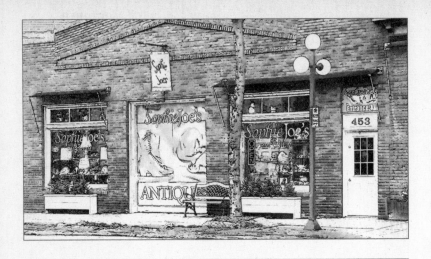

26 Friday

Zoo Boo
page 288

27 Saturday

Zoo Boo
page 288

Downtown Saint Paul Farmers' Market
page 281

28 Sunday

Great Pumpkin Festival

Day of the Dead Family Fiesta

Zoo Boo

Downtown Saint Paul Farmers' Market

pages 281 and 288

Escape the Clouds

Flint Keller

The windows were filthy, but the day was dismal and gray so it didn't matter much. I'll have to clean these windows next spring, I thought, looking through the grime at the whiteness outside. It was not yet winter and already the temperatures were in the teens, and snow covered everything.

Snow had fallen for two days, and in places it was almost four feet deep. The tree swing tried to sway in the wind but the bottom had been buried in the snow. The lack of green and color depressed me more than the thought of driving or shoveling. Next door the brown garage listed even more without the shrubs to steady it. Frozen at its precarious angle, it seemed only the cold now held it from falling into my yard.

The blaring "doodle-dee-du-du-da-doodle-dee-du" of the Nintendo game had been going on for hours in the living room, and my children were silent in its powerful grasp. They did not fight, they did not whine, they did not move. Their grandmother had purchased the toy for them and brought it when she came from California for Thanksgiving. I'd given up on trying to monitor their use of the machine, and I'd noticed their father was as addicted to it as they. I wondered if he was in there with them or if he was watching the game on the TV upstairs instead: helmets crashing, men grunting, and thousands cheering if I ventured up.

My children and husband would spend five to twelve hours straight adhered to the TV; its inane noises pursued and annoyed me. I dreaded the coming winter break with my kids out of school and my husband taking vacation time, too, especially if the Sundays since Nintendo 64 had come into our house were any precursor of things to come. And I had no reason to believe they were not. I longed for the days that produced the drawings on the wall to my left: simple A-frame houses with bright suns in the corners of the pages, flowers that looked like lollipops on green sticks, trees that looked like giant green lollipops on brown sticks; hearts and people, birds and dogs, words scribbled to me or my husband: "I love you Mom." "I love you Dad."

I took the dog for a walk, and realized when I returned that my absence had not been noticed. I went to the kitchen to scratch together a dinner that would not be appreciated, merely eaten. I walked into the living room. The plane on the TV dived and zoomed through a loop, and the three watched in silence; only my son's hands moved on the gray controls. "Dinner," I said for the third time.

"Okay Mom, be right there."

"Now please, I called three times."

"Mom, wait a sec." His eyes didn't flinch from the screen.

I turned to my husband for help. "Phil?"

"Just a sec, Hon, he's just finishing his turn—he's on a . . . Whoa! Go low Benny, go low, atta boy. Sher, why don't you go in with your mom, we'll be in in a sec."

"It's my turn next."

"After dinner, Sher."

"Jeezz. All right, Mom."

"Wash up, Sherri."

Sherri and I were putting Parmesan cheese on our spaghetti when Phil and Ben came in.

"Gold medals on four now!" Ben beamed with delight.

This caused Sherri great concern and she held the Parmesan in mid-shake, looking up incredulously at her brother and father. "You got it?"

"Yeah, it was awesome."

"Jeezz, I missed it, for this." She gestured at the table.

"It's on replay."

"Can we discuss something else during dinner, please? My ears are ringing from that machine."

Silence fell like the quiet that overcomes a room when someone whistles loudly for attention. All I could see of my family was the tops of their heads as they refueled on spaghetti and garlic bread. Through the silence came the sucking, slurping, and whipping sounds of the long noodles.

"Good dinner, Hon." He barely glanced up.

"Yeah, Mom."

I tried to think of something to say to my kids, my husband. How was school? would reap a "fine." How was work? could garner the same—or lists of complaints about troubled kids I didn't really care to listen to. It was Sunday anyway. I waited. Would anyone ask me about me? My day? How I felt? I looked at them all, the kid's eyes were glassed over from video overload, Phil's from his naps, the beers, the game. The usual Sunday.

**I think they actually breathed a sigh of relief to see me go.
I felt like some interloper in their group,
like I didn't have the password or something.**

The kitchen windows were fogged from the warm room. My reflection in the window was distorted, and as condensation began to dribble down the panes of glass, the streaks twisted the face even more.

"So, anybody up for a bit of fresh air after dinner?" I asked.

"Nah," said Ben.

Sherri kind of shrugged. She was the weak link. I thought if I could work on her I might be able to get one of them away from the TV. "Sherri?"

"It's my turn next, Ma."

Phil helped himself to seconds. "I don't think so, babe, not tonight. I just feel like staying in."

"You've been in all day." I could feel the kid's eyes on us waiting for another argument over the Nintendo. But I didn't want that, I didn't have the energy. "I just thought maybe . . . it's really beautiful out."

"It's cold, dark, and snowy, Mom." That ugly sarcasm had crept into his voice.

"You used to love walking in the snow, Ben. It's better than that stupid game."

"No thanks."

Suddenly the smell of my favorite spaghetti made me nauseated. "Okay. I'm going up for a hot bath." And I left them at the table. I think they actually breathed a sigh of relief to see me go. I felt like some interloper in their group, like I didn't have the password or something. I took a warm bath and looked at my swollen belly. I remembered my other swollen bellies before. The excitement of the first. The nightly walks with Phil around the dirt track and baseball diamonds at Balboa Park. The handholding. The warmth. The glow. The whispers into my stomach, "Hello in there, this is your daddy." The excitement seemed to double with my second. A child now placed little hands all over my belly: "Come out so we can play," Sherri would say over and over. She would lay her ear on my belly trying to hear, to listen, to tune in.

Now everyone seemed tuned out. My husband worked from seven in the morning to almost seven each night. The kids came home from school, ate a snack, and left. The garden bloomed and no one watched.

Christmas lights lit the other end of the street and I headed that direction, oblivious of the cold numbing my toes, bare in the house slippers. The quiet of the still night washed over me and I looked up to see the moon trying to escape the clouds.

I spread oil over my round stomach and sang to my new forming babe. I came downstairs in sweatpants and a sweatshirt. And now my daughter's hands scrambled over the controls.

I belonged in the room in the back of the house with the artwork from days gone by taped to the wall, the piles of books on the desk, and the now unused kid's art table in the corner. The lamp illuminated a section of the desk and I stood in the doorway inspecting what it lit up: a *Parent* magazine with a small Chinese baby on the cover, a dictionary of American Sign Language on top of that, a dying spider plant in a handmade Popsicle-stick holder, a stack of mail and assorted documents waiting to be gone through. The baby kicked me. The living room filled with a mild cheer as some milestone must have been overcome in the world of the TV. And a tear rolled down my cheek. The cat purred for food in the kitchen where the dinner plates were still on the counter and the dog scratched to go out.

It was dark and cold, yet when I opened the door, I followed the dog out. It must have been very cold for I felt my damp hair stiffen. The cold didn't creep up on me like it did when I was skiing, slowly edging its way into gloves and boots, then chilling the whole body. It bore into the rubber soles of my slippers instantly and sent a quick chill through my body. But the air felt so fresh in my lungs as I took another deep breath. I walked around to the front of my house. My slippers had decent traction in the new fallen snow and I had beaten down a path on my earlier walk. The shades had not been drawn and the glow from the TV filled the living room. I could not see the people I knew were there, dodging planes or bullets or whatever.

Christmas lights lit the other end of the street and I headed that direction, oblivious of the cold numbing my bare toes in the house slippers. The quiet of the still night washed over me and I looked up to see the moon trying to escape the clouds. The dog ran ahead and back—thrilled to be out again, uncaring that the ritual of boots and coat and gloves and leash draped around his neck had been skipped.

Santa's nose blinked on and off, and across the street another Santa waved at me. The good people in the neighborhood had already shoveled their sidewalks and piles of snow lay pushed off to the sides.

I made my way to the nearby golf course, where the kids and I used to sled. I came to some drifted snow that I chose to wade through rather than go around; my sweatshirt rode up and wet snow tickled my extended belly. There were no cross-country skiers out and no sledders. The new snow would first need to be packed down. The dog danced in the deep snow, up and down, back and forth, head covered in a white mane. I pushed my hands up into opposite sleeves, realizing that my fingertips were beginning to tingle. The clouds pulled back like a sheet on a bed to reveal an almost full moon. The snow glowed white and from here the world did not seem so gray at all.

Above the trees to my right, the conservatory that houses plants of all kinds was lit up. The glass dome of the building glowed, mirroring the moon in the sky. Years before I had pulled the kids in the sled to the conservatory for our first picnic lunch and walk through the eternal summer housed there. "Mom, look at this! What is it?" But before I could catch up to read the tag and tell him that it was a purple dendrobium orchid, Ben had moved on to an anthurium plant, its red waxlike bloom mocking the winter outside. Sherri moved more slowly through the buildings, quietly taking the flowers and plants in—but discussing them at length hours later.

Once, I dug into my old art materials in the basement—art had been my major in college—and had brought a pad for myself, to sketch sunflowers. I had also brought paper and a box of crayons for Ben and Sherri. Before going, I had told them about the great artists and showed them some of Renoir and Cézanne's work.

"I'm . . . who am I, Mom?"

"Cézanne?"

"No, the other."

"Renoir?"

"Yeah," his face lit up in glee, "I'm Renoir."

"Who can I be then, Mom?"

"Cézanne?"

"No, he's dumb."

"How about Mary Cassatt? She was a wonderful artist."

"Yeah, I'm her."

They placed their paper on a bench and began their work. Sherri took on the role of the artist with ease; tossing her head of brown hair back and carefully eyeing her subject before meticulously putting crayon to paper. Ben ripped through page after page, filling them either to satisfaction or flinging them aside to start anew. They didn't last long at their artistic efforts, so neither could I. But we all enjoyed the conservatory immensely each time we went, which was often in the winter.

Going there even prompted us to plant our own gardens at home. I knew nothing about gardening, but we visited the library and spent time picking out plants in the nursery. That was two years ago. I remember Benny often digging half a hole, then running off to play with the neighbors. But while the work in the garden didn't always appeal to the kids, blooming time always did. Watching bud change to flower, the blooming succession from bulbs to perennials. Each morning Ben would run outside to see if anything new had pushed up through the ground, and then run in with a report, "It's coming up, Mom! The watchamathingy! You can see the bud in the middle! Come and see, c'mon!" And out he'd drag me in my robe and bare feet to see a tulip just getting some color deep within the green leaves.

I thought of my lovely children back home, awash in the luminescent glow of the TV, and how the passion was still within each of them—it had just changed. That this obsession with video games would pass. And others would come to take its place. How they might never again revel in the delight of spring in quite the same way they did when they were young, but that was okay.

I thought of Phil, the ups and downs our marriage had gone through, the lovely tender man I knew inside. And I thought of the baby soon to share our bed, the light and life that would surely be added to our family when it came.

I turned to head home. I had walked the dog through the golf course many times, but never before in slippers. My slippers by now were quite filled with snow and my ankles were iced. Never before did I remember it being quite so peaceful and serene out here. It all seemed to be going in slow motion. Each beauty—the quiet, the moon, the glowing conservatory, the white white world—seemed to slowly enter my senses and bathe me in its brilliance.

My body began to shiver and my teeth chattered. I've always loved the sound of my teeth chattering in the cold bed at night before warmth

fills the sheets. How I could make them stop or go faster, or hum to make it sound louder. Now I could not stop them; they were responding to a power higher than me. I made them chatter all the louder and it made me laugh and laugh. But then I was tired.

The snow was deep and a cloud was covering the moon. The wolves howled in their yard at the nearby zoo, and I answered them with chattery teeth. I leaned against a tree in the middle of two fairways and slid down to the ground. The dog came over and licked my face. I tried to lift my hand to pat his face but found I could not. My body chattered and felt cold and warm all at once. I closed my eyes and pictured myself, years before, at my desk, looking out the windows at my children swinging and playing in the backyard. They were cheerful, happy, and full of energy. And sunlight streamed through clean windows.

November

Capital City Lights from mid-Nov.–March

Minnesota State High School League

   Girls' Volleyball Tournament Nov. 8–10

Minnesota Hmong New Year Nov. 22–25

Holiday Bazaar Nov. 29–Dec. 1

Downtown Saint Paul Farmers' Market Through Nov. 11

See page 288 for more information on November events.

S	M	T	W	T	F	S
				1	2	3
4	5	6	7	8	9	10
11	12	13	14	15	16	17
18	19	20	21	22	23	24
25	26	27	28	29	30	

Alexander Ramsey was Minnesota's governor at the start of the Civil War. He later became a U.S. senator and Secretary of War.

29 Monday

30 Tuesday

31 Wednesday

Halloween

1 Thursday

All Saints' Day

Golden Thyme Coffee Shop

2 Friday

Day of the Dead

3 Saturday Downtown Saint Paul Farmers' Market
page 281

4 Sunday Downtown Saint Paul Farmers' Market
page 281

Parting

Gordon Parks

Two roads passed my father's house,
paved with roses and thorns.
They went everywhere, with tolls
unfixed on unmarked distances,
paved with roses and thorns.
Papa said a few things when I was packed to go:
The feel of your feet will reconcile the differences
in which road you take.
Signposts along the way will give devious directions.
It is your right to question, but don't ignore them.
Each one is meant for something.
Summer grass underfoot will be kinder than weeds.
Yet during winter storms, it will be the taller stalks,
leaning above the snow, that will catch your eye.
And you will learn that all things are not the same.
You must select your friends with the same care
I gave to selecting your mother.
Avoid things that die too easy, and get your soul ready
to die well.
As you grow older, you will pray more and worry less.

Well, what I've told you might amount to everything,
or maybe nothing.
Just be thankful if, in autumn, you can still manage a smile.

River Prayer

Linda Back McKay

The old man was not really in a rowboat
under the Mississippi River bridge.
He was in the process of turning
inside himself, as we all will do one day.

Inside, he was finalizing the finished
and unfinished business of his life.
I just made up the part about him in a rowboat,
fishing being some of his best times.

In the rowboat, he tied a hook on a line,
fashioned a slab of plywood into an oar,
nailed, plugged, chopped, and welded
all the materials of his backbreaking years.

This was great work for him and his face
was pinched with effort. Beads of sweat
glinted on his forehead as he gently laid
each of the items back into the water

from which they came, I imagine. The river
was grateful and in return rocked him
in its faithful current downstream
toward home,

which was a warm house filled with sisters
and all his old friends and Ma right there.
There, baking bread in the wood stove
from a recipe in her head.

Saint Paul is considered one of the top ten most livable mid-size cities in the United States. Saint Paul is consistently named one of the healthiest places to live and boasts one of the top ten largest concentrations of creative people, according to Carnegie Mellon University's research.

NOVEMBER

S	M	T	W	T	F	S
				1	2	3
4	5	6	7	8	9	10
11	12	13	14	15	16	17
18	19	20	21	22	23	24
25	26	27	28	29	30	

5 Monday

6 Tuesday

7 Wednesday

8 Thursday

Girls' Volleyball Tournament
page 288

Downtown Saint Paul at Sunset

9 Friday	**Girls' Volleyball Tournament** *page 288*

10 Saturday	**Girls' Volleyball Tournament** *page 288* **Downtown Saint Paul Farmers' Market** *page 281*

11 Sunday	**Downtown Saint Paul Farmers' Market** *page 281*

This Rock Rocks

John O'Brien

I like to think of it as my Saint Paul urban retreat. My rock is an ancient chunk of limestone that juts out above the Mississippi, where I can sit alone, or with others, and take in the scenery. It's located at the west end of Summit Avenue, beyond the tall Celtic-looking cross, through the fence, down the stone staircase, and past the gnarled stump. That's my rock. It's not a very private place; someone is often there when I arrive. They usually don't stay for too long, so we share the view.

I last visited there in mid-November, a very mild fall afternoon it was, record breaking in fact. I watched people on the Minneapolis side walking along the beach, dragging a stick in the sand, skipping stones. Not far away from them, in the woods above, a boy and his dog careened, maneuvering through the trees, both standing and fallen, stirring up the leaves as they ran. They must have been in heaven. It didn't feel too bad on my side, either.

This rocky outpost splits down the middle like a forked tongue. Stones and pebbles surround it as if it's slowly going to pieces. All the visitors over the years and the elements are taking their toll, but there's still plenty of room to sit or lie on my rock.

I saw the bushes rustling on the Saint Paul side. Someone in colorful running gear was racing downhill through the woods, managing somehow to stay on that narrow, dusty path. Most people have trouble just walking on it. He was doing laps, running down, then up and out onto the grass, then back down into the woods again and again. Now that's what I'd call a workout.

I saw the Witch Tower of Prospect Park peaking through the trees. It's supposed to be the highest point in the city of Minneapolis. Two radio towers blinked noiselessly to the right. The two arches of the Lake Street Bridge gracefully spanned the river. Above, cars glided across the bridge, quietly and continuously. Soon they'd be climbing the hill past the golf course. Then along came the number 21 bus all the way from Uptown with three cars trailing very closely behind, not very patiently.

Trees on both sides of the river were almost bare, the lush green of summer and the brilliant yellows and reds of fall all gone. Instead, dull brown leaves carpeted the ground everywhere, all the way to the

Big Rock on the Edge of the Mississippi

water's edge. Just then one solitary leaf blew into the river, drifting away, beginning a brief journey before sinking to the bottom.

Every few minutes the sound of a jet broke the quiet, flying high above, maybe to California or Colorado. A lone gull soared, too, first right, then left, then down and out of sight. I looked across the river again, at graffiti above a drainage pipe, sprayed at an almost impossible angle. Calling all contortionists! How do they do it? When do they do it?

I heard the water lapping the shore gently. Just then, two late-season canoeists paddled by, down below my perch. We waved to each other as they headed southward. Some people say you can see faces in the rocks along the river; it's up to your imagination. Water dripped mysteriously from the rocks next to me. What was the source? Some huge underground lake?

The November clouds, gray and heavy, lingered, barely moving. Crows called out greetings or warnings. What looked like a convoy of a dozen or so cars passed along the West River Road, like a funeral procession. There went the 21 again across the bridge, coming from Saint Paul with another three cars following close behind.

Upon rising from my rock, I climbed toward the cross standing above, through the fence, and into the parking lot. This was my last visit of the year; the cold weather was moving in. No need to worry; my rock will be there come spring.

The Irish in Saint Paul created the Saint Paul Saint Patrick's Association in 1967. This association is a nonprofit organization that plans the yearly parade downtown. Even the Vulcans participate in the parade, changing their colors from red to green.

NOVEMBER

S	M	T	W	T	F	S
				1	2	3
4	5	6	7	8	9	10
11	12	13	14	15	16	17
18	19	20	21	22	23	24
25	26	27	28	29	30	

12 Monday
Veterans Day (observed)

13 Tuesday

14 Wednesday

15 Thursday

The High Bridge over the Mississippi

16 Friday

17 Saturday

18 Sunday

Saint Paul's Caves

Cary Griffith

In late November I drive through downtown Saint Paul and turn across the river on Wabasha Street, in search of the city's caves. The river banks are saw-toothed with jagged edges of ice. A ceiling of gray clouds threatens snow. It is twenty degrees and forecast to drop another five by the end of the day.

The temperature reminds me of just one of the reasons the sandstone bluffs along Saint Paul's Mississippi riverfront are dotted with dark openings. Shelter. Places to turn to when Minnesota's weather makes its seasonal plunge. Over the years Saint Paul's natural and man-made caves have been used for numerous purposes: Indian ceremonies, hideouts, speakeasies, tourist attractions, novel restaurants, storage areas, naturally air-conditioned or heated abodes, mushroom farms, places to age cheese and brew beer and whiskey, and on rare occasion, killing dens.

Saint Paul's first caves formed naturally. Water erosion wore through the sandstone on either side of the Mississippi, creating caverns in the soft rock. By the time the first settlers came to the region, the indigenous people were already familiar with and using a large cavern in what is now Saint Paul's Dayton's Bluff area.

In 1766, Captain Jonathan Carver, a Connecticut native working in the British fur trade, came to the upper Mississippi River. From the local Dakota tribe he learned about Waukon Teebee, or "House of Spirits," a large cavern with an underground lake. In Captain Carver's November 14 journal entry he writes, "The mouth of the cave fronting the river [is] on an ascent near forty-five [degrees], the enterence about ten feet broad and three feet high. I went in and measured the room upwards of thirty feet broad, and about sixty feet from the enterence of the cave [to] where I came to a lake. . . . I tasted of this water and found it very good."

Because Carver was the first to describe it, the name stuck. Carver Cave still resides in the bluff, though over the years it has been boarded up and blocked off, and today a pair of heavy steel doors cover its entrance.

Across the river between Drake and Randolph streets, the same geologic process cut into the sandstone and limestone riverbanks to create another spacious cavern. In 1829 Pierre "Pig's Eye" Parrant (nicknamed because of one blind eye) came into America from Canada. After several years and scrapes with the law he settled in the area just north of Fort Snelling. In 1838 he built a cabin in front of a large cavern with clear water running out of it—Fountain Cave. There he built a whiskey still and began selling his product to American Indians, soldiers, and fellow settlers—at least until the military authorities evicted him two years later.

Fountain Cave was subsequently used as a storage area and tourist attraction. According to Greg Brick ("Saint Paul Underground—What Happened to Fountain Cave?" *Ramsey County History,* vol. 29:4 [Winter 1995]) the cave "was described as 'a marble temple,' issuing water so pure it resembled 'a shower of diamonds.' A pavilion was opened nearby offering refreshments and lights for exploring the cave. Fountain Cave was featured in the Tourists' Guide to the Health and Pleasure Resorts of the Golden Northwest."

In subsequent years the Omaha Railroad and the city transformed the cave into a cesspit, ruining the attraction. Then the construction of Shepard Road covered over its entrance, and today it can no longer be explored.

One of the best examples of man-made caves can be found at the Wabasha Street Caves, where the owners offer tours every Thursday and Saturday. When seen from across the river on Wabasha Street, the cave entrance looks more like the front of a Summit Avenue mansion than a door to caverns.

In the late 1840s, Lyman Dayton (for whom the bluffs are named) noticed the fine quality of the area's sand. He began mining and selling the sand, and after several years his efforts created several huge caverns in the bluffs. After the sand was mined, the caverns were abandoned but not filled in.

Then in the 1880s, Louis Lambert, Charles Etienne, and Albert Mouchenotte came to Saint Paul from France. In France, Louis had learned the fine art of growing mushrooms on manure. The caverns turned out to be ideal for the process, and their location along Wabasha Street, one of Saint Paul's historic roads, provided a constant source of manure. Lambert, Etienne, and Mouchenotte grew rich growing and selling the button-sized fungi.

On one late night bullets flew (some of which can still be seen in the walls) from a Thompson submachine gun, and three mobsters lay dead on the floor.

Albert had a daughter named Josie, who eventually married William Lehmann. Tiring of the mushroom growing business, the two set out to create one of Saint Paul's finest restaurants and in 1932 they opened Castle Royal (in what is now the first cavern of the Wabasha Street Caves). Over the next decade they wined and dined some of Saint Paul's finest and most notorious citizens, including John Dillinger and probably members of the Ma Barker gang.

After Prohibition, Castle Royal was one of the first establishments to be issued a liquor license. And at least on one late night, bullets flew (some of which can still be seen in the walls) from a Thompson submachine gun, and three mobsters lay dead on the floor. The mobsters' bodies and blood disappeared, and the gunman escaped—leading some to speculate that bodies are still buried deep in the bluff.

While bullets have sometimes flown into the sandstone cliffs, accidents have accounted for more cave deaths. In large part these misfortunes are because most of Saint Paul's caves are not true natural caves.

Move up to one of the sandstone walls with a pen knife and you'll discover what the city's earliest inhabitants found. Plunge your blade into the river bluff and its tip will bury itself about an inch. Twist the blade and fine sand will crumble out of the hole, starting the first clear mark of penetration. After a few hours of hard labor with the right tools you could probably curl up in a cave-like space. An intermittent few days of labor might yield a nice large room with a flat floor and storage closet. And it would be a comfortable hobbit-hole. Warm in the winter and cool in the summer—a constant fifty-two degrees—with only one small disadvantage. No ventilation.

These man-made caves differ from most of their natural cousins by being air tight. Natural caves carved by eons of water pouring over and through limestone karst are honeycombed with small openings and jagged breaches. These holes enable the earth to breath. They ventilate most caves, making them safe to turn into. Saint Paul's man-made sandstone caves are surrounded by tons of hermetically sealed earth. While their peculiar features have made them ideal for many uses, they have also made them extremely dangerous.

The Wabasha Caves

Walking along these cliffs at the corner of Wabasha Street and Plato Boulevard, I'm reminded of just one of the tragedies that occurred in Saint Paul's caves. On April 27, 2004, five teenagers visited one of these hillside openings barely large enough for a body to squeeze through. They uncovered its feeble opening, crawled inside, and found a maze-like playground. Like many of these caves, this one had plenty of underground passageways, including areas large enough in which to stand.

But it was cold, and they found enough sticks and rubble to build a fire. Fire produces heat and carbon monoxide. One of the four teenagers managed to remain conscious long enough to climb out of the cave to safety. He alerted the authorities, who started an immediate search and rescue. Three of the teenagers didn't survive.

Between 1988 and 1992 five people died in the caves, including two girls who died in the same cave as the 2004 victims.

Over the years Saint Paul's caves have been places of spiritual retreats and fine restaurants. The caves have produced whiskey and beer, fine cheeses, mushrooms, sand, and stored wines, gunpowder, building supplies, and much more. And they have staged the scenes of numerous unexpected tragedies. But in the end, Saint Paul's caves continue to awe and attract us.

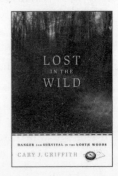

Lost in the Wild: Danger and Survival in the North Woods is Cary Griffith's new book of two wilderness trekkers' extreme survival experiences in the north country. Order at borealisbooks.org.

The Saint Paul Chamber Orchestra is the only full-time chamber orchestra in the United States; going on its 47th year, the chamber orchestra is world renowned.

NOVEMBER

S	M	T	W	T	F	S
				1	2	3
4	5	6	7	8	9	10
11	12	13	14	15	16	17
18	19	20	21	22	23	24
25	26	27	28	29	30	

19 Monday

20 Tuesday

21 Wednesday

22 Thursday

Thanksgiving Day

Minnesota Hmong New Year
page 288

Lake Harriet Pavilion and *Jonathan Padelford* Paddleboat

23 Friday	Minnesota Hmong New Year *page 288*

24 Saturday	Minnesota Hmong New Year *page 288*

25 Sunday	Minnesota Hmong New Year *page 288* Fall Flower Show ends *page 287*

Film *The Time Is Right For Mee*

Rare Glimpse Behind
the Scene of Political Campaign

Sao Sue Jurewitsch

Due to a lack of funding, it took producer Foung Heu and cinematographer Noel Lee almost four years to finish *The Time Is Right For Mee*. With a total budget of only $28,000, the duo produced not only a refreshingly honest look behind the scenes of Mee Moua's 2002 state senate campaign, they do so in a surprisingly entertaining and even moving way. To craft his film, Foung Heu had to condense over 100 hours of raw footage into a one-hour documentary. Ask how he did it, he answers that he "built little stories that included the climactic moments of the campaign." Judging from the reaction of the audience at the Minnesota History Center, his little stories add up to a film worth watching.

When Mee Moua decided to run in the special election for the State Senate seat vacated by then newly elected Saint Paul Mayor Randy Kelly in January 2002, the odds were clearly against her. No Hmong American had been elected to state office in Minnesota, and fellow Democratic-Farmer-Labor (DFL) party member Tim Mahoney seemed to be a shoe-in after receiving the support of Randy Kelly. Foung Heu's documentary shows how Mee Moua secured the support of some DFLers, especially Sheldon Johnson, and then built a grassroots organization that helped her overcome the odds.

One of the strengths of Foung Heu's documentary is that he does not just focus on Mee Moua's campaign. Heu also gained the cooperation of Moua's political opponents. Some of the more telling moments of his film come when Tim Mahoney, Jim Kielkopf, and Michelle Ford share their thoughts during the campaign. Mr. Heu's very sparing use of narration—he leaves most of the talking to the political actors—is another strength of the film. Hearing the different campaigns react in real time gives the documentary a more immediate and honest feel. It also allows the audience to make up their own mind about the merits of the stated positions.

At times the struggle between the political campaigns resembles an ultimate fighting match, like when Tim Mahoney blindsides Mee Moua during a televised debate and then justifies his attack by saying "politics is a tough arena." Despite the no-holds-barred campaigning he

Foung Heu

covers, Foung Heu succeeds in showing even Mee Moua's opponents in a most human light. The film also documents how Mee Moua raised grassroots support through hard work and her enormous talent communicating with very different parts of her constituency. In this regard, the film deserves to become required training material for any political campaign.

The film has many memorable moments, from Mee Moua's interaction with her campaign staff, to the televised debates, to the December 17 DFL Caucus, when Mee Moua was able to prevent a party endorsement for Tim Mahoney despite the fact that she had no delegates of her own and that the only Hmong-American delegate at the caucus supported Tim Mahoney. One of the most moving moments came when Senator Paul Wellstone, who died the following fall, walked into the picture to greet Mee Moua at the 2002 Saint Paul Hmong New Year. The scene was also poignant as it showed fellow DFLer Randy Kelly leaving the New Year without even stopping at Mee Moua's booth.

Reaction to the film was very positive. After the screening Senator Mee Moua said that the film gave her a first chance to look back at the events that led to her election. "I am still caught up in the emotion. The special election came up so fast, and the last four years have been so packed, I haven't really had time to reflect on it." She also thinks that the film captures the highlights and the feel of the campaign. Ask if she would run again in the fall, the senator gave a two-word answer: "Yes, definitely."

With no money to spend on post-production, Foung Heu had to edit the film in his spare time, mostly on weekends. It took him four years. Looking at the result—a film that is as enlightening as it is entertaining—it was worth the wait.

Foung Heu recently sold distribution rights to The Time is Right For Mee.

Since 1910 the Saint Paul Hotel has been home to many famous people, including Calvin Coolidge, Woodrow Wilson, Bill Clinton, Bing Crosby, and Bill Murray, to name a few.

NOVEMBER

S	M	T	W	T	F	S
				1	2	3
4	5	6	7	8	9	10
11	12	13	14	15	16	17
18	19	20	21	22	23	24
25	26	27	28	29	30	

26 Monday

27 Tuesday

28 Wednesday

29 Thursday

Holiday Bazaar
page 288

Downy Woodpecker in Winter in Swede Hollow Park

30 Friday

Holiday Bazaar
page 288

1 Saturday

Holiday Bazaar
page 288

Grand Meander
pages 289

2 Sunday

Rondo Oral History

Oral History is the spoken word in print. Oral histories are personal memories shared from the perspective of the narrator. By means of recorded interviews, oral history documents collect spoken memories and personal commentaries of historical significance. These interviews are transcribed verbatim and minimally edited for readability. The greatest appreciation is gained when one can read an oral history aloud.

Kate Cavett, oral historian,
HAND in HAND Productions

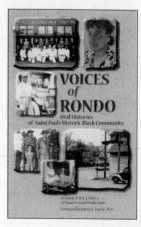

The following oral history is excerpted from Voices of Rondo: Oral Histories of Saint Paul's Historic Black Community *and is used by permission.* Voices of Rondo *won a 2006 Minnesota Book Award.*

William Kelso "Corky" Finney

I'm Bill Finney. I grew up at 437 Rondo. My home would have been between Western Avenue and Arundel on Rondo, north side of the street. This is Corn-meal Valley, a wonderful, diverse community. It was a community of people who knew each other, every house. People lived in those houses for generations. Doors were left unlocked and open. Everybody on the block was an adjunct parent of yours. There were some people that were the

Bill Finney

old characters on the block that the parents would just as soon you not associate with, and so you didn't. They were adults, and adults didn't interact with kids, especially adults that knew the parents wouldn't want you talking to their child, so they stayed their distance. They weren't bad people, but people that had maybe bad habits.

Bill Finney with Lady Pontess

My dog was an old female Springer spaniel. Lady Pontess. And Lady Pontess was guardian for the kids in about a square-block radius. She would pull kids out of the street. She would step in between children and adults she didn't know. She just mothered everyone and so that was that.

Rondo had a streetcar that went down the middle of Rondo. I rode on a streetcar, you know, the trolley, and I think they took them out of business in about 1954. I was born in 1948, so I would have been a kindergartener riding on the thing, my recollection. But I mean it was a wonderful experience, you know, because it was a train. And trains were the big thing. My dad was a railroad man, and so a lot of the Black middle-class were professionals, railroad men. And there were more railmen than probably the other professionals. When I say professionals—doctors, lawyers, teachers and other civil servants, postmen, and then the railroad guys. You either worked at the railroad, on the trains, or you worked as a Redcap or in one of the little concessions at the depot. And then there were the guys that worked for the packinghouse in South Saint Paul, and so that was a little bit on the lower social economic scale, although those people were hardworking and made good livings.

The rough cut would be people from Cornmeal Valley and Oatmeal Hill, and Oatmeal Hill is generally considered those that are middle class, the professionals. And generally, most of that attitude eroded in my generation, the baby boomers, but the pre-baby boomers were really familiar with it. And I'm just cursorily familiar with it through my family. But basically it was like this: people that live west of Dale Street were considered Oatmeal, okay, because it was on the hill and it was the back and that was the newer part. People below, east of Dale Street on Rondo, would have been considered Cornmeal Valley, although you had many Oatmeal people living in Cornmeal Valley.

We lived in Cornmeal Valley because of our geographical location. But my dad was definitely and my mother was definitely Oatmeal. Our house was also a business. My mother ran Finney's Beauty Parlor out of the house, so I grew up seeing many people from the neighborhood. The beauty parlor was separate. You came in the side door of our house. I remember that the side door had a porch off of it, and then inside it was a one-room beauty shop. It had a couple chairs.

My mother graduated from high school at sixteen. She was very, very bright. If she would have been a White child, she would have gotten a scholarship to go to school. They didn't give them to Black kids then. So she went to Chicago to a school of cosmetology for Black hair. She got her degree there and came back and did hair. I remember the wonderful relationships that were made, the respect that people in the community had for my mother because she did their hair. And hairdressers are very, very important to the fabric of the Black community, very important. It's a social experience.

One of the processes for Black women back then—they didn't use cold perms, it was the hot comb. My mother was really good at hot combing and curling, so on Saturday she'd have just lines of customers because they wanted to look nice for church on Sunday. We call it fryin', hair–fryin'. So I remember the smells. I remember the women that came there. You know, when you're a boy of eight, nine, ten years old, they all look old to you because they might be in their twenties, they might be in their thirties, but they look old and you're young. And then I can remember some of the teenage girls, which you kinda looked at, and used to like, or the girls our age that had to get their hair done because of African American hair.

My mom didn't cut hair. It was against the law for beauticians, hairdressers to cut hair. You had to have a barber's license to cut hair, and they used to check that. She could style, straighten, she could trim. Couldn't cut hair. You had to have a barber's license and you had to go to the Barber Academy to get that.

Boys didn't sit in women's beauty salons to get their hair cut, no, no, no, no. I went to Clarence's barbershop, down there where my dad got his hair cut. As a real little boy, I went in with my dad, so I wasn't really paying attention to adult conversation. When you got to be ten, eleven, twelve, thirteen, that's when you listen to the old boys talkin'. And it was kind of funny. It would make you giggle. "You boys quit listening." Okay, you'd listen harder then. You wouldn't say nothing, you wouldn't show any expression on your face, 'cause they'd put you out. "I'm gonna send you home, young Finney." It was funny.

I was the only child in my household, and I grew up with my mother, my father, and my aunt, who's like my sister—my mother's baby sister, Petey Vassar, who was sixteen years older than me, but my big sister.

I had my first gun when I was seven years old. Not a BB gun, a live gun, a 410 single-shot shotgun, which I still have. And my dad always taught me about weapons and the proper use of them. I always wanted a .22 rifle. And he said, "No, I won't give you a .22," he says, "because people think .22s are toys. They're a very, very deadly gun. Very dangerous. And because people think it's a minor firearm they use them recklessly, and I won't allow you to have one." So I had big-caliber guns. I didn't get a .22 until I was sixteen. And we had places to shoot them because of our lake cabin. We had forty acres at Big Round Lake, Wisconsin. We had that property from 1952 until 1977. We sold it after my father had passed. And so I always was familiar with guns. I always shot them, knew them and shot them well. My dad taught me. He was a crack shot. Not a hand-gunner, but a rifleman and shotgun. I had to learn hand gunning a different way, although we had four handguns and he could shoot them, but he didn't like handguns much.

I can remember we were victims of the Ku Klux Klan in Wisconsin in 1952 or '54. I've got the *Jet* magazine that has that in it. We had bought forty acres on the lake from a guy named Schilling, German guy. My dad and another guy by the name of Emmett Searles bought his old farm. Anyway, we were up there and they had bought one of these old World War II Quonset huts. So our family is on the one side, their family is on the other side. We always closed up for the winter. They burned us out. They burned all the Black families out of there. The property was right next to a reservation. They blamed it on Indians. It wasn't Indians. They had the FBI investigating that one. It was the Ku Klux Klan deal. And you know Wisconsin has a fair amount of Ku Klux Klanners, especially during that time. It was the McCarthy era. Never caught the guy or charged anybody, but the guy burned his own place down and left the state. He owned a tavern down the road.

And so this is where I get my dedication, commitment, and tenacity from. My parents said, "We're rebuilding. Instead of having one building, we're gonna have two. Searles is gonna build over here. We're gonna build this one." They got three other Black families, they all built. My dad sold them property and they built. "So now we're here. Sheriff, you protect our property." Never had any more trouble after that. That's why they taught me to shoot young. I told you I got my first gun at seven.

Shooting a gun was not as a statement for protection. They never talked that stuff. "These are skills you may need to know." Never shot anything that even looked like a human target, never. Shot at cans, shot at a board on the edge, a board with a round bull's-eye target on it. But I never shot at a human target until I became a police officer. My parents were not militants. My parents were conservative African Americans who believed that "we're doin' it by the American way, and by God we'll protect it the American way."

"Corky" is a nickname that has been with me ever since I was a child, when I was just beginning to speak. My name is William Kelso Finney. Black mothers like to nickname their children. And so my mother wanted to nickname me Kelly. And I never could pronounce the "L." So I would say, "Corky." So after a while they said, "You want to be called Corky? That is your nickname."

I was Corky until I made chief and people decided that they shouldn't call me Corky. The news media asked me how would I like to be known as. And so I said, "Bill Finney." "So you don't want to be called Corky anymore?" I said, "People that know me as Corky can call me Corky. It is part of me. It is my name and I certainly will answer to it. But if you ask me how I want to be referred to in the press, Bill Finney." When I ran for school board I ran as Bill "Corky" Finney, on the ticket for school board. A lot of people from the old community, that's how they know me, as Corky. Now people know me in all areas as Bill Finney. Fewer people call me Corky now.

And so chief is what I do. I love it. I loved being your chief, your police officer. Did I ever just seek the title? No. I sought the job. The title went with it. My nickname seems to be Chief. It is one of those things that come with certain jobs. It is like once you become senator or you become governor or the mayor—if you're the mayor you're always, "Your Honor." Or a judge, it always, "Judge." It just goes with your name. Once you've been a chief, especially if it's a successful chiefdom, people will always forever call you Chief. I've been a cop most of my life. I've been a cop since I was twenty years old, so it's hard to separate. Corky is a rich life outside of it, but it is very much a part of my personality. I had it when I became a police officer, "Corky," "Corky the Cop." So now it's Chief, and it's been an honor to be Police Chief of Saint Paul.

December

Holiday Bazaar Nov. 29–Dec. 1

Grand Meander Dec. 1

Holiday Flower Show Dec. 1–mid-January

SKANDIA: Scandinavian Festival Dec. 9

Kwanzaa Celebration Dec. 30

Five Star New Year Dec. 31

See page 288–289 for more information on December events.

The Junior League of Saint Paul, Inc., has been a dedicated force in assisting Saint Paulites since its creation in 1917. Its first prominent project was managing the World War I Red Cross Campaign in 1917.

DECEMBER

S	M	T	W	T	F	S
						1
2	3	4	5	6	7	8
9	10	11	12	13	14	15
16	17	18	19	20	21	22
23/30	24/31	25	26	27	28	29

3 Monday

4 Tuesday

5 Wednesday

Hanukkah

6 Thursday

7 Friday

8 Saturday

9 Sunday   SKANDIA: Scandinavian Festival
page 289

Roof Work in Saint Paul

Mary Gardner

1. The Football Fan Handyman

Every crack in the asphalt
bisects the field.
He tamps the patching tar
into each end zone.
His head, with its gray curls,
is a helmet against the blue.
When he heads homeward,
the Vikings salute him.

2. The Roofers

Below fifteen degrees
their glue freezes.
In Minneapolis,
it's too cold already.
With the skylight pried loose,
every "shit" echoes.
Knowing she can hear them,
the old one says, "Shhh."

3. The Crows

Twin Cities winters,
and last night the ponds froze.
A flock of giant crows
has attacked the skylight
pile-driving the edges
of the unyielding plexiglas.
Selby, Western, Arundel—
no street provides entrance.

4. The Anxious Cat

From below, where he walks,
come the good things:
the down Bibelot pillow,
milk creamy from Kowalski's,
the rug's swirled nap,
resplendent litter.

But from the Saint Paul sky,
harsh caws are resounding,
claws, bills, and shrill eyes
seeking small furred creatures.

All Saint Paulites can thank a certain New York reporter for the Saint Paul Winter Carnival. In 1885, after a New York reporter called Saint Paul "another Siberia, unfit for human habitation," the Saint Paul Chamber of Commerce wanted to prove the nation wrong.

DECEMBER

S	M	T	W	T	F	S
						1
2	3	4	5	6	7	8
9	10	11	12	13	14	15
16	17	18	19	20	21	22
23/30	24/31	25	26	27	28	29

10 Monday

UN International Human Rights Day

11 Tuesday

12 Wednesday

13 Thursday

14 Friday

15 Saturday

16 Sunday

World Champion

Mark Connor

On Friday, December 18, 1998, Will Grigsby, a lifelong native of Saint Paul, did something staggeringly rare. He became a Minnesota-based World Champion professional boxer.

That night the twenty-eight-year-old fighter climbed into the ring in Florida to fight for the International Boxing Federation (IBF) Junior Flyweight (108 lbs.) title. His opponent, twenty-five-year-old Ratanapol Sor Vorapin of Thailand, was naturally favored, with thirty-seven wins against three losses and one draw,

Will Grigsby, World Champion

and twenty-nine knockouts. Grigsby had only fourteen fights in a ten-year professional career, compiling a record of 12-1-1. But he dominated Vorapin, winning a unanimous decision. It surprised many, but not those who knew Grigsby's talent and determination and the story behind his lack of activity.

An Upper Midwest Golden Gloves Champion in 1987 and 1988, Grigsby turned professional at eighteen. Debuting with a third-round technical knockout, he then faced 1988 Junior Flyweight Olympic Silver medalist Michael Carbajol on February 24, 1989, in Atlantic City, New Jersey. It was a daring step so early in Grigsby's career. Olympians command a greater amount of attention and income, so Grigsby was brought in as the expected loser. "I knew I had to beat him up pretty bad, or knock him out," Grigsby said of the fight. "I thought I could knock him out." While Grigsby fought impressively, he lost a four-round decision. His celebrated opponent went on to become the first million-dollar-earning Junior Flyweight in history, while over the next few years Grigsby's dream of a world title seemed to drift away, carrying him with it.

Grigsby experienced troubling personal issues, including the loss of his mother to a form of multiple sclerosis. But lifelong trainer Dennis Presley was always there, working with amateurs and willing to train him if he got serious again. Also standing stoically in the background was Gene "Rock" White, founder of the Inner City Youth League boxing gym on Selby Avenue, who had trained and mentored both Grigsby and Presley as amateurs. "And Lalo Sanchez kept bugging me to box again," Grigsby says.

Sometimes an amateur coach and sometimes an assistant cornerman in the professional game, Sanchez persuaded Grigsby to train at Jim Glancey's gym on the East Side of Saint Paul. Grigsby got hold of Presley and signed a contract for Glancey, a boxing photographer who for many years has assisted amateurs and professionals, to manage.

"I never took any money from him," Glancey explains, knowing that until a boxer reaches the level of title fights, the purse is rarely enough to live on. "I've known Willie since he was thirteen. The fighters, they're the ones that get the punches. I always try to do the best I can for them."

After Grigsby knocked out an opponent at the Prom Expo Center, Boxing Commissioner Jim O'Hara compared him to the legendary Willie Pep. "He said, 'Dennis, he reminds me of Willie the Wisp'," Presley recalls with a smile.

Rory Rowe became co-manager, and eventually sole manager. In 1996 Grigsby got a shot at the United States Boxing Association (USBA) Flyweight (112 lbs.) title. He won, becoming world ranked, while Rowe negotiated a world title shot. Then came that memorable night in 1998. It was a great accomplishment for Grigsby, who never forgot the city of Saint Paul in his glory. While interviewed in the ring, he dedicated the fight to the memory of White, who'd died of pancreatic cancer in January that year, and "Jumpin'" Johnny Montantez, a Saint Paul Lightweight who'd died in a Las Vegas fight in 1997.

Grigsby defended the title successfully in March 1999 with a twelve-round decision over Carmello Carceres of the Philippines, then lost it in a twelve-round decision in October to Ricardo Lopez of Mexico, one of the greatest pound-for-pound boxers at any weight during the nineties. He defeated Nelsen Dieppa of Puerto Rico for the World Boxing Organization Championship in 2000, but the fight was later declared a no decision and the title taken from him. On May 14, 2005, at the age of 35, Grigsby dominated José Victor Burgos of Mexico, regaining the IBF Junior Flyweight Championship with a twelve-round unanimous decision. He lost a twelve-round unanimous decision and the title to Ulises Solis of Mexico on January 7, 2006, after which it was unclear if he would fight again. With eighteen wins, three losses, one draw, and seven knockouts, Grigsby has proven himself a true champion, making Saint Paul proud.

The Saint Paul Neighborhood Network (SPNN) was created in 1985 as a one-channel cable network called Cable Access Saint Paul. Thanks to continuous support, the nonprofit organization has grown to five different channels reaching 52,000 homes.

DECEMBER

S	M	T	W	T	F	S
						1
2	3	4	5	6	7	8
9	10	11	12	13	14	15
16	17	18	19	20	21	22
23/30	24/31	25	26	27	28	29

17 Monday

18 Tuesday

19 Wednesday

20 Thursday

Eid-al-Adha

Morelli's Market on the East Side

21 Friday

22 Saturday

Winter Solstice

23 Sunday

District Energy

Amy Siqveland

I was very aware of where I stood politically when I started working at District Energy Saint Paul, Inc,. in 2004. It was quite a shock to my network of progressive friends on the West Coast when I took a job at a power plant. Although everybody uses energy on a daily basis, power plants are especially symbolic, conjuring images of belching stacks and smog. I was surprised to discover later how congruent District Energy's mission was with the work I was doing in social activism.

District Energy heats and cools all of downtown Saint Paul using a central location and a series of well-insulated underground pipes that weave their way under the buildings of the city. District Energy does not believe that there is a dichotomy between environmental stewardship and economic growth, but instead asserts that development and eco-logical conservation can be achieved simultaneously. Located on the craggy bluffs of the Mississippi waterfront, the power plant originated as a steam heat franchise in 1904, originally using barges and the adja-cent railroad to bring oil and coal from distant suppliers. Electrical in-stallation was added in 1906, and then Northern Heating and Electric Company purchased the American District Steam Company in 1910, and changed its name to Northern States Power (NSP) in 1916.

District Energy is a private corporation that was founded in response to the energy crisis of the 1970s. District Heating Development Corpora-tion purchased the plant from NSP in the early '80s after a national study was completed analyzing the feasibility of urban hot water. They changed their name and began to provide heating service to downtown customers. In 1993 District Cooling was added when the company began to offer air conditioning services and then, in the late '90s, District Energy partnered again with Trigen-Cinergy Solutions to construct a new cogeneration plant. The plant's goal was to create heat by burning excess wood waste and at the same time produce electricity for the NSP power grid.

The process of capturing the heat from the wood chips is safe and re-newable, and, although DE still uses fossil fuels, it has begun a slow move over from dependence upon these materials. The company has cut coal use by 80 percent and soot emissions by 50 percent since adding biomass

Steaming District Energy Headquarters on Kellogg Boulevard

to the mix. In this sense, they aim to significantly reduce the greenhouse gases that lead to global warming.

District Energy wants to be held accountable to its 450-plus customer base by being reliable, conscientious, and efficient. It also means they need to stay in the forefront of the energy market and continue to seek innovative and ecologically sound ways to serve their community.

Environmental issues cannot be separated from social issues. Humankind's use of nature has disrupted how natural habitats function and these shifts have long-term consequences. Because District Energy strives to be a model in energy management, they view the investment of their employees as their greatest asset. They are interested in creating the ideal surroundings for employees from the inside out.

Employees know their coworkers and their commitment to this type of dialogue is one of the benchmarks of their success. I was completely welcomed into all their activities even though I was only a temp for three short months. This was best illustrated when one of the engineers fixed my car on a blustery winter day and wouldn't take money, even for the supplies. "It's Saint Paul," he said. "That's just how things work here."

I was an ethnographer of sorts while I was there—a social worker and journalist who felt out of my element in numerous ways. District Energy helped me remember that true social activism starts where you currently are with creating a vision and then acting upon it. If DE can continue to hone some of their current strategies, their leadership will be a uniting force in the changing face of Saint Paul in the coming years.

Every Saint Paulite should know about Saint Paul native Charles M. Schulz's creation, Snoopy, but what not everyone knows is that Snoopy had seven siblings: Andy, Belle, Marbles, Molly, Olaf, Rover, and Spike.

DECEMBER

S	M	T	W	T	F	S
						1
2	3	4	5	6	7	8
9	10	11	12	13	14	15
16	17	18	19	20	21	22
23/30	24/31	25	26	27	28	29

24 Monday

25 Tuesday

Christmas

26 Wednesday

Kwanzaa begins

27 Thursday

28 Friday

29 Saturday

30 Sunday/
31 Monday

New Year's Eve

Kwanzaa Celebration
Five Star New Year

page 289

Until They Bring
the Streetcars Back

(an excerpt)

Stanley Gordon West

I don't know why but we always sat seven rows back on the right side of Immanuel Lutheran Church unless someone beat us to the punch, but we usually got there early enough to stake out our pew like it wouldn't count if we sat anywhere else. We rode the streetcar four blocks to Snelling, and most Sundays we could've walked it by the time we waited, but riding the Grand-Mississippi was as much a part of our Sunday tradition as the sacraments.

On the streetcar, my dad always rode shotgun and talked with the motorman on the short ride and most of the time it was Andy Johnson, a thin nervous guy who'd lost twin boys in the war—one in Italy, one in the Phillipines—and he'd volunteer for every extra hour on the board. My dad said you could always count on Andy to take your run, as though Johnson figured if he drove a big yellow streetcar far enough, his brain would go numb and he'd forget what happened to his boys. I really felt sorry for the guy and I always gave him a big cheery hello.

Pastor Ostrum was a tall rangy guy who impressed me most with the fact that he played basketball in college but he looked as out of place in the pulpit as a giraffe in a phone booth. I'd usually kind of day dream during the sermon but that morning he preached on the meaning of love and I perked up and took notice when he used that magic word. While the six-foot-six minister flipped through his notes like a deck of cards and said things like Love is not something we wait to have happen to us, but something we *do,* I remembered the first time I saw Lola.

She came strolling past me in the hall, talking with two other girls, and when she laughed, I stopped in my tracks and forgot to breathe. I'd never seen anyone so delicious and as I watched her walk away, I hurt inside because that gorgeously shaped girl didn't know I was on the planet. Jeez, it was like I'd been run over by a truck or something. It had just happened, I didn't make any decision, I didn't even know her name. Was that love? Or insanity? And what was that ache I lugged around in my chest that only she could stop? If I didn't love Lola, what strange disease made my heart pound whenever I saw her or heard her voice or someone mentioned her name?

When church was over, we'd walk two blocks home after riding the streetcar and my father always went ahead with my mother while Peggy and I trailed behind, usually ragging each other or something.

"Dad, when did you first know you loved Mom?" I said.

Without turning around and without missing a step, my dad answered, "When she had her knee on my throat."

"Oh, Horace," my mother said and pretended to swat him. So much for romance.

We huddled around the cooler in the drugstore on Dunlap and Selby after football practice, comparing bloody shins and jammed fingers and seeing who could swill the most O-So Grape.

"If we don't beat Mechanic Arts, Kascoe will make us run tackling drills all next week," Jerry said.

"Yeah, and all afternoon I kept getting Fred," I said. "I tried to switch places in line, but every time I looked up, there was madman Walker, ready to break both my legs. Darn it, he tries to kill you every time."

"If I don't get my grades up in English, my dad will break both my legs," Jerry said. "I flunked the last M.R."

Jeez, every Friday we had an English test called Minimum Requirements, and it had all this stuff with spelling and punctuation and grammar, a short test we had shoved at us the minute we showed our face in English and it always took some of the fun out of Fridays because you had to get past the M.R. before you could start thinking about the weekend. M.R.s about drove me nuts, they really did. There were questions like He said lie/lay down to his dog. Everyone knows since the beginning of time that you tell your dog to lay down, but do you think that's the right answer? No, you're supposed to say Lie down according to the M.R.s. Huh! There isn't a dog in the universe that'd know what you meant if you told him to *lie* down. There were all kinds of questions like that and you could never figure them out with logic, and anything below seventy-five was failing. The boys thought it was unfair in English to be graded with the girls because girls were born knowing all that stuff.

The streetcar glided up the hill and we found one unoccupied strap to hang onto in the jammed car. She leaned against me as we swayed and bumped together and I could smell her hair.

Someone shouted that the streetcar was coming, and the place emptied as if a skunk had trotted in the back door. I'd walk over to Summit and hitchhike, saving a dollar a week and hoping I'd get a ride in a Hudson or Packard or something. When the gang boarded the streetcar and it rolled away, I had a clear view up Dunlap where a girl came strolling from school. I'd recognize Lola if she were walking on the moon. I chug-a-lugged my O-So Grape and scrambled across Selby, acting like I hadn't seen her coming.

"Hi Cal, where's Tom?" she said as she got to the corner. Jeez, she was wearing a gray pleated skirt and a pink cardigan sweater, and just to see her was like getting hit by madman Walker in tackling drills but in a pleasant way if you know what I mean.

"Hi, they must have caught a streetcar, I'm slow today."

"I've been at a *Cehisean* meeting." She snapped her gum and smiled.

The *Cehisean* was our year book and it was one of those words made with the first letters of other words and I forgot what you call it but I was betting it would show up on an M.R. before long. My throat went dry standing there alone with her, and I nonchalantly fished in my pocket to see if I had eleven cents left after four O-So Grapes and a Nut Goodie at five cents a crack. I'd take the streetcar home and have Lola to myself for that short breathtaking ride.

"Are you going to the dance?" she said as we peered down Selby for any sign of a streetcar.

She held her books with both arms, snuggling them against her pink sweater, and I felt kind of hot and sweaty and my arms were about to reach out and hug her without even checking with me first.

"Yeah, I better. With Skull and Keys putting it on, Steve would pound me if I didn't."

"Who are you taking?"

"I'm going stag."

A streetcar appeared down the street.

"Cal, there are so many girls who would love to go with you."

It was like she touched me with her eyes and I felt brave.

"Not the right one, though."

"You mean you have a secret heartthrob?" she said.

The streetcar glided up the hill and we found one unoccupied strap to hang onto in the jammed car. She leaned against me as we swayed and bumped together and I could smell her hair.

"Now tell me, who is she?"

She was so close I could kiss her and I felt blood rush to my face and I turned and looked out the window.

"*You* ought to know," I said and my Adam's apple felt like a popcorn ball.

"I don't, Cal, tell me. Does Tom know?"

The streetcar dropped off people at every intersection and little by little the aisle cleared and I lost my excuse to stand leaning against her.

"They took pictures of the cheerleaders Monday," she said. "My dad said he'd watch me cheer sometime, but he never has."

"Aw, that's nothing, we won the city championship last year in JVs and my dad's never seen me play football."

"Why not?"

"He works a lot . . . but he's coming one of these days."

"My dad lives in Baltimore. That's a long way to come, and his work is awfully important."

Sharing confidences in the crowd of the homeward bound, I felt so good I wanted to do cartwheels. Like sweethearts, we got off the streetcar together, and the afterglow looked like God had a huge bonfire going somewhere out in South Dakota. I planned to ride as far as Saint Clair, which wouldn't be far enough out of the way to make her suspicious, and though it'd be an extra half-mile walk after my body had been a tackling dummy for madman Fred Walker all afternoon, it would be worth ten more minutes with Lola.

Excerpted from Until They Bring the Streetcars Back *by Stanley Gordon West. Published by Lexington-Marshall Publishing. Available at your independent bookstore.*

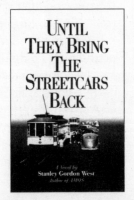

The Hill Where Many People Gather

A Very Brief Account of Pilot Knob's Long History, in Which a Small Bit of an Historic and Sacred Site Is at Last Protected

Judith Niemi

Long before there was Saint Paul, or Minneapolis, or Fort Snelling, many trails around here led to *Mdo-te,* or Mendota (the Meeting Place of the Waters), and to a prominent bluff topped with a small distinctive knob. *Oheyawahi* is what they called it, "the hill where many people gather." Oheyawahi was not a settlement, but (since perhaps 1500) the people who lived in villages along the rivers and out on the prairies came there for ceremonies, for large gatherings, and often they buried their dead there.

As white settlers arrived, the Dakota continued to meet there, and Oheyawahi as a burial and ceremonial site is well recorded in early settlers' writings, and in many paintings by Seth Eastman at Fort Snelling, showing the beautiful oak savannah, the tipis, the burial scaffolds. Pilot Knob is what the whites generally called it—a handy landmark for riverboat captains. When in 1851 the Dakota signed treaties transferring thirty-five million acres, the treaty with the Mdewakanton and Wahpekute bands was signed somewhere on Pilot Knob. Negotiations had begun at Henry Sibley's American Fur Company Warehouse, but it was too small—and too warm. Wabasha asked that the negotiations be held "in the open air," out where the Dakota encampments and ceremonies were taking place.

Oheyawahi/Pilot Knob was so notable a landmark that in 1849 it was proposed as the appropriate site for the territorial capital. Saint Paul won out because Henry Sibley opposed the idea.

Oheyawahi is an attractive place, particularly noted for its magnificent views. Sibley, who first arrived in Minnesota in 1834, wrote, "I was struck with the picturesque beauty of the scene," and his eye traced the course of the Mississippi eastward to where Saint Paul now stands. By 1849 one writer's description of the "delightful view" included not only verdant plains and groves, but "the town of Saint Paul, with its new buildings gleaming in the sun." An exuberant account in the *Saint Paul Democrat* (1854) says, "Standing upon the Knob amidst its Indian graves, viewing like the Egypto-Jew Moses from Pisgah's top, 'the land-scape o'er'. . . . a more beautiful spectacle can hardly be conceived."

The view is still great. As the twenty-first century came around, those verdant plains and wide prairies were replaced by a lot more buildings gleaming in the sun, but the river valleys are still green. Sub-urbs have grown up around Pilot Knob, and the distinctive little knob has been removed (in 1926), but the scenic hill and bluff area is still undeveloped. Much of the area is owned by Acacia Cemetery, which seemed to many to be an appropriate and respectful use of the old burial site. Of course, by now a half-million planes a year are taking off from the airport across the river, many flying right over—and at peak traffic hours thousands of cars streak over the Mendota Bridge, just north of the site. But noise or not, the site is a sacred one, and where many ancestors are, so the Dakota still visit for occasional ceremonies. On his 1999 Unity Ride, Chief Arvol Looking Horse conducted a pipe ceremony there, and another in 2004, with Chris Leith, a spiritual ad-visor from Prairie Island.

> Oheyawahi/Pilot Knob was so notable a landmark
> in 1849 that it was proposed as the appropriate site
> for the territorial capital. Saint Paul won out
> because Henry Sibley opposed the idea.

In 2002, however, a new use was proposed for this land: high-den-sity housing. A developer proposed luxury townhomes on twenty-five acres, many with this magnificent view. (Unlike some nineteenth-cen-tury development proposals, or Acacia Cemetery brochures, the devel-opers did not highlight the historic significance of the site.) The first stage of The Bluffs was proposed to include a particularly scenic eight and a half acres owned by two private persons. The Mendota Heights City Council granted conditional approval.

The Dakota, of course, opposed the plan; letters came from many communities. Bob Brown, the chairman of the Mendota Mdewakan-ton Dakota Community, was instrumental in first sounding the alarm and gathering support. A soft-spoken man dedicated to preserving Dakota language and culture, Brown was able to find friends and al-lies among many people. Beth Jacob Congregation, near neighbors in the Pilot Knob area, sent letters opposing digging up anyone's bones. The Sierra Club led a spring birdwalk there. The Metropolitan Airport

Pilot Knob Covered in Snow

Commission thought it was a bad place for housing. In the 1970s they acquired and demolished housing—at taxpayers' expense—just south of this area, in the airport noise zone. (Apparently people buying in The Bluffs would be expected to sign a disclaimer recognizing the noise, and enjoy the spectacular view from indoors.)

Historians wrote up the rich history of the area and submitted an application to the National Register of Historic Places (which soon approved its eligibility; a site is not actually listed, however, without the okay of the landowners). Bob Brown died in August 2003, but not before The Pilot Knob Preservation Association was formed. A public lecture series was offered in his memory, "The Importance of Place."

The first step was taken when the lawyer for the Mendota Mdewakanton Dakota filed a petition signed by many local people for an Environmental Assessment Worksheet. The Mendota Heights City Council (a new council and new mayor, after elections) agreed. In the coming months, some of the arguments got pretty ugly. Exactly on what bit of ground the treaty had been signed wasn't clear—probably not where the Daughters of the American Revolution had put plaques. What proof was there, lacking written records, that there actually were any bones there? asked the developers. They argued that the bones had already been disturbed and destroyed by scraping off of soil, by highway widening. (When bodies were traditionally put on scaffolds, and later buried without caskets, the Dakota asked how the presence of intact skeletons—which in any case they would not want dug up— was necessary. Their ancestors were in that earth.) It may also have been in some people's minds that the unmarked graves of Pilot Knob may include those of many children who died of measles in the internment camp below Fort Snelling following the 1862 Dakota Conflict. It was also argued that because of a few previous developments—a gas station, a motel, since removed—the site was already compromised, pointless to preserve now. In late 2003 the city council ordered a full Environmental Impact Statement; the developer and landowners then filed suit against the city, and lost.

Preservationists had been able to stop or slow down the immediate threat, but the real challenge was to come up with a better plan. Members of the Pilot Knob Preservation Association recall a night when after one of the early meetings, they stood on a dark street in Mendota and had a desperate conversation that, reduced to its essentials, ran:

"We'll do whatever it takes! Put our bodies on the line." (They would have, too. Many were veterans of the bitter Highway 55/Camp Coldwater controversy.)

"No. What this project needs is maza-ska (white metal). A whole lot of money."

"The money is out there. We're going to find it."

In the long run, the problem of these eight acres was solved to the satisfaction of most parties: the Dakota, other preservation advocates, the city of Mendota Heights, and the landowners. The site was purchased (for $1.9 million) and made public land.

It took a coalition of state, county, city, and private agencies to pull this off, "an extraordinary example of inter-governmental and private sector cooperation," according to Wayne Sames of the

Pilot Knob in Winter

Minnesota Department of Natural Resources (DNR). The Trust for Public Land took a leading role, negotiating with all parties, orchestrating the sale, and securing some grants from the McKnight Foundation and the Saint Paul Foundation. Dakota County Farmland and Natural Areas made the first public contribution: $400,000. One million fifty thousand dollars came from three programs of the Minnesota DNR: the Metro Greenways Program, the Remediation Grant Fund, and the Natural and Scenic Area program, funded by the Minnesota Environment and Natural Resources Trust Fund. The final step was taken when the Mendota Heights City Council voted unanimously to appropriate $400,000 for the purpose and take on ownership and management for public use.

> "We walked right in, past that huge 'No Trespassing' sign that had stood there, an affront to those claiming sacred space," said Gail Lewellan. "There was such joy in being there, we were laughing and hugging each other, and saying miracles do happen."

The city plans to leave the land in a natural state, restoring native vegetation. There will be an observation area, and a few unpaved paths, connecting to the Big Rivers Regional Trail.

Pilot Knob should have been protected long ago. In 1925 some in the legislature proposed securing it as an historic site; it was instead bought by Acacia Cemetery, and many seemed to believe it was then protected. The site has been listed by various preservation groups. The eight-acre private plot had been up for sale for years, and the Mendota Mdewakanton Dakota Community had attended city council meetings earlier, but they are a small group, without a land base, and they had been busy as well with their struggle for federal recognition as a tribe, and, with many others, by the Highway 55 controversy.

What made saving it possible this time? "Just the right people coming together, each with a passion for preserving this site. Everyone was needed," says Gail Lewellan, president of the Pilot Knob Preservation Association. "A whole web of concern and action developed around a compelling area, and that created the opportunity for visionary leaders to do the right thing."

On December 22, 2005, word went out that the deal was complete. That night the people of Pilot Knob Preservation Association (PKPA) were on the phone to each other; by noon several were gathering at the hill. Bob Brown was there in vivid memory; he was buried in Acacia Cemetery after a pipe ceremony in his honor held on Pilot Knob. His widow and co-worker Linda Brown was there; just a month earlier she had been honored with a Virginia McKnight Binger Award in Human Services, for her work in rekindling the traditions of the Mendota Mdewakanton Dakota and helping preserve their historic sites. Its president Gail Lewellan, and Bruce White, who had written the history of Pilot Knob and had first sent out a call for a Pilot Knob Preservation Association, were there. Also present were another half-dozen historians, and friends of the Dakota, and believers in the sanctity of burial grounds—the people who'd been at every meeting for three years.

"We walked right in, past that huge 'No Trespassing' sign that had stood there, an affront to those claiming sacred space," said Gail Lewellan. "There was such joy in being there, we were laughing and hugging each other, and saying miracles do happen." The sun was shining; they stood in a circle in the snow in jeans and warm coats. Someone offered tobacco and a brief prayer in Dakota—a language Gail Lewellan had studied in the classes Bob Brown had started in Mendota. They talked about what the day meant and their gratitude, and then went to Linda's house for chili; a feast always follows a ceremony.

They'll probably go on seeing a lot of each other, though. What was saved were just the eight and a half acres. An area twice as big was up for sale by Acacia Cemetery, and development plans have already been drawn up. The whole round of meetings seemed likely to start up again soon. The part preserved is the area of greatest scenic value; it connects with existing trails, and has the greatest impact on the view from Fort Snelling. But to those whose ancestors lived and died here, the whole hill is a burial ground, all sacred.

Drive east across the Mendota Bridge, and turn south on Acacia. There will be new signs replacing "No Trespassing," and gradually a rare bit of tallgrass prairie will be reborn. It's a good place to enjoy the view of the meeting of great rivers and to look down toward the buildings of Saint Paul catching sunset light, and to think about what we want our cities to be.

A detailed history of the Pilot Knob site can be found in the feature article, "Oheyawahi/Pilot Knob: A Hill of State and National Significance in Dakota County" by Bruce White and Alan Woolworth, in Over the Years, vol. 45:2 (June 2004), pp.1–24. The Pilot Knob Preservation Association is at PO Box 50823, Mendota, MN 55150. A phone contact is Jim Rogers 651.962.5662.

Listings

Events

January

HOLIDAY FLOWER SHOW
Dec. 2–Jan. 21
Marjorie McNeely Conservatory
Como Park
651.487.8200
www.comozooconservatory.org

Elvis at the Winter Carnival Parade

**SAINT PAUL
WINTER CARNIVAL**
Jan. 26–Feb. 4
Downtown Saint Paul
651.223.4700
www.winter-carnival.com
Tons of winter events—parades,
ice skating, ice sculpture, coro-
nation, Medallion hunt.

**THE SAINT PAUL
CHAMBER ORCHESTRA**
Jan. 12, 13
Various locations
651.292.3248
www.thespco.org

**VIETNAMESE TET
NEW YEAR FESTIVAL**
Jan. 27
Saint Paul RiverCentre
651.265.4800
www.vietnam-minnesota.org
Vietnamese music, dancing, con-
tests, food, and celebration.

February

**SAINT PAUL
WINTER CARNIVAL**
Jan. 26–Feb. 4
Downtown Saint Paul
651.223.4700
www.winter-carnival.com
Tons of winter events—parades,
ice skating, ice sculpture, coro-
nation, Medallion hunt.

WINTER FLOWER SHOW
Feb. 2–18
Marjorie McNeely Conservatory
Como Park
651.487.8200
www.comozooconservatory.org

The Saint Paul Chamber Orchestra
Feb. 3, 22, 23, and 24
Various locations
651.292.3248
www.thespco.org

Scottish Ramble
Feb. 10–11
Landmark Center
651.292.3225
www.landmarkcenter.org
Scottish music, dancing, food, and celebration.

The Minnesota Opera
The Grapes of Wrath
Feb. 10, 13, 15, 17, and 18
Ordway Center for the Performing Arts
612.333.6669
www.www.mnopera.org
If you love music, give opera a chance. It's sexy. It will make your toes wiggle. Save up for a ticket.

Minnesota Home and Patio Show
Feb. 15–18
Saint Paul RiverCentre
651.265.4800
www.rivercentre.org
Check out the newest in home-related products.

Minnesota State High School Leagues—

Dance Team Competition
Feb. 16–17
Xcel Energy Center
763.560.2262
www.mshsl.org

Girls' Hockey Tournament
Feb. 22–24
Xcel Energy Center
763.560.2262
www.mshsl.org

Girls' Gymnastics Tournament
Feb. 23–24
Legendary Roy Wilkins Auditorium
763.560.2262
www.mshsl.org

March

The Saint Paul Chamber Orchestra
March 2, 3, 17, 23, and 24
Various locations
651.292.3248
http://www.thespco.org

Saint Patrick's Day Parade
Mar. 17
Downtown Saint Paul
651.256.2155
www.stpaulassoc.org
Once the biggest parade in Saint Paul, and it's still a big one.

Irish Celebration

Dance—Mar. 11
Saint Patrick's Day—Mar. 17
Landmark Center
651.292.3225
www.landmarkcenter.org
Irish food, lively music, Irish
dancing, and art vendors.

Saint Patrick's Day 33rd Annual Irish Ceili Dance

Mar. 17
7–10 p.m.
Randolph Heights Elementary
School, 378 Hamline Ave.

Saint Patrick's Day Irish Ceili Dance

Mar. 17
7–10 p.m.
CSPS Hall, 383 Michigan St.
651.290.0542
www.mnfolkfestival@aol.com

Minnesota State High School Leagues—

Boys' Wrestling Tournament

Mar. 2–3
Xcel Energy Center
763.560.2262
www.mshsl.org

Boys' Hockey Tournament

Mar. 7–10
Xcel Energy Center
763.560.2262
www.mshsl.org

Spring Flower Show

Mar. 24–Apr. 29
Marjorie McNeely Conservatory
Como Park
651.487.8200
www.comozooconservatory.org

The Minnesota Opera

Lakmé
Mar. 31
Ordway Center for the
Performing Arts
612.333.6669
www.mnopera.org
Music lover's delight.

April

The Minnesota Opera

Lakmé
Apr. 1, 3, 5, and 7
Ordway Center for the
Performing Arts
612.333.6669
www.mnopera.org
If you love music, try opera.
It's sexy. It will make your toes
wiggle. Save up for a ticket.

American Craft Council Craft Show

Apr. 13–15
Saint Paul RiverCentre
651.265.4800
www.craftcouncil.org
Stunning handcrafted art for
sale: clay, fiber, glass, metal,
wood, and other materials.

THE SAINT PAUL CHAMBER ORCHESTRA
Apr. 14, 20, 21, 22, 27, and 28
Various locations
651.292.3248
http://www.thespco.org

SAINT PAUL ART CRAWL
Apr. 20–22
Downtown Saint Paul
651.292.4373
www.artcrawl.org
More than 200 artists open their studios to the public.

25TH ANNUAL MINNEAPOLIS–SAINT PAUL INTERNATIONAL FILM FESTIVAL
Mid-Apr.
612.331.3134
www.mspfilmfest.org
The largest film festival in the upper Midwest. Over 150 films from more than 50 countries. Various locations.

MINNESOTA DANCE FESTIVAL
April 26–29
Fitzgerald Theater
651.290.1496
www.balletminnesota.org
Variety of dance performances.

DOWNTOWN SAINT PAUL FARMERS' MARKET
APR. 28–NOV. 11
Saturdays, 6 a.m.–1 p.m.
and Sundays, 8 a.m.–1 p.m.
290 East Fifth St.
651.227-8101
www.stpaulfarmersmarket.com

May

COMO MEMORIAL JAPANESE GARDEN
May 1–Sept. 30
Marjorie McNeely Conservatory
Como Park
651.487.8200
www.comozooconservatory.org

FESTIVAL OF NATIONS
May 3–6
Saint Paul RiverCentre
651.647.0191
www.festivalofnations.com
Over 90 ethnic groups share the foods, crafts, and traditions that form the mosaic of our American culture.

Festival of Nations

Cinco de Mayo Festival

CINCO DE MAYO FESTVAL
May 5–6
District Del Sol
651.222.6347
www.districtdelsol.com
Celebrate with live music, food, children's area, community wellness village, parade, vendors..

THE MINNESOTA OPERA
The Marriage of Figaro
May 5, 6, 8, 10, and 12
Ordway Center for the
Performing Arts
612.333.6669
www.mnopera.org

**THE SAINT PAUL
CHAMBER ORCHESTRA**
May 5, 11, 13, 17, 18, 19, 25, and 26
Various locations
651.292.3248
http://www.thespco.org

**MINNESOTA BONSAI
SOCIETY SHOW**
May 12–13
Marjorie McNeely Conservatory
Como Park
651.487.8200
www.comozooconservatory.org

LIVING GREEN EXPO
May 5–6
10 a.m.–5 p.m.
State Fairgrounds
651.215.0218
www.livinggreen.org
Environmental fair—66 workshops, live music, food, kids' activities.

SUMMER FLOWER SHOW
May 5–Sept. 30
Marjorie McNeely Conservatory
Como Park
651.487.8200
www.comozooconservatory.org

June

**CAPITAL CITY
CLASSIC CRUISERS**
June 2–Sept. 28
Every Saturday night, 6–10 p.m.
Kellogg Blvd., between Wabasha
Ave. and Robert St.
651.266.8989
Come downtown and see beautifully restored classic cars from 1965 and earlier, right on the banks of the Mississippi River. Food and gift vendors, and Kellogg Mall will have sounds of classic cruising music.

Flint Hills International Children's Festival
June 2–3
Ordway Center for the
Performing Arts, Rice Park
651.224.4222
www.ordway.org
Parade, performances, dancing,
international foods, and hands-
on workshops.

Grand Old Day
June 3
Grand Avenue—
Dale to Fairview
651.699.0029
www.grandave.com
Sporting events, parade, family fun area, teen battle of the
bands, live music, festival gardens, and over 140 outdoor food
and merchandise vendors.

Saint Paul Sommerfest
June 8–10
Downtown Saint Paul
651.489.9623
www.saintpaulsommerfest.org
A weekend of European splendor.

Sommerfest includes:

Sommerfest River Cruise
June 8
6–10 p.m., Harriet Island
"The best happy hour in town!"
A fun-filled evening of dining and
dancing on an elegant Mississippi
River paddleboat with jazz, polka,
and choral music. Casual dress,
$55 per ticket. Purchase tickets at
saintpaulsommerfest.org

12th Annual German Carfest
June 9
9 a.m.–2 p.m.
Rice Park
952.937.1822
www.mbca-tc.org
Rice Park comes alive with music, food, and classic German
automobiles: Mercedes-Benz,
Porsche, Audi, BMW, and
Volkswagen.

The Fourth Annual Emperor's Ball
June 9
6 p.m.–12 a.m.
Landmark Center
651.489.9623
www.saintpaulsommerfest.org
A Viennese ball is recreated.
Performances by the Saint Paul
City Ballet, a five-course ban-
quet, a 50-piece orchestra, jazz
and swing music, café, beer hall,
plus carriage rides in Rice Park.
Black tie. $155 per ticket. Dinner
excluded—$75 per ticket.

Concours d'Elégance
June 10
9 a.m.–2 p.m., Rice Park
952.937.1822
www.mbca-tc.org
Vintage cars in Rice Park for a
juried car show. Music and food.

Sommerfest Promenade and Picnic

June 10
2:30 p.m., Saint Paul Cathedral parking lot
www.gai-mn.org
Horse-drawn wagons, carriages, and car show winners parade to Summit Avenue for music, food, and fun.

Twin Cities Hot Summer Jazz Festival
June 15–16
Mears Park
612.343.5943
www.hotsummerjazz.com

Saint Paul Blues Festival
Dates to be anounced
Raspberry Island
651.266.6400
800.55.BLUES
www.stpaulbluesfest.com
Beer, food, and gift vendors. Come and go as you please. No coolers, but bring your lawn chair.

Solstice Film Festival
June 20–24
Fitzgerald Theater
10 East Exchange Saint
651.290.1496
www.solsticefilmfest.org
Get off the couch and experience a film festival unlike any other. Five days of film at downtown venues, with outdoor music and wrap parties at local restaurants.

Minnesota Crafts Festival
June 22–24
Minnesota History
Center Museum
345 West Kellogg Blvd.
651.296.6126 or 800.657.3773
www.mnhs.org

Back to the '50s Car Show
June 22–24
Minnesota State Fairgrounds
651.641.1992
www.msra.com
Over 10,000 cars registered last year, over 300 vendors and crafters, over 350 swappers, plus '50s dances Friday and Saturday nights.

Taste of Minnesota
June 29–July 4
Harriet Island and Downtown
651.772.9980
www.tasteofmn.org
Includes four music stages, multiple food vendors, and fireworks every night.

July

Taste of Minnesota
June 29–July 4
Harriet Island and Downtown
651.772.9980
www.tasteofmn.org
Twenty-fifth anniversary. Four stages, fireworks every night, and lots of food vendors.

Hmong Sports Festival
July 7–8 (tentative)
Como Park
651.266.6400
Largest Hmong community sporting event in the nation. Volleyball, soccer, kato, and tops tournaments; food, retail, and music.

Dragon Festival and Dragon Boat Races
Dates to be announced
Lake Phalen
651.646.7717
www.dragonfestival.org
Asian cultural festival with performances, food vendors, and Dragon Boat races where paddlers follow the drumbeats.

Rondo Day
July 21
www.rondodays.org
Rondo Day is a central gathering place for celebrating the unique heritage of Saint Paul's historic Black community. The festival remembers Rondo with a senior citizens' dinner, one-day festival, famous drill team competition, parade, music, food, and art.

Highland Fest
July 20–22
Highland Village
651.699.9042
www.highlandfest.com

Rondo Day Drill Competition

Three-day outdoor festival. Food, art vendors, and live entertainment on two stages. Fireworks Friday and Saturday.

Car Craft Summer Nationals
July 20–22
Minnesota State Fairgrounds
317.236.6515
www.carcraft.com
Showcases over 4,000 street machines and muscle cars.

Circus Juventas
July 27, 28, and 29
651.699.8229
www.circusjuventas.org
Youth performers create a spectacular Cirque du Soleil-like show.

Sixteenth Annual Rib America Festival
July 26–29
Harriet Island
www.ribamerica.com
Minnesota's largest barbeque.

Minnesota State Fair

August

CIRCUS JUVENTAS
Aug. 2, 3, 4, 5, 9, 10, 11, and 12
651.699.8229
www.circusjuventas.org
Youth performers create a spectacular Cirque du Soleil-like show.

IRISH FAIR
Aug. 10–12
Harriet Island
952.474.7411
www.irishfair.com
Upper Midwest's largest Irish festival. Lots of music, dance, history, food, and theater. Free.

JAPANESE LANTERN LIGHTING FESTIVAL
Aug. 19
4 p.m.–dusk
Marjorie McNeely Conservatory, Como Park
651.487.8200
www.comozooconservatory.org
Lanterns float in the Japanese garden ponds to celebrate *Obon*, the Japanese festival honoring one's ancestors. Japanese food and entertainment.

TWIN CITIES BLACK FILM FESTIVAL
Aug. 17–19
Various locations in Saint Paul
www.tcbff.com
Opening and closing night premieres, panel discussions, festival parties, a Hollywood fashion show, 25 independent film projects, plus much more.

MINNESOTA STATE FAIR
Aug. 23–Sept. 3
Minnesota State Fairgrounds
651.288.4400
www.mnstatefair.org
The biggest state fair in the Midwest. Lots of food on sticks.

September

MINNESOTA STATE FAIR
Aug. 23–Sept. 3
Minnesota State Fairgrounds
651.288.4400
www.mnstatefair.org
The biggest state fair in the Midwest. Lots of food on sticks.

Minnesota American Indian Festival

Dates to be announced
Harriet Island
612.870.4533
www.maicc.org
Three-day family festival with traditional American Indian dance, music, and artists, as well as nationally known American Indian entertainers. Food, retail, and business area.

Selby Avenue JazzFest

Sept. 8
12–8 p.m.
Corner of Selby and Milton
Outdoor festival celebrating jazz music. Lots of things for kids to do, so bring the whole family. Delicious food, including lots of southern-style cuisine along with wine and beer sales. Local artisans and businesses too.

Wild River Music, Comedy, and Film Festival

Dates to be announced
Harriet Island, various downtown locations
www.wildriverfestival.com
With its inaugural year in 2006, the Wild River Music, Comedy, and Film Festival features eclectic music, skit and improv troupes, and films from around the world.

Ramsey Hill House Tour

Sept. 16
651.222.0200
www.ramseyhill.org

A self-guided tour of 15–20 lovely houses in the Victorian neighborhood of Ramsey Hill, located by the Saint Paul Cathedral.

October

Fall Flower Show

Oct. 6–Nov. 25
Marjorie McNeely Conservatory
Como Park
651.487.8200
www.comozooconservatory.org

Saint Paul Art Crawl

Oct. 12–14
Downtown Saint Paul
651.292.4373
www.artcrawl.org
More than 200 artists open their studios to the public.

Sur Seine

Oct. 12–21
Black Dog Café and other various locations
651.292.9746
www.surseine.org
International music festival. Jazz, rock, folk, and Celtic music.

"La Familia" Latino Family Festival & Expo

Dates to be announced
Saint Paul RiverCentre
651.265.4800
www.rivercentre.org
A one-day expo catering to the needs and interests of the Latino community.

Zoo Boo
Oct. 20, 21, 26, 27, 28
5–7:30 p.m.
Como Park Zoo
651.487.8200
www.comozooconservatory.org
Annual dress-up family Halloween festival.

Great Pumpkin Festival
Oct. 28
Landmark Center
651.292.3225
www.landmarkcenter.org
An autumn celebration for the
whole family: includes costume
contests, music, and art projects.

**Day of the Dead
Family Fiesta**
Oct. 28
Minnesota History
Center Museum
345 West Kellogg Blvd.
651.296.6126 or 800.657.3773
www.mnhs.org

November

**Minnesota State High
School League—**

Girls' Volleyball Tournament
Nov. 8–10
Xcel Energy Center
763.560.2262
www.mshsl.org

Capital City Lights
Mid-Nov.–March
Downtown Saint Paul
651.291.5600
www.capitalcitypartnership.com
Come downtown and enjoy the
holiday lights every winter.

Minnesota Hmong New Year
Nov. 22–25
Saint Paul RiverCentre
651.265.4800
www.rivercentre.org
Celebrate the Hmong New Year
with dance, food, music, entertainment, and more.

Holiday Bazaar
Nov. 29–Dec. 1
Landmark Center
651.292.3225
www.landmarkcenter.org
More than 80 exhibits featuring
local artists' work and gift items.

December

Holiday Bazaar
Nov. 29–Dec. 1
Landmark Center
651.292.3225
www.landmarkcenter.org
More than 80 exhibits featuring
local artists' work and gift items.

GRAND MEANDER
Dec. 1
Grand Ave.
651.699.0029
www.grandave.com
Trolley and hayrides, free breakfast for seniors, carolers, pancake breakfast with Santa. Free soup tasting.

HOLIDAY FLOWER SHOW
Dec. 1–Mid-January
Marjorie McNeely
Conservatory Como Park
651.487.8200
www.comozooconservatory.org

SKANDIA: SCANDINAVIAN FESTIVAL
Dec. 9
Landmark Center
651.292.3225
www.landmarkcenter.org
Celebrate Scandinavian traditions through music, dance, and food. Lutefisk available. Children's activities too.

KWANZAA CELEBRATION
Dec. 30
12–5 p.m.
Minnesota History Center
651.296.6126
www.minnesotahistorycenter.org
Annual Kwanzaa celebration with crafts, stories, and music—for all ages.

Dancers at the
SKANDIA Festival

FIVE STAR NEW YEAR
Dec. 31
Landmark Center
651.292.3225
www.landmarkcenter.org
Champagne, music, and magic. Tickets are $30 in advance and $40 at the door.

Health and Fitness Events
Saint Paul's Recreation Enthusiasts Can Choose from a Calendar of Activities

Teri J. Dwyer

Saint Paul can be a little slice of heaven to outdoor recreation enthusiasts. It has all of the conveniences of an urban setting, but also offers many hidden (and not-so-hidden) treasures. Paved paths along the river, bike lanes on major roads, parks, and lakes, as well as sidewalks, paths, and trails throughout the city, provide wonderful venues to enjoy many different outdoor recreational activities. Through snow, ice, rain, heat, and humidity—Saint Paul's most active citizens participate in a number of events throughout the year.

Here's a month-by-month look at some of the health and fitness events that make this city a great place to live, work, and work out.

January

THE FRIGID 5
www.tslevents.com
There's not much going on at the Minnesota State Fairgrounds in late January—so it's the perfect place to stage a running event! The Frigid 5 is a 5K and 10K race circling the fairgrounds. There are also shorter races (¼ mile and ½ mile) for the kids. The permanent booths and wide-open roadway look quite different covered in snow with hundreds of people around you rather than with the thousands who attend the State Fair daily in August.

THE BATTLE CREEK 10K CLASSIC NORDIC CHALLENGE
www.co.ramsey.mn.us/parks
A cross-country ski race fits the bill for January quite nicely—at least for those winters when we have enough snow on the ground to ski! The Battle Creek 10K Classic Nordic Challenge takes place on a late-January weekend in this park on the eastern edge of Saint Paul.

TWIN CITIES BICYCLING CLUB (TCBC)
www.mtn.org/tcbc
People who participate in the events of the Twin Cities Bicycling Club (TCBC) are not willing to hang up their bikes just because of a little snow and cold. Join them for their Winter Warmup, Think Spring, We Don't Need No Stinkin' Winter, and Fridays on the Bike events. They meet in various locations throughout the winter in Saint Paul.

February

Saint Paul Winter Carnival's Half Marathon and 5K

www.winter-carnival.com
Nothing says Minnesota like winter—at least to folks in most of the rest of the U.S. So we heartily embrace that notion by throwing a Winter Carnival each winter in Saint Paul. One of the many events of the Winter Carnival includes a health and fitness component—the "Coolest Race on Earth," Saint Paul Winter Carnival's Half Marathon and 5K starts and ends in the heart of Downtown. The course(s) follow the Mississippi River for the mid-portions of each race.

Heart of Saint Paul

www.tslevents.com
TCBC events (see January)
www.mtn.org/tcbc
New to the running scene in 2006, the Heart of Saint Paul showcases one of the jewels of Saint Paul—Como Lake on the city's north end. Planned to coincide with Valentine's Day—or the weekend closest to it—this race is truly family friendly with a 5K run and youth run options (¼ mile and ½ mile)

March

Human Race

www.tslevents.com
For more than 30 years, runners and walkers in Minnesota have equated the Human Race run and walk event with the start of the spring racing season in Saint Paul. This event has been a Saint Patrick's Day tradition throughout its history. The event offers an 8K run, a 5K run/walk, and youth runs from ¼ to ½ mile.

April

Saint Paul Parks' Annual Spring Parks Clean-Up

www.stpaul.gov/depts/parks.
Perhaps you wouldn't consider the Saint Paul Parks' Annual Spring Parks Clean-Up a health and fitness event, but if you come out and participate, you can get a good workout. And you'll feel good about cleaning up the environment—making a safer, less-polluted, and better-looking city for all to enjoy! Each year, Saint Paul Parks and Recreation hosts this event for families, groups, and individuals to help clean up the trash in Saint Paul's Parks and Recreation centers. The clean-up is generally held on a Saturday in April.

Challenge Obesity 5K
www.charitieschallenge.org
Sponsored by Charities Challenge, this is the first in a Summer Series of five events at Como Lake. Run, Race Walk, Fitness Walk, and "Walk By My Side" 2.5K.

May

Menudo 5K
www.districtdelsol.com/cinco.html
Saint Paul's West Side, with a large Hispanic/Latino population, hosts a Cinco de Mayo (Fifth of May) celebration each spring on the weekend closest to May 5th. On the Saturday of this celebratory weekend, they host the Menudo 5K.

Run Walk for Every Body
www.melpomene.org
If it's the first Saturday in May—it must be time for Melpomene! Cleverly dubbed the "Run Walk for Every Body," this 5K run benefits Melpomene, an organization with goals of promoting active, healthy lives for girls and women. The race offers separate women's and men's 5K runs, a co-ed 5K walk, a 3K family walk, and half-mile and one-mile kids' fun runs. This family-friendly event is run along the beautiful Mississippi River.

Bark in the Park and Run for Animals Walk & Run
www.hsca.net
Both events are hosted by the Humane Society for Companion Animals. This event kicks off the national "Be Kind to Animals Week" at Como Park.

Mississippi 10 Miler
www.runmdra.org
Starts and ends at Summit Avenue and East Mississippi River Blvd. This long-standing event is sponsored by MDRA (Minnesota Distance Running Association). The course is out and back along the Saint Paul side of the Mississippi River.

Challenge Hearts and Minds 5K
www.charitieschallenge.org
Sponsored by Charities Challenge, this is the second in a Summer Series of five events at Como Lake. Run, Race Walk, Fitness Walk, and "Walk By My Side" 2.5K.

June

Grand Old Day on the Go!
www.tslevents.com
We love to celebrate our lovely summer weather in Saint Paul by hosting outdoor festivals of all sizes. The largest one-day music, food, and entertainment festival in the U.S., Grand Old Day falls

on a Sunday in early June. To kick off this annual tradition, Grand Old Day on the Go! offers an 8K inline skate, 8K run, 5K run/walk ,and youth run events (¼ mile and ½ mile).

CHALLENGE CANCER 5K
www.charitieschallenge.org
Sponsored by Charities Challenge, this is the third in a summer series of five events at Como Lake. Run, Race Walk, Fitness Walk, and "Walk By My Side" 2.5K.

TIME TO FLY 10K AND 5K
www.childrenscancer.org/news_details_events_timetofly.html
Children's Cancer Research Fund hosts the Time to Fly 10K and 5K at Harriet Island. Besides the 10K and 5K races, there's a 2K and 1K kids' run.

GREAT RIVER ENERGY BICYCLE FESTIVAL
www.minnbikefestival.com
Come during the day to watch the professionals race, stay to take part in the Amateur and Kids' Fun Race in the evening.

July

LANGFORD PARK RACES
These very low-key races (runners choose a 2- or 4-mile option) have had an entry fee of 50 cents for their entire history—since 1974. The course is a 2-mile

loop on the streets of Saint Paul's picturesque Saint Anthony Park. Races begin and end at Langford Park. This race is a fun way to kick off your Fourth of July celebration.

ROCKIN' EASTSIDE 5K
Both 5K and 1K around beautiful Lake Phalen on Saint Paul's East Side.

RICE STREET MILE
Race starts at the intersection of Rice Street and Front Avenue. The course is flat and point-to-point. Don't miss this opportunity to run one of the shortest road races offered in Saint Paul.

CHALLENGE DIABETES 5K
www.charitieschallenge.org
Sponsored by Charities Challenge, this is the fourth in a Summer Series of five events at Como Lake. Run, Race Walk, Fitness Walk, and "Walk By My Side" 2.5K.

August

MINNESOTA STATE FAIR MILK RUN 5K
www.mnstatefair.org
Participants receive an admission ticket to the fair and a coupon for a free malt!

Saint Paul Inline Marathon

Aug. 19, Downtown Saint Paul
651.238.2651
www.saintpaulinlinemarathon.com
First-time marathoners share the road with the world's top skating professionals. A chance for inline skaters from beginners to professionals to skate along the beautiful Mississippi River. The race ends at Mears Park.

Highland Fest 5K

www.highlandfest.com
This low-key, family-friendly fun run is part of the annual Highland Fest celebration. The course is out and back along the Mississippi River.

MDRA Cross Country Runs

www.runmdra.org
Since 1974, the Minnesota Distance Running Association (MDRA) has sponsored this series of cross country races held every Wednesday evening in August at Como Park. The races are open to all ages and abilities.

September

Saint Paul Classic Bike Tour

www.spnec.org
A rare opportunity to bicycle around and throughout the city of Saint Paul on streets free of car traffic. This family friendly event offers a 15-mile tour of Saint Paul or a 30-mile ride.

West Fest Jalapeño 5K

Another race showcasing the city's West Side. This event is family friendly and includes a Chile Chase that is free for runners 10 years of age and younger.

Challenge Arthritis 5K

www.charitieschallenge.org
Sponsored by Charities Challenge, this is the fifth in a Summer Series of five events at Como Lake. Run, Race Walk, Fitness Walk, and "Walk By My Side" 2.5K.

Sharing Life Walk/Run (3 miles)

This Lake Phalen all-ages event includes special races and games for the kids. Support organ donation education and raise money for families going through the organ transplant process.

October

The Twin Cities Marathon (TCM)

Oct. 7
763.287.3888
www.twincitiesmarathon.org
A Twin Cities tradition for over 30 years crosses the Mississippi River. On the Saturday before Sunday's big marathon, TCM hosts their Saturday running events exclusively in Saint Paul. The TCM 5K and Family Events offer something for all ages and abilities. The races start and end near the State Capitol.

The Paul Mausling Cross-Country Run (4K & 6K)
www.tslevents.com
Named after former Saint Paul resident (and graduate of Saint Paul's Macalester College) Paul Mausling, this race offers another opportunity for runners of all ages and abilities to run a cross-country race at Saint Paul's Como Park.

The Grand Tour
www.tslevents.com
A Halloween-themed event, this race showcases one of the great streets in Saint Paul—Grand Avenue. The race is run on an out and back course from Avon to Snelling.

The Monster Dash
www.jlsp.org
Billed as "A Race to Erase Domestic Violence," this 5K Run/Walk and Kid's Fun Run is sponsored by the Junior League of Saint Paul. The event takes place at Harriet Island.

November
Rocky's Run
www.tslevents.com
This cross-country race offers the public a rare opportunity to run the same course the University of Minnesota men's and women's cross-country teams race on (at the Les Bolstad University Golf Course). The 8K and 5K races benefit a scholarship in Rocky Racette's name for the women's track and field and cross-country teams at the U of M.

Turkey Run
www.mtn.org/tcbc
A tradition for the Sunday before Thanksgiving each year, this family-friendly fun run encircles Como Lake, beginning and ending at warm indoor headquarters at Como Elementary School.
www.tslevents.com
TCBC events (see January).

December
TCBC Events
(see January)
www.mtn.org/tcbc
Year-'round Saint Paul Activities

The Saint Paul Hiking Club
This group meets regularly at various locations throughout Saint Paul. Everyone is welcome. Check your local newspapers' recreation/events calendar for current hike locations and contact information.

Winter Activities

CROSS-COUNTRY SKIING

Saint Paul grooms trails at three sites each winter: Como Golf Course, Phalen Golf Course, and the Highland Nine-Hole Golf Course.

CLASSIC AND SKATE SKIING

www.stpaul.gov/depts/parks
Tuesday night lessons are available through the City of Saint Paul's Parks and Recreation.

ICE SKATING RINKS

www.stpaul.gov/depts/parks
www.capitalcitypartnership.com
There are a variety of outdoor ice skating rinks located throughout the city. Amenities, including rental skates, vary by location.

KEY:

4K (2.5 miles)
5K (3.1 miles)
6K (3.75 miles)
8K (4.97 miles)
10K (6.2 miles)
Half marathon (13.1 miles)
Marathon (26.2 miles)

Restaurants

128 CAFE
128 Cleveland Ave.
651.645.4128
It's cozy. Broc and Natalie's cooking will warm you all over.

ABU NADER
2095 Como Ave.
651.647.5391
Small deli serves satisfying falafel sandwiches.

ANDY'S GARAGE
1825 University Ave.
651.917.2332
www.andysgaragecafe.com

ARTISTS' QUARTER
408 Saint Peter St.
651.292.1359
Jazz club too.

AWADA'S ON PLATO
199 E. Plato Blvd.
651.293.9111

BARBARY FIG
720 Grand Ave.
651.290.2085

BABANI'S
544 Saint Peter St.
651.602.9964

BLACK DOG CAFE AND WINE BAR
Suite 100, 308 Prince St.
651.228.9274
Nice digs and great Lowertown location.

Black Sea on N. Snelling

BLACK SEA
737 N. Snelling Ave.
651.917.8832
Turkish. Run by Ali and Sema. Neighborly, cozy, delicious, and comfortable.

BLONDIES CAFÉ
454 S. Snelling Ave.
651.204.0152

BOCA CHICA RESTAURANTE
11 Concord St.
651.222.8499
Patio. Mariachi music every fourth Saturday of the month.

BUI'S ASIAN CUISINE
422 West University Ave.
651.222.1333

Cafe Latté
850 Grand Ave.
651.224.5687
www.cafelatte.com
Join the crowds at Cafe Latté.

Café Minnesota
Minnesota History Center
345 West Kellogg Blvd.
651.297.4859
www.minnesotahistorycenter.org
Outdoor patio. Breakfast and
lunch only.

Caffe Biaggio
2356 University Ave.
651.917.7997
Italian bistro. Delicious. Pricey.

Carousel
Crowne Plaza Hotel
11 East Kellogg Blvd.
651.292.1900
Enjoy a panoramic view of Saint
Paul and the Mississippi River at
this revolving restaurant. Expensive.

Cecil's Delicatessen and Bakery
651 Cleveland Ave. South
651.341.0170
Best reubens in town.

Cheng Heng
448 West University Ave.
651.222.5577
Cambodian.

Cherokee Sirloin Room
886 South Smith Ave.
651.457.2729

Chico Chica
242 West Seventh St.
651.209.9210
Mexican.

Christo's
214 Fourth St. East
651.224.6000
Greek food in the restored Depot. Lunch buffet.

**Cossetta Italian Market
and Pizzeria**
211 West Seventh St.
651.222.3476

Cravings
271 West Seventh St.
651.224.1554
Inexpensive. Killer carrot cake.

Danny Boy's Cheeseburgers
1026 West Seventh St.
651.287.0270
Inexpensive. Classic cheeseburgers, fries, and malts.

**Dar's Double Scoop Ice Cream
and Coffee Shop**
1046 Rice St.
651.487.4073
Check it out.

Day By Day Café
477 West Seventh St.
651.227.0654
Good for breakfast.

Degidios
425 West Seventh St.
651.291.7398
Italian. Classic Saint Paul eatery.

DIXIE'S ON GRAND
695 Grand Ave.
651.222.7345
www.dixiesongrand.com

**DOWNTOWNER
WOODFIRE GRILL**
253 West Seventh St.
651.228.9500

EVEREST ON GRAND
1276-78 Grand Ave.
651.696.1666
Tibetan. Terrific curries and
momos (dumplings).

FASIKA
510 North Snelling Ave.
651.646.4747
Ethiopian. Tasty.

FHIMA
6 West Sixth St.
651.287.0784
www.fhimas.com
Mediterranean and French.

FOREPAUGHS
276 Exchange St. South
651.224.5606
www.forepaughs.com
Victorian mansion built by its
namesake in 1870. French. Pricey.

FRENCH PRESS JAZZ CAFÉ
213 Fourth Street East
651.224.2732

FUJI YA
Japanese
465 North Wabasha St.
651.310.0111

Degidios on West Seventh

GRAND OLE CREAMERY
750 Grand Ave.
651.293.1655
Homemade ice cream.

GRANDMA RITA'S CAFÉ
327 West Seventh St.
651.224.9235
Part coffee shop, part Mexican
restaurant.

GRANDVIEW GRILL
1818 Grand Ave.
651.698.2346
Gleaming '50s-decor malt shop.

**GREAT WATERS
BREWING COMPANY**
426 Saint Peter St.
651.224.2739
www.greatwatersbc.com
Brew pub and restaurant.

HEARTLAND
1806 Saint Clair Ave.
651.699.3536
Local ingredients, superb.
Expensive.

HIGHLAND GRILL
771 Cleveland Ave. South
651.690.1173
Good sweet potato fries.

ITALIAN PIE SHOPPE & WINERY
1670 Grand Ave.
651.221.0093
www.italianpieshoppe.com
Established in 1976.

IZZY'S ICE CREAM CAFE
2034 Marshall Ave.
651.603.1458

Jay's Cafe on Raymond Avenue

JAY'S CAFE
791 Raymond Ave.
651.641.1446
Yum, yum. Attractive.

JERABEK'S NEW BOHEMIAN COFFEEHOUSE AND BAKERY
63 Winifred St. West
651.228.1245
Best soups ever. Cozy. It's home-town Saint Paul at its finest. Vegan options.

KEY'S CAFÉ
767 Raymond Ave.
651.646.5756

KHYBER PASS
1571 Grand Ave.
651.690.0505
Afghan. Delicious and friendly.

KRUA THAILAND
432 West University Ave.
651.224.4053
Thai. Expensive.

KUM GANG SAN
694 North Snelling Ave.
651.645.2000
Classic Korean.
Inexpensive.

LA CUCARACHA
36 Dale St. South
651.221.9682
Mexican. Since the 1960s.

Jerabek's New Bohemian Coffeehouse and Bakery

La Grolla
452 Selby Ave.
651.221.1061
Expensive. Great ambience and lovely food.

The Lexington
1096 Grand Ave.
651.222.5878
A classic.

The Liffey
Irish Pub
175 West Seventh St.
651.556.1416
www.theliffey.com
New outdoor patio

The Little Oven
1786 East Minnehaha Ave.
651.735.4944
Italian.

Los Tejanos
287 North Ruth St.
651.730.7303
Family-run Mexican restaurant.

LoTo
380 Jackson St., Galtier Plaza
651.209.7776
David Fhima's restaurant.

Luci Ancora
2060 Randolph Ave.
651.698.6889
Italian.

M St. Café
Saint Paul Hotel
350 Market St.
651.228.3855

Mañana
828 East Seventh St.
651.772.6866
Chinese, Mexican. Inexpensive.

Mancini's Char House
531 West Seventh St.
651.224.7345
www.mancinis.com
Great food and entertainment in a unique lounge.

Mickey's Dining Car

MARGAUX
486 Robert St. North
651.407.6438
A new restaurant in Saint Paul
serving French food.

MICKEY'S DINING CAR
36 West Seventh St.
651.222.5633
On National Register of Historic
Places. Thirties art deco architecture. Open 24 hours a day, 365
days a year.

MIM'S
1435 North Cleveland Ave.
651.646.0456
Middle Eastern.
Mahmoud Shahin owns Lori's
Coffee House next door too.

MISS CHINA
704 University Ave.
651.225.8080
Chinese.

MOSCOW ON THE HILL
371 Selby Ave.
651.291.1236
Russian. Great back yard patio.

MUDDY PIG
162 North Dale St.
651.290.2041
Neighborhood bar and grill.

MUFFULETTA
2260 Como Ave.
651.644.9116

**NEW HONG KONG KITCHEN
CHINESE PALACE**
1192 Dale St.
651.489.8681
Chinese. Inexpensive.

NINA'S COFFEE CAFÉ
165 Western Ave. North
651.292.9816

THE NOOK
492 Hamline Ave. South
651.698.4347
Classic neighborhood bar
and grill.

Pad Thai Grand Café
1659 Grand Ave.
651.690.1393
Thai. Cozy neighborhood
restaurant.

**Padelford Packet
Boat Co., Inc.**
Harriet Island
651.227.1100
Prime rib dinner cruises every
Friday in Saint Paul. Expensive.

**Pastor Hamilton's
Bar-B-Que**
1150 East Seventh St.
651.772.0279

Patrick McGovern's Pub
225 West Seventh St.
651.224.5821

Pazzaluna
360 Saint Peter St.
651.223.7000
www.pazzaluna.com
Dinner only. Complimentary
valet parking.

Piñeda Tacos 3
1304 South Robert St.
651.455.6833
Deli-style Mexican. Way better
than Chipotle.

Porky's Drive-In
1890 University Ave. West
651.644.1790
The best onion rings. Classic-
car-watching hangout on summer weekends.

Punch Woodfire Pizza
704 S Cleveland Ave.
651.696.1066
Neighborhood bistro.

**Que Nha Vietnamese
Restaurant**
849 University Ave.
651.290.8552
Vietnamese.

**Ray's Mediterranean
Restaurant**
1199 West Seventh St.
651.224.3883
Mediterranean. Good food.
Friendly. A favorite.

À Rebours
410 Saint Peter St.
651.665.0656
French.

Red's Savoy Inn and Pizza
421 East Seventh St.
651.227.1437

Ristorante Luci
470 Cleveland Ave. South
651.699.8258
Italian. Expensive.

River Boat Grill
Harriet Island riverfront
651.353.0576

Ruam Mit Thai Cafe
475 Saint Peter St.
651.290.0067

Triêu Châu on University Avenue

SAIGON
601 West University Ave.
651.225.8751

SAJI-YA
695 Grand Ave.
651.292.0444
www.sajiya.com
Japanese restaurant and bar.

ST. CLAIR BROILER
1580 Saint Clair Ave.
651.698.7055

SAINT PAUL GRILL
www.stpaulhotel.com
The Saint Paul Hotel
350 Market St.
651.292.9292
Classic Saint Paul eatery.

SAKURA
350 Saint Peter St.
651.224.0185
Japanese.

SPANKY'S BAR AND GRILL
825 Jefferson Ave.
651.227.6315
Karaoke on Thursdays and
Saturdays.

SUPATRA'S THAI CUISINE
289 East Fifth St.
651.222.5859
Open for lunch Monday through
Saturday, dinner only on Sunday.

SWEDE HOLLOW CAFÉ
725 East Seventh St.
651.776.8810
Lunch place. Good sandwiches,
salads, and soups.

SWEET WILLIAM AND TEA
142 East Fifth St.
651.222.4767

TAMALANDIA
935 South Robert St.
651.554.7703
Mexican. Great tamales.

TANPOPO NOODLE SHOP
308 Prince St.
651.209.6527
Simple and elegant Japanese
food. Inexpensive.

TAQUERIA LOS OCAMPO
895 Arcade St.
651.774.7623
Mexican.

TASTE OF THAILAND
1671 Selby Ave.
651.644.3997

Tavern on Grand
656 Grand Ave.
651.228.9030
Famous for walleye.

Tay Ho Restaurant
302 West University Ave.
651.228.7216
Chinese, Vietnamese.

Trieu Chau Restaurant
500 University Ave. West
651.222.6148
Outstanding soups and tasty sandwiches. Best egg rolls.

Trattoria da Vinci
400 Sibley St.
651.222.4050
Italian.

Village Bistro
2012 Ford Pkwy.
651.698.6335

Vintage Restaurant and Wine Bar
579 Selby Ave.
651.222.7000

W. A. Frost & Company
Dacotah Building
374 Selby Ave.
651.224.5715
www.wafrost.com
A favorite destination since 1975. Incomparable ambiance and Old World character. Fireplaces, a charming bar, and a European-style garden patio.

Wild Tymes
33 West Seventh Place
651.224.8181

Yarusso's
637 Payne Ave.
651.776.4848
Italian. Since 1933. Classic. Stop by for the sauce, stay for the bocce ball.

Yours Truly Café
201 East Fourth St.
651.298.0173

Z Café
518 Selby Ave.
651.222.5224
Greek, Mediterranean.

Zander Café
525 Selby Ave.
651.222.5224

Yarusso's on Payne Avenue

Theater

Jami Shoemaker

It has been said that, outside of New York City, there are more theaters per capita in the Twin Cities than any other place in the U.S., and Saint Paul has its share of them. Whether you're looking for cutting-edge original works or the classics, you'll find it all in Saint Paul. The city's diversity can be seen in its many offerings, including dinner theater, music theater, opera, and theater with African-American, Latino, and Jewish themes.

ACTORS THEATER OF MINNESOTA
1043 Grand Ave., Suite 291
651.227.2464
www.actorsmn.org
This professional theater company presents an annual season at the Minnesota Centennial Showboat and at the Lowry Theater in downtown Saint Paul.

ANODYNE THEATRE
825 Carleton St.
Saint Paul, MN 55114
651.646.8242
Anodyne Theatre produces conventional and unconventional works and continues community building by supporting emerging performing artists. Upcoming productions include *It Could Be Worse* or *Love at Frostbite, Fused Compositions,* and *Divine Feminine.*

COMMEDIA BEAUREGARD
585 Van Buren Ave.
Saint Paul, MN 55103
651.214.2905
www.soulsofwit.com/cb/

"Theatre that is beautiful in expression." Commedia Beauregard presents original workshop productions and modern classic comedies.

GREMLIN THEATRE
509 Sibley St.
Saint Paul, MN 55101
651.228.7008
www.gremlintheatre.org
This dynamic and exciting small professional theater focuses on bringing you a wide range of styles and works in an intimate, urban venue.

GREAT AMERICAN HISTORY THEATRE
30 East Tenth St.
Saint Paul, MN 55101
651.292.4323
www.historytheatre.com
The Great American History Theatre is a nonprofit, professional theater in downtown Saint Paul devoted to creating and producing plays about Minnesota, the Midwest, and the diverse American experience.

In the Basement Productions

P.O. Box 65861
Saint Paul, MN 55165
651.224.2603
www.itbp.org

Working out of the Fourth Street Theatre, this nonprofit company produces original, classic, and contemporary works, emphasizing the unique talents and contributions of each individual artist.

Lex-Ham Community Theater

1184 Portland Ave.
Saint Paul, MN 55104
651.644.3366
www.LexHamArts.org

The Lex-Ham Community Theater offers a variety of ways for novice and experienced theater lovers and performers in the Saint Paul and Twin Cities area to become involved: Shakespeare Reading Series, acting classes, and main stage theater productions throughout the year.

Lowry Theater

16 West Fifth St.
Saint Paul, MN 55102
651.290.2290
www.wegottabingo.com

Professional dinner theater presenting interactive comedies.

Lowry Theater

Minnesota Jewish Theatre Company

P.O. Box 16155
Saint Paul, MN 55116
651.647.4315
www.mnjewishtheatre.org

Telling stories of our common search for identity in a multicultural world.

Mounds Theatre

1029 Hudson Rd.
Saint Paul, MN 55106
651.772.2253
www.moundstheatre.org

The Mounds Theatre Company is committed to the cultural enrichment of Saint Paul's ethnically and economically diverse East Side neighborhoods.

Nautilus Music-Theater

308 Prince St., Suite 250
Saint Paul, MN 55101
651.298.9913
http://www.wesleybalk.org/nautilus.html
Nautilus supports the creation, development, and production of new operas and music theater pieces, working with writers, composers, performers, and directors. Works in progress are presented in a monthly ROUGH CUTS program, and occasional full productions include world premieres and innovative presentations of existing works.

Park Square Theatre

North Star Opera

Landmark Center, Suite 414
75 West Fifth St.
Saint Paul, MN 55102
651.292.4309
www.northstaropera.org
Founded in 1980, North Star Opera presents a wide-ranging repertoire of opera, operetta, and musical theater emphasizing strongly balanced musical and theatrical values. North Star Opera stresses accessibility by performing works in English in intimate venues at moderate prices.

Park Square Theatre

20 West Seventh Place
Saint Paul, MN 55102
651.291.7005
www.parksquaretheatre.org
This professional theater in downtown Saint Paul produces a perfect balance of familiar favorites and fresh new stories.

Penumbra Theatre Company

270 North Kent St.
Saint Paul, MN 55102
651.224.3180
www.penumbratheatre.org
Celebrating its thirtieth season, Penumbra Theatre Company is Minnesota's only professional African-American theater company, performing at the Martin Luther King/Hallie Q. Brown Center in the heart of the Selby-Dale neighborhood. Performances

for 2007 include *Blue*, Feb. 15–March 11; *I Just Stopped by to See the Man*, April 12–May 6; *Get Ready*, June 7–July 1.

STARTING GATE PRODUCTIONS
P.O. Box 16392
Saint Paul, MN 55116
651.645.3503
www.startinggate.org
Performing at the Mounds Theatre, this small professional theater group produces primarily classic and contemporary dramas and comedies. The 2006-2007 season includes *A View From the Bridge, P.S. Your Cat is Dead, Amadeus, True West,* and *King Lear.*

STEPPINGSTONE THEATRE FOR YOUTH DEVELOPMENT
75 Fifth St. West
Saint Paul, MN 55102
651.225.9265
www.steppingstonetheatre.org
Celebrating its twentieth season in 2007, SteppingStone Theatre is known as Saint Paul's premier youth-centered arts organization, producing six fully staged productions each year.

TEATRO DEL PUEBLO
209 Page St. West, Suite 208
Saint Paul, MN 55107
651.224.8806
www.teatrodelpueblo.org

Teatro del Pueblo

Teatro is a fun-loving, hardworking theater company devoted to raising awareness of Latino issues, artists, and culture. Located on the West Side, Teatro is currently in its fourteenth year and continues to serve many communities across the state with its educational residencies, touring shows, and the Annual Political Theater Festival.

THE THEATRICAL MUSIC COMPANY
152 Hurley Ave. East
West Saint Paul, MN 55118
651.554.7794
www.mnartists.org
The focus of this innovative, award-winning performance ensemble is on re-imagining how music tells stories.

Music

ARNELIA'S
1183 University Ave. West
651.642.5975
Mon.: Twin Cities Open Stage
Show, $2, 10 p.m.

ARTISTS' QUARTER
Seventh Place and Saint Peter
651.292.1359
Jazz most nights.

BIG V'S
1567 University Ave. West
651.645.8472

FRENCH PRESS JAZZ CAFÉ
213 East Fourth St.
651.224.2732
Jazz most nights.

GINGKO COFFEESHOP
721 Snelling Ave. North
651.645.2647
Jazz and folk.

HALF TIME REC
1013 Front Ave.
651.488.8245
Irish, Celtic, and Cajun.

HAT TRICK LOUNGE
134 East Fifth St.
651.488-8245

MINNESOTA MUSIC CAFÉ
499 Payne Ave.
651.776.4699

NEUMANN'S BAR
2531 East Seventh Ave. North
651.770.6020

O'GARA'S GARAGE
164 Snelling Ave. North
651.644.3333

OLD MAN RIVER CAFÉ
879 Smith Ave.
651.450.7070

OVER THE RAINBOW
719 North Dale St.
651.487.5070

SPANKY'S BAR AND GRILL
825 Jefferson Ave.
651.227.6315

STARTING GATE
2516 West Seventh St.
651.698.6407

STUDIO Z
275 East Fourth St., Suite 100
651.698.6407

TURF CLUB
1601 University Ave. West
651.647.0486

**THE SAINT PAUL
CHAMBER ORCHESTRA**
408 Saint Peter St., Third Floor
651.292.3248
www.thespco.org

Dance

Swing Night on Thursdays
Wabasha Caves
215 Wabasha St. South
651.224.1191
Doors open at 6 p.m. Lesson at
6:15. Live music from 7–9 p.m.
All ages event. Password: "Gus
sent me." $7.

Black Dog Café and Wine Bar
308 Prince St.
Friday Argentine Tango, 8 p.m.
Lesson at 7:30. $3.

First Saturday New England Contra Dance
Oddfellows' Hall
Corner of Hampden and
Raymond avenues.
651.222.5475
8 p.m. Lesson at 7:30 p.m.
Upstairs entrance is on the side
of the building on Hampden
Avenue. Various bands. $7.

Sunday Night Social Dances
Half Time Rec
1013 Front St.
8–11 p.m. Band varies weekly.
Usually couples dancing, currently
mostly Cajun and Zydeco. Dance
lesson before the dance. $5.

Alternate Tuesdays Ceili Dancing and Lessons
Nickel Joint
501 Blair Ave. (NW corner Blair
and MacKubin).

7:30–9 p.m. Recorded music.
Every second and fourth Tuesday
of the month.

Wednesday Ceili Dancing and Lessons
The Dubliner
2162 University Ave. West
7–9 p.m. Lesson at beginning of
dance. Free.

Wednesday Ceili Dancing and Lessons
The Conway Recreation Center
2090 Conway St.
7–8:45 p.m. The center is alcohol
free. Lessons at beginning of
dance. Free.

Third Saturday Ceili
Oddfellows' Hall
Corner of Hampden and
Raymond avenues.
651.222.5475
8–10 p.m. Lesson at 7:30. Dancers, $2. Musicians, free.
Alcohol free.

First Saturday Ceili
The Dubliner
2162 University Ave. West
2–5 p.m. The first Saturday of
each month, ceili and session
(live music). Free.

Art Galleries

ART RESOURCES GALLERY
494 Jackson St.
651.222.4431

AZ GALLERY
308 Prince St.
651.229.0819

CATHERINE G. MURPHY GALLERY
College of Saint Catherine
2004 Randolph Ave.
651.690.6644

EVOKE GALLERY
355 Wabasha St.
651.224.6388
www.evokegalllery.com

FIVETWOSIX GALLERY
526 Selby Ave.
651.222.3839

GALLERY PRINT
253 East Fourth St.
651.224.7056

GRAND HAND GALLERY
611 Grand Ave.
651.312.1122

IMAGES UNDER GLASS
1085 Grand Ave.
651.224.3801

9TH STREET ENTRY GALLERY
Rossmor Building
500 North Robert St.
651.638.6527
www.bethel.edu/galleries

OXYGEN GALLERY
253 East Fourth St.
651.224.7056
www.o2gallery.com

RAYMOND AVENUE GALLERY
761 Raymond Ave.
651.644.9200

Books

RED BALLOON BOOKSTORE
891 Grand Ave.
651.224.8320

SIXTH CHAMBER USED BOOKSTORE
1332 Grand Ave.
651.690.9463

MICAWBER'S BOOKS
2238 Carter Ave.
651.646.5506
www.micawbers.com

MIDWAY BOOKS
1579 University Ave. West
651.644.7605
www.midwaybooks.com

Museums

AMERICAN ASSOCIATION OF WOODTURNERS
222 Landmark Center
75 West Fifth St.
651.484.9094
www.woodturners.org
Spectacular wood art pieces.

THE GOLDSTEIN MUSEUM OF DESIGN
University of Minnesota
240 McNeal Hall
1985 Buford Ave.
612.624.7434
www.goldstein.che.umn.edu
Art in everday life.

JACKSON STREET ROUNDHOUSE
193 East Pennsylvania Ave.
651.228.0263
www.mtmuseum.org
Working railroad museum.

MINNESOTA CHILDREN'S MUSEUM
10 West Seventh St.
651.225.6000
www.mcm.org
Lots of fun for kids of all ages.

MINNESOTA HISTORY CENTER MUSEUM
345 West Kellogg Blvd.
651.296.6126 or 800.657.3773
www.mnhs.org
Rotating exhibits. Good library.

MINNESOTA MUSEUM OF AMERICAN ART
50 West Kellogg Blvd.
Small but stunning.

SCIENCE MUSEUM OF MINNESOTA
120 West Kellogg Blvd.
651.221.9444
www.smm.org
Includes Imax Theater.

THE SHUBERT CLUB'S MUSEUM OF MUSICAL INSTRUMENTS
Lower level and second floor of
Landmark Center, 75 West Fifth St.
Mon–Fri. 11 a.m.–3 p.m.
Sun. 1–5 p.m. free.

TWIN CITY RAILROAD MUSEUM
Suite 222
1021 East Bandana Blvd.
651.647.9628
www.tcmrm.org
State-of-the-art miniature railroad, reproduced in ¼" scale.
Call for hours. Ages 6 and up: $3.

Historical Sites

Alexander Ramsey House
265 South Exchange St.
651.296.0100
www.mnhs.org/ramseyhouse
Home of Alexander Ramsey completed in 1872. Guided hourly tours 10 a.m. to 3 p.m. Fridays and Saturdays.

Assumption Church
51 West Seventh St.
651.224.7536
Roman Catholic church built in 1871. On National List of Historic Places. Guided or self-guided tours available.

Cathedral of Saint Paul
239 Selby Ave.
651.228.1766
www.cathedralsp.org
Construction completed in 1915. Guided tours Mondays, Wednesdays, and Fridays at 1 p.m.

Governor's Residence
1006 Summit Ave.
651.297.2161
www.admin.state.mn.us/buildings/residence
Limited public tours available.

Historic Fort Snelling
Highways 5 and 55
612.726.1171
www.mnhs.org/fortsnelling
Open May through October. Reconstructed 1820s military post. Costumed guides and demonstrations.

James J. Hill House
240 Summit Ave.
651.297.2555
www.mnhs.org/hillhouse
The red sandstone residence was completed in 1891. Art exhibit and tours. Tours $8 adults, $6 seniors.

Julian H. Sleeper House
66 South Saint Albans St.
651.225.1505
Nine exhibition rooms of the Gilded Age. Includes President James A. Garfield memorabilia. Tours available by appointment.

Minnesota Korean War Veterans' Memorial
State Capitol Grounds
Dramatic sculpture honoring troops who fought in Korea.

Minnesota State Capitol
75 Rev. Dr. Martin Luther King Jr. Blvd.
651.296.2881 (tours)
www.mnhs.org/statecapitol
Cass Gilbert's masterpiece. Guided tours offered on the hour. Free.

Minnesota Vietnam Veterans' Memorial
State Capitol Grounds
www.mvvm.org

Granite memorial recognizes and honors the 68,000 Minnesotans who served in Vietnam, 1,077 of whom were killed, 43 who are still missing.

Old Muskego Church

Luther Seminary
2375 Como Ave.
651.641.3456
www.luthersem.edu/events
First church built by Norse immigrants in America in 1844 in Wisconsin. Moved to Luther Seminary in 1904. Self-guided or guided tours available upon request.

Ramsey County Courthouse and Saint Paul City Hall

15 West Kellogg Blvd.
651.266.8500
www.co.ramsey.mn.us
Built in 1932; art deco architecture. The "Vision of Peace" statue was designed by Carl Milles, is three stories high, and sculptured in onyx.

Roy Wilkins Memorial

State Capitol Grounds
www.tccom.com/wilkins/
Honors Minnesota native and civil rights leader Roy Wilkins. Designed by Curtis Patterson.

Saint Paul Public Central Library

90 Fourth St. West
651.266.7000
www.stpaul.lib.mn.us
Italian Renaissance revival building built in 1917.

Wabasha Street Caves

215 South Wabasha St.
651.224.1191
www.wabashastreetcaves.com
Swing dancing, tours.
Cave tours—5 p.m. Thurs., 11 a.m. Sat. and Sun.

Old Muskego Church

Tours

DOWN IN HISTORY TOURS
Wabasha Street Caves
215 South Wabasha St.
651.292.1220
www.wabashastreetcaves.com
Cave tours—5 p.m. Thurs.,
11 a.m. Sat. and Sun.
Gangster Tour—12 p.m. Sat.
Call for info.

**PADELFORD PACKET
BOAT COMPANY**
Harriet Island-Wharf Boat Office
651.227.1100
www.riverrides.com
Saint Paul is a whole different
world viewed from the river.

SUMMIT BREWING COMPANY
910 Montreal Circle
651.265.7800
www.summitbrewing.com
Tours Tues., Thurs., and Sat. at
1 p.m. Reservations required for
Saturday tour.

**WALKING TOUR—HISTORIC
SUMMIT AVENUE**
651.297.2555
www.mnhs.org
May through September.
11 a.m and 2 p.m. Sat.,
2 p.m. Sun. Adults $8, seniors
$6, children ages 6–17, $4.
Reservations recommended.

Food Co-ops

**MISSISSIPPI MARKET
FOOD CO-OPS:**
1810 Randolph Ave.
Saint Paul, MN 55105
651.690.0507
www.msmarket.coop
Small and friendly.

622 Selby Ave.
Saint Paul, MN 55104
651.310.9499
www.msmarket.coop
Superb deli and attractive layout.

HAMPDEN PARK FOOD CO-OP
928 Raymond Ave.
Saint Paul, MN 55114
651.646-6686
www.hampdenparkcoop.com
Working member discounts,
friendly staff, great prices, strong
neighborhood feel, terrific soups.

Sports

BOCCE BALL
Half Time Rec
1013 Front Ave.
651.488.8245

**MINNESOTA STATE HIGH
SCHOOL LEAGUE**
2100 Freeway Blvd.
Brooklyn Center, MN 55430
763.560.2262
www.mshsl.org

MINNESOTA SWARM
317 Washington St.
888.MN.SWARM
www.mnswarm.com
Lacrosse

**MINNESOTA THUNDER AND
MINNESOTA LIGHTNING**
2124 University Ave. West
Suite 215
651.917.8326
www.mnthunder.com
Professional soccer teams

MINNESOTA WILD
317 Washington St.
651.222.WILD box office
www.wild.com
Hockey

SAINT PAUL CURLING CLUB
470 Selby Ave.
651.224.7408
www.stpaulcurlingclub.org

SAINT PAUL SAINTS
1771 Energy Park Dr.
651.644.6659
www.saintsbaseball.com

Other Activities

RAPTOR CENTER
University of Minnesota
1920 Fitch Ave.
612.624.4745
www.theraptorcenter.org
Check out the hawks and owls.

OMNITHEATER
Science Museum
120 West Kellogg Blvd.
651.221.9444
651.221.4585 TDD

Contributors

GeGe Youngdahl Anderson is a retired grandmother living in northeast Minneapolis. When she can't be with her incredible grandchildren and grand-nieces and nephews, she reads, writes, sews, quilts, makes dolls, and generally pretends she's no longer a responsible adult. It's a formula that works for her.

Heidi Annexstad could probably ride up Ramsey Hill if her kids pushed her. She lives in Golden Valley, where she prefers riding downhill.

Daniel Bachhuber was born in Milwaukee and now teaches at a Montessori school in Saint Paul. His poetry has appeared in many places, including The *Christian Science Monitor,* The *Atlantic Review,* and the *Southern Review.*

Kelsey Bour-Schilla is a young photographer from Saint Paul who is about to embark on the greatest adventure yet: four months in Glacier National Park, Montana, working and photographing the spectacular scenery and wildlife. She aspires to become a Forest Service Ranger specializing in conservation.

Patricia Bour-Schilla is a nanny/freelance photographer from Saint Paul who loves long bicycle rides with her husband. She reads constantly but would never purchase a skinny book—she wants to get her money's worth. The skinny ones she checks out from the library.

Carol Caouette is a freelance writer, singer, and musician. She was once a Saint Paul Winter Carnival Queen candidate but secretly coveted the title of Bouncing Blanket Girl. Carol lives in Stillwater with her husband but visits Saint Paul often.

Mark Connor is a freelance journalist, creative writer, and professional boxing trainer from Saint Paul. His work has been published nationally and internationally, much of it focusing on life in Saint Paul.

Anisha Dawan was married to Cliff Comb for forty-seven years before his death. She worked at Ramadan Meat and Seafood and the Urban League, and has volunteered at United Hospital and continues to volunteer with the National Association for the Advancement of Colored People (NAACP).

Teri J. Dwyer is a Saint Paul-based freelance writer. For years she has run, walked, biked, and inline-skated around Saint Paul's lakes and parks. She has been a published writer for over fifteen years.

William Kelso "Corky" Finney served on the Saint Paul School Board from 1989 to 1992 and in 2005. He served with the Saint Paul Police Department beginning in 1971 and as chief of police, 1992–2004. Corky has had a lifelong appreciation of vintage cars and Harley-Davidson motorcycles, and he is an Old West history buff.

Mary Gardner lives on the third floor of a 110-year-old condo building in the Cathedral Hill area of Saint Paul. She is a novelist. Her fourth novel, *Salvation Run,* was released in 2005. During the winters she teaches novel writing at The Loft, and she spends summers at her cabin in northwestern Minnesota.

Jennifer Gehlhar of Minneapolis has been playing music for over twenty years. She currently plays bass for a local band and publishes a local zine, *Atomic TC,* in support of the wildly independent punk rock scene here in the Twin Cities.

Cary Griffith is a freelance writer from Rosemount, Minnesota, and the author of *Lost in the Wild: Danger and Survival in the North Woods* (Borealis Books; March, 2006).

Moira F. Harris is the author of *Fire and Ice: The History of the Saint Paul Winter Carnival,* (Saint Paul: Pogo Press, 2004). Vulcanus Rex LXVII Tom Barrett named Ms. Harris as his "Matriarch of Carnival Memories."

Vernon Holmberg made sculpture for thirty-four years, funding his work by employment with Univac, Sperry, and Unisys. Now he writes fiction and has published one novel, *Mulcahey's Meatheads,* creates small movies, and still works as a technical writer for the military-industrial complex.

Ronnie Howell moved to Minnesota from New York in 1977. She is a mother, accomplished cook, published author/writer, and executive director of Dreams and Visions, a National Heritage Foundation nonprofit that helps others achieve their dreams of owning/operating their own businesses. Contact her at dreamsnvisionsnhf@yahoo.com.

Sao Sue Jurewitsch was born Andreas Jurewitsch in Hamburg, Germany. He's been married to Blia Thao Jurewitsch for twelve years and they have two children. He was honored with his Hmong elder name, Sao Sue, by his wife's family in 2005. He has been writing for the *Hmong Times* in Saint Paul since 2004.

Patrick Kahnke is a freelance writer and pastor of Saint Paul Fellowship Church in Frogtown. He has written numerous articles, poems, and songs, writes a blog (www.frogtownpastor.com), and plans to spend at least the next thirty years tinkering with an unfinished novel set in various Saint Paul neighborhoods.

Flint Keller loves spending time with his family. A fourth grade teacher in Saint Paul, Flint recently finished his first young adult novel, *Millikin Home*. He is currently working on an M.F.A in creative writing at Hamline University. Email at Flint.Keller@spps.org.

Nathaniel Abdul Khaliq is president of the Saint Paul branch of the National Association for the Advancement of Colored People (NAACP). Mr. Khaliq owns a construction company and Malcolm Shabbaz Apartments. He has been married to Victoria A. Alexander Davis for thirty years.

Evelyn Klein publishes regularly. Her most recent award is from the Family Housing Fund for the poem "A Place Called Home," touring the Twin Cities in an exhibit. She edited and contributed to the multicultural anthology *Stage Two: Poetic Lives.* Her book of poetry *From Here Across the Bridge* was published last year (Saint Paul: Nodin Press, 2006).

Kelly LaBrosse (aka Artemis the Huntress) was born in Saint Paul in 1972, grew up in South Saint Paul, and graduated from South Saint Paul High School. Although she currently lives up north in the Mille Lacs Lake area, Saint Paul will always be "home." She has self-published two volumes of poetry and is working on a third.

Susan Larson and Tom Lewis (aka the Larson/Lewis Project) have lived in Saint Paul since 1999. They were both born in California, but they relocated to the Upper Midwest because of the "healthy climate," easy access to cheese curds, and opportunities to explore the region's wealth of visionary environments.

May Lee is a writer aspiring to get paid for it. Instead of listing generic statistics, May believes in revealing more important things about a person, such as her idiosyncrasy for eating plain pho, her insistence on defending the legitimacy of reading romance novels, and her penchant for perpetuating Asian stereotypes by perfecting her skills as a karaoke singer. She is a former member of the spoken-word group F.I.R.E. (Free Inspiring Rising Elements) and has been published in *Paj Ntaub Voice, Unarmed Journal, and Bamboo Among the Oaks,* the first anthology to explore the creative voices of Hmong Americans. She is a winner of the 2005 Loft Mentorship Program in Non-Fiction, a recipient of the 2004 Minnesota State Arts Board Artist Initiative Grant, and of a 2002-2003 Playwright Center Many Voices Fellowship.

Jami Leigh is a writer who lives in Minneapolis but has for years secretly adored her hometown of Saint Paul.

Meridel Le Sueur (1900–1996) used her words to dig through our reserved Midwest façades and open up our tormented, tender, cruel hearts. The author and poet of many books, she challenged the status quo and spent her life championing the rights of women and the oppressed in the U.S. and overseas. Her work won numerous awards.

Virginia L. Martin, a writer and editor all her professional life, completed her M.A. in Mass Communications. Her varied workplaces have included the Minnesota Historical Society and hi-tech local companies. She has now returned to history, researching and writing a book on urban renewal, historic preservation, and Summit-University.

Linda Back McKay is a Saint Paul-born writer and teaching artist. Her books include *Choppers* (youth nonfiction), *Ride That Full Tilt Boogie* (poems), *Iron Horse Cowgirls: Around the World with Women Bikers,* and *Shadow Mothers: Stories of Adoption and Reunion* (both nonfiction). She lives in (gasp) Minneapolis.

Deborah McLaren is a travel writer who lives with her family in Merriam Park—dangerously close to Izzy's Ice Cream. Contact her at Deborah@mm.com.

Tasha Merritt loves to cook southern-style meals, has an admiration for art, believes there is nothing compared to sledding in the winter, and is a sight to see on roller skates.

Melissa Mierva is an avid gardener, artist, and freelance editor specializing in herbs. She attended Minneapolis College of Art and Design where she received her B.F.A., and is currently working toward certification in botanical illustration at the Marjorie Neely Conservatory. She resides in a vintage cottage with her daughter and two cats in Saint Paul.

Deborah Louise Gilbreath Montgomery received her B.A. from the University of Minnesota, an M.A. from Saint Thomas University, an M.A. from the Humphrey Institute, and is a graduate of the Senior Police Management Institute at Harvard University. She and her husband, Robert, have been married thirty-eight years.

Judith Niemi is a freelancer with a home base on Saint Paul's West Side and another on Lake Vermilion. She runs Women in the Wilderness trips, writes articles, essays, and books, teaches occasionally at Hamline and elsewhere, and canoes and rambles with her gun-shy German shorthaired pointer.

Kimberly Nightingale conceived and edited the Saint Paul Almanac. Kimberly is a Saint Paulite who has worked for many years as a book editor. Prior to that, she taught high school English, worked on a salmon processor in the Bering Sea, and hosted several radio shows. When she's not seeing Bob Dylan or Billy Bragg live, she spends her time traveling, getting involved in her community, and riding her recumbent bicycle. She lives with her sweetheart and two teenagers in a 1928 bungalow in the heart of Saint Paul.

John O'Brien was born in the Bronx, New York, and moved to Minnesota in 1990. From 1998–2002 he worked as a freelance writer in Caracas, Venezuela. John is currently writing about his experience driving a cab in New York from 1985–1990, before it became Trumpatized.

Eva Palma is a Chilean journalist currently working as the Spanish acquisitions editor at Llewellyn Worldwide. She was the editor of *La Prensa de Minnesota* and one of the writers of *Viceversa* magazine in the Twin Cities. She also worked for The Resource Center of the Americas as the assistant editor of *The Connections*.

Gordon Parks (1912–2006) was a photographer, filmmaker, writer, and poet who blazed an incredible path of artistic brilliance. He was born in Kansas and moved to Saint Paul at fifteen years old. After working as a porter, against all odds he made a name for himself as a fashion photographer in Saint Paul and later became a photographer and reporter for *Life* magazine, famous for his gritty photo essays about the grinding effects of poverty in the U.S. and abroad. He wrote several books, poetry, and screenplays. He wrote and directed *The Learning Tree* (1969) and *Shaft* (1971). His work won numerous awards.

Liz Pasch is a Twin Cities-based writer who left a twenty-year corporate career to cruise on a boat with her husband. She now writes feature articles for several marine and travel magazines.

Ron Peterson ended up getting a Ph.D. in physics and technology and worked at Honeywell through much of the 1990s. He's retired now, finishing up a science fiction novel (tentatively called *Children's Chrysalis*), playing with his grandson Peter, and generally goofing off. This is his first non-technical publication.

Thien-bao Thuc Phi was born in Sai Gon, Viet Nam, and raised in the Phillips Neighborhood in Minneapolis. A multiple Minnesota Grand Poetry Slam champion and National Poetry Slam individual finalist, Bao Phi is one of the premiere performance poets in the nation, and has been a featured performer in venues from the Nuyorican Poets Café to Stanford University. He was a featured poet on season three of HBO's *Russell Simmons Presents Def Poetry Jam* and remains an active member of the national Asian American spoken word community. One of his poems was recently selected by former U.S. Poet Laureate Billy Collins to appear in 2006's prestigious *Best American Poetry* anthology. www.baophi.com

Russ Ringsak was a registered architect in Minnesota when he bought an over-the-road semi tractor in 1977, a career move that ultimately led him to driving the trucks and writing for the *Prairie Home Companion* radio show. He has now been with the show for more than twenty years—and about half a million miles. He lives in Stillwater, Minnesota.

John Rosengren is an award-winning journalist whose work has appeared in over seventy-five publications, ranging from *Reader's Digest* to *Sports Illustrated*. John lives in Minneapolis with his wife and their two children.

Larry Schilla was born in Saint Paul and has lived near and worked on West Seventh Street most of his life. He's fifty years old and prides himself in knowing a little about Saint Paul.

Jami Shoemaker has lived in Saint Paul since 1999. She works as a freelance writer and editor, and has a great fondness for the theatrical arts.

Karin Simoneau is a book editor and longtime resident of Saint Paul. Born in California, she has lived in the city since 1997 and continues to marvel at the new places and things she happens upon in the beautiful city she calls home.

Amy Siqveland is a social worker and a freelance writer. She grew up in Minnesota and works for the University of Minnesota Press and writes for msNBC.com in Seattle.

Dr. Ivar E. Siqveland was born in Michigan in 1872 and practiced dentistry in Saint Paul from 1891 until he retired in 1943. In 1899, after having saved some money from his dental practice, he was presented with a decision of whether to buy stock in his friend Henry Ford's new company, or buy the first gasoline-powered car, a one-lunged Winton. He chose the car.

Vic Tedesco started out life in Swede Hollow and went on to become a Saint Paul City Council member for eleven consecutive terms. Vic is one of the best-loved and most colorful politicians in the city's history.

Seanne Thomas lives in Saint Paul and enjoys reading and jumping on the trampoline with the sprinkler on because she's the biggest kid in her house.

David Tilsen resides in an extensive fantasy world, where he is a brilliant writer, a pundit whose thoughts are widely sought after, and the best-looking man in the Cities. He lives with the happiest married woman in the world, installing software for the most satisfied customers in the galaxy. His wisdom can be obtained at www.dtilsen.net/blog

Drew Tilsen is the new owner of Magic's Automotive Repair and Towing in Saint Paul. He spends his days working on cars and learning all the new automotive technology, and spends his nights thinking of new cars to build and new projects to work on.

Bradley Wakefield stays out of trouble.

Stanley Gordon West was born in Saint Paul and graduated from Central High School in 1950. He attended Macalester College and the University of Minnesota. His novel *Amos* was a CBS *Movie of the Week* starring Kirk Douglas and Elizabeth Montgomery.

James Wright (1927–1980) pried open seams of the world and ourselves with his writing. His poetry is deeply loved. Born in Ohio, he taught at the University of Minnesota and Macalester College. He won the Pulitzer Prize in 1971 for his *Collected Poems.*

Beadrin (Pixie) Youngdahl is a lifelong resident of Minneapolis with a deep curiosity about the city "over there." She works as a registered nurse and has recently completed a novel that is currently visiting the slush piles of publishing houses and agency round files. Sometimes her writing is funny. Sometimes the editors just laugh at it. Beadrin@aol.com.

Allen Zumach captures everyday Twin Cities scenes through digital photos—skylines, parks, neighborhoods—and extracts from them very striking, almost romantic, images. These images, available as notecards and prints, awaken memories and inspire awareness of the beauty found in our ordinary lives. For more information visit www.zumach.net.

Permissions

Resources for Peace and Justice

This is a very difficult time. Please help promote peace and justice in the world, in the country, in Minnesota, in Saint Paul, and in your neighborhood.

SAINT ANTHONY PARK NEIGHBORS FOR PEACE
Karen Lilley
651.644.3927
Email: web@parkpeace.org

COMO PARK NEIGHBORS FOR PEACE
David List
651.489.1965
Email: listtesdell@earthlink.net

CROCUS HILL/WEST SEVENTH NEIGHBORS FOR PEACE
Linda Winsor
651-224-6004
Email: ljwinsor@yahoo.com
Join us. We have a passion for peace and justice, and provide opportunities for people to make a difference.

HAMLINE-MIDWAY NEIGHBORS FOR PEACE
Barb Spears
651.646.5568
Email: hmpeace@attbi.com

MACALESTER-GROVELAND NEIGHBORS FOR PEACE
Mark Johnson
651.699.6086
Email: mark-r-johnson@attbi.com
We pursue peaceful means for solving conflicts.

MERRIAM PARK NEIGHBORS FOR PEACE
Krista Menzel
651.641.7592
Email: web@mppeace.org
www.mppeace.org
Dedicated to pursuing peaceful, nonviolent alternatives in every area where conflicts arise.

MINNESOTA NEIGHBORS FOR PEACE
Krista Menzel
651.641.7592
Email: web@mppeace.org
mnneighbors4peace.org

Other Resources in Saint Paul

NONVIOLENT PEACEFORCE (RECENTLY RELOCATED FROM SAINT PAUL)
425 Oak Grove Street
Minneapolis, MN 55403
612.871.0005
www.nonviolentpeaceforce.org

PEACE AND JUSTICE COMMITTEE
Aaron Gerhardt
651.635.2278
Email: geraar@mac.com
We seek to take personal action on issues relating to peace and justice through events, protests, and other actions.

SISTERS OF SAINT JOSEPH OF CARONDELET
Margaret L. Kvasnicka
651.696.8644
Email: mlkcsj@aol.com

STUDENT COALITION FOR SOCIAL JUSTICE
Mike Klein
651.962.5337
Email: mcklein@stthomas.edu
SCSJ is a coalition of justice-oriented action groups at the University of Saint Thomas.

PEACE IN THE PRECINCTS
1050 Selby Ave.
651.917.0383
Email: info@peaceintheprecincts.org

The *Saint Paul Almanac*

Subscribe to it

Three annual issues for $30

(price includes tax, shipping, and handling)

To order

online: www.saintpaulalmanac.com

mail: Subscriptions
          Saint Paul Almanac
          PO Box 16243
          Saint Paul, MN 55116

If mailing, please fill out and send the info below.

....

❏ Begin with *2007 Saint Paul Almanac* (available now)

❏ Begin with *2008 Saint Paul Almanac* (available August 2007)

❏ Check or money order enclosed

❏ Charge: __ Visa __ MasterCard

_____

CARD NUMBER

_____

EXPIRATION DATE

_____

SIGNATURE OF CARDHOLDER

_____

MAILING ADDRESS

_____

EMAIL

For gift orders

_____

SHIP TO NAME

_____

MAILING ADDRESS